THE SPCK HANDBOOK
of
ANGLICAN THEOLOGIANS

THE SPCK HANDBOOK
of
ANGLICAN THEOLOGIANS

Edited by Alister E. McGrath

First published in Great Britain 1998
Society for Promoting Christian Knowledge
Holy Trinity Church
Marylebone Road
London NW1 4DU

British Library Cataloguing-in-Publication Data
A catalogue record of this book is available from
the British Library

ISBN 0-281-05145-3

Typeset by Pioneer Associates, Perthshire
Printed in Great Britain at
The University Press, Cambridge

CONTENTS

CONTRIBUTORS

Revd Dr Alister E. McGrath, editor (AM)
Principal, Wycliffe Hall, Oxford: Research Lecturer in Theology, Oxford University; Research Professor of Systematic Theology, Regent College, Vancouver, Canada and serves on the Doctrine Commission of the Church of England

The initials in brackets following each contributor's name are the form of abbreviation used at the end of articles in the Survey of Anglican Theologians.

Revd Dr Paul Avis (PA)
Vicar, Stoke Canon, Exeter

Canon Maurice Betteridge (MB)
Ridley College, Melbourne, Australia

Professor John Booty (JB)
University of the South, Sewanee, Tennessee

Revd Dr Timothy Bradshaw (TB)
Regents Park College, Oxford

Professor David Brown (DB)
Department of Theology, University of Durham

Professor William Crockett (WC)
Vancouver School of Theology

Most Revd Brian N. Davies (BND)
Archbishop of Wellington, New Zealand

Rt Revd Timothy Dudley-Smith (TDS)
Bishop of Thetford (retired)

Professor Walter V. L. Eversley
Virginia Theological Seminary

Professor R. William Franklin (RWF)
General Theological Seminary, New York

Professor James Griffiss (JG)
Anglican Theological Review

Revd Dr Tudor Griffiths (TG)
Bishop Tucker Theological College, Uganda

Professor Ann Loades (AL)
Department of Theology, University of Durham

Rt Revd Henry McAdoo (HM)
Archbishop of Dublin (retired)

Professor John Macquarrie (JM)
Oxford University

Rt Revd Michael Nazir-Ali (MNA)
Bishop of Rochester

Professor James I. Packer (JIP)
Regent College, Vancouver

Professor Robert Prichard (RP)
Virginia Theological Seminary

Professor David Scott (DS)
Virginia Theological Seminary

Revd Dr Charles Sherlock (CS)
Melbourne College of Divinity, Australia

Rt Revd Kenneth Stevenson (KS)
Bishop of Portsmouth

Professor John Suggitt (JS)
Rhodes University, South Africa

Dr Mark Thompson (MT)
Moore College, Sydney

Professor John Webster (JW)
Oxford University

Revd Dr Peter Williams (PW)
Vicar, Eccleshall, Sheffield

Rt Revd Rowan Williams (RW)
Bishop of Monmouth

Professor J. Robert Wright (JRW)
General Theological Seminary, New York

Shorter unsigned articles have been compiled by Revd Ronald D. Kuykendal and Revd Daniel Dunlap, students researching in the development of Anglican theology at Oxford.

PREFACE

Anglicanism remains a significant presence in the Christian world and continues to offer important opportunities for consolidation and expansion in the next millennium. An essential resource for the renewal of Anglican theology is access to the theological riches which are part of its heritage. This volume aims to survey the heritage of Anglican theology, not as a matter of historical or antiquarian interest, but on the assumption that future theological reconstruction and reformulation will need to engage with that heritage.

The work opens with a global survey of Anglicanism, providing in-depth analysis of the evolution of Anglican theology in eight major regions of the world. This section aims to acquaint its readers with the richness and diversity of the Anglican heritage in the various regions of the world in which it has established a significant presence, as Anglican theologians struggled to state and justify their theological tradition in a range of historical and cultural contexts. While it is inevitable that a substantial part of this survey should be devoted to the development of Anglicanism in Britain, every effort has been made to ensure that the development of Anglicanism in other regions is represented and recorded. This section of the work will be an indispensable resource for all those concerned with the theological identity, consolidation and renewal of Anglicanism, or the study of its tasks and traditions.

The second major section of the work provides an analysis of a selection of nearly one hundred Anglican theologians who are held to be of continuing relevance to the Anglican Communion in its pastoral, teaching, ecumenical, apologetic and evangelistic tasks. It is impossible, and in any case not particularly helpful, to provide an exhaustive list of Anglican theologians. The writers to be presented here have been identified on the basis of a worldwide consultation, in which the primary consideration was the potential of such theologians to be a resource to Anglicanism in the future. The present work is not intended as an historical guide, although it may have some value in that respect. It is primarily concerned to identify theologians who are likely to be of continuing value as dialogue partners in the continuous task of revising, extending and renewing the Anglican theological vision in the future. Each entry provides appropriate bibliographical resources to allow users to take matters further.

Alister E. McGrath

INTERNET RESOURCES

The Internet is now a major source of material relating to Christianity in general, including Anglicanism. This section lists some of the more important Anglican Web sites. You are also recommended to explore other Web sites of importance, such as the following, all of which have extensive hypertext links, sometimes with powerful search engines, allowing direct access to a wide range of important resources:

http://www.bakerbooks.com/ccc/
http://www.iclnet.org/pub/resources/christian-resources.html
http://www.yahoo.com/Society_and_Culture/Religion/Christianity/
http://galaxy.einet.net/galaxy/Humanities/Religion.html

ANGLICAN RESOURCES

The Church of England Home Page contains details of Anglicanism in England, and of the Anglican Communion in general. It also features links to the Archbishop of Canterbury.

http://www.anglican.org.uk/

Anglicans Online

http://www.infomatch.com/~haibeck/anglican.html

an excellent starting-point for information relating to Anglicanism in North America, although with some information relating to England.
For direct access to news items relating to the United States, go to

http://www.infomatch.com/~haibeck/anglican/usa.htm

For access to the Episcopal News Service, which provides up-to-date information on the Episcopal Church of the United States of America, see

http://www.dfns.org/ens/

For news of Anglicanism worldwide, see

http://www.infomatch.com/~haibeck/anglican/world.htm

PART ONE

A Regional Survey of Anglican Theology

GREAT BRITAIN

Paul Avis

Although a self-conscious 'Anglicanism' emerged only in the second half of the seventeenth century, the Church of England came into being when King Henry VIII renounced the canonical authority of the Pope in the early 1530s. In doing so, Henry was taking the tensions and power-struggles, that had been endemic in Europe during the medieval period between rulers (emperor, kings and princes) and the papacy, to their ultimate conclusion. The authority of the papacy in England stemmed from Pope Gregory the Great's initiative of 597 in sending Augustine (of Canterbury) to convert the English to the Roman obedience. Augustine's mission was able to capitalize on the presence of the Christian Church in Britain since the earliest years of the Christian era. Roman soldiers had probably been the first Christians to set foot in England. The indigenous Christian Church was first Celtic, then – thanks to the Celtic monastic missionaries from Ireland and Scotland – Saxon, and only then Roman Catholic.

It was central to Anglican apologetic during the Reformation and subsequently to claim that the realm of England had originally been independent of Rome and that the throwing-off of papal jurisdiction was simply restoring the inherent autonomy of the English church – which, it was frequently claimed, had been founded by Joseph of Arimathea. Between 664 (the Synod of Whitby) and 1533, the English church was part of the patriarchate of the West which, after the decisive breach between the West and the East in 1054, regarded itself as identical with the Christian Church.

Thus the term 'Anglicanism' is anachronistic if used of developments before the English Civil War, and the expression itself only comes into use in the early nineteenth century. Similarly, the term 'Church of England' is anachronistic before the Reformation, though the integrity and rights of the English Church (*Ecclesia Anglicana*) were contended for long before then. We now turn to survey the development of Anglicanism in the British Isles in three fairly arbitrary historical periods.

Primary sources

G. R. Evans and J. R. Wright (eds.), 1991. *The Anglican Tradition* (London: SPCK).

The Church of England Yearbook (London: Church House Publishing) provides statistical and other information on the Church of England and on the Anglican Communion, including the other British Anglican churches.

Secondary studies

J. Robert Wright, 1988. 'Anglicanism, *Ecclesia Anglicana*, and Anglican: An Essay on Terminology', in S. Sykes and J. Booty (eds.), *The Study of Anglicanism* (London: SPCK; Philadelphia: Fortress Press, 1988), 424–9; rev. edn 1996. (This volume is an essential resource for the nature of Anglicanism.)

FROM HENRY VIII TO JAMES I

Was the Reformation wanted?

The Reformation in England is now recognized to have been more imposed from above than demanded from below. The symbolic world of late medieval piety and liturgy retained its power. The Church still attracted enormous loyalty and generosity. The pre-Reformation Church in England was suffering neither decline nor decay. If anything, the vigour of lay piety pointed to further development and demanded the reform of glaring abuses along Erasmian lines, i.e. without revolution and without schism. Naturally, there were secular forces at work also, envious of ecclesiastical power and covetous of ecclesiastical wealth.

On the other hand, the scholarly return to the original texts of the Western tradition by the Christian humanists of northern Europe had generated a theological renewal which called into question some traditional theological assumptions behind current practice. For example, Martin Luther's teaching on justification by faith had radical implications for that definitive doctrine of late medieval Catholicism, purgatory, and with it for eucharistic theology, the understanding of priesthood and the power of the papacy (propitiatory sacrifice, masses for the dead, the mass as a meritorious work, the treasury of merits, indulgences, etc.). The corollary of justification by faith in Luther – the universal priesthood of the baptized – lent itself to arguments which sought to legitimate the claims of the laity to intervene in ecclesiastical affairs and so lay behind the supreme governership of the sovereign and the role of Parliament as the lay synod (bishops excepted) of the Church.

The role of the sovereign

It is true to say that in the sixteenth and early seventeenth centuries, the Church of England owed its whole existence to the royal supremacy. But that supremacy was a developing concept. Henry VIII substituted royal for papal authority, titling himself 'Head' of the Church and assuming many of the functions of the pope in England. He effectively exercised jurisdiction over the Church and claimed the right to define doctrine, hear appeals, collect revenues and appoint bishops. Archbishop Cranmer and the canon lawyers encouraged Henry in these aspirations. Like the German princes who had defended Luther, they regarded the English sovereign as the 'godly prince', modelled on King Josiah in the Old Testament, who reformed worship and protected the people of God. Henry also toyed with the notion of royal sacramental power but never put this into practice: it would have been the litmus test of Reformation ecclesiology. Henry VIII, Elizabeth I and James I were capable theologians and assumed the direction of the official theology of their reigns (Henry and James publishing theological works in their own names).

Henry's supremacy was essentially personal, but under Elizabeth supremacy became vested, at least in theory, in the sovereign in Parliament. Elizabeth was content to style herself simply 'Supreme Governor', but there was an equivalence between her governorship in temporal or secular matters and her governorship in spiritual or ecclesiastical matters (this remains the canonical position today: Canon A7). Elizabeth effectively silenced one of her Archbishops of Canterbury (Grindal). Just as much as Henry, she was regarded as the providential protector and reformer of the Church. The sovereign continued to be what he or she had always been, a sacred figure, neither quite lay person nor priest, whose authority could be expanded or contracted to suit the circumstances.

Church and State

At the Reformation, the sovereign was the only source of an authority powerful enough to challenge the papacy. The emphasis on national churches, which had been important in the conciliar movement of the previous two centuries, was strengthened by incipient nationalism. The official theology of Henry's reign, which could not be described as Protestant, insisted on the integrity of national churches and claimed that being in communion with the pope was not a condition of being a church.

Until the late seventeenth century no practical distinction was made, in law or in theology, between the state and the Church. The common-wealth of England and the Church of England were coterminous. To be born into the commonwealth and to be baptized into the Church were two sides of the same coin. All citizens of the realm were *ipso facto* members of the Church of England. The Elizabethan puritans also accepted this assumption, though they made great play of the distinc-tion between the visible and the invisible Church. Only the radical Protestants, the Separatists of the late sixteenth century who harked back to the continental Anabaptists, and the recusant Roman Catholics for whom Elizabeth was a heretic and an outlaw, operated with such a distinction. Both groups did so at peril of their lives.

Episcopacy

The threefold ministry in historic succession and the continuity of bishops in the historic sees survived the upheavals of the Reformation, as did the pastoral ministry of the clergy in the parishes of the land. The bishops continued to have a civil and political function as well as an ecclesiastical function. Their presence was required at court, and they ruled in their dioceses on behalf of the sovereign. Though their spiritual authority came from God, their jurisdiction and temporal privileges were dispensed by the monarch.

The early English Reformers, up to and including Archbishop Whitgift, were pragmatic about episcopacy. The outward form of ministerial order was not an issue until the Presbyterians (who at this time were still with-in the Church of England) raised it in the last quarter of the sixteenth century. Until the late 1580s, episcopacy was defended on the grounds that it was 'primitive' (i.e. it went back to the early, undivided Church), not contrary to Scripture and ordained by the 'magistrate' (the sovereign). While the Presbyterians claimed divine right (*jure divino*) for the elder-ship, Anglicans declined to raise the stakes in a corresponding way for episcopacy. From 1597, a succession of apologists for episcopacy began to resort to divine-right arguments, though in Hooker this is tempered by an acknowledgement that the Church, by united action, has the authority to adapt its polity to changing circumstances. Certainly there is no suggestion at this stage that the episcopate – least of all the historic episcopate – was necessary to the existence of a church.

The Church of England and other churches

The English Reformers and their successors until the Laudians in the

1630s regarded Rome as the Antichrist, but this designation is not reflected in the Church of England's official formularies. Though Rome was the enemy, the Reformers did not deny that she retained some semblance or residue of a church. The pope is demoted to be merely Bishop of Rome, but he is also feared as a foreign prince with designs upon the realm of England. Because the sovereign had sacred authority and the pope wielded temporal power, the distinction between them was one more of degree than of kind: in the temporal context they were rival princes; in the spiritual context they were rival vicars of Christ. The pope excommunicated Elizabeth, purported to depose her and encouraged her subjects to rebel. This had the effect of making all recusant Roman Catholics suspect as traitors.

The English Reformation was influenced first by Christian humanist ideas, associated with Erasmus and Colet (Dean of St Paul's in the early 1500s), as well as by the radical tradition of Jan Hus in Bohemia and of John Wyclif at home (leader of the Lollard movement in the late fourteenth and early fifteenth centuries). The influence first of Martin Luther and then of John Calvin supervened on this background. The reformed Church of England regarded the continental Protestants as sister churches and their own church as equally Protestant. Cranmer engaged in pan-Protestant ecumenism, and the Church of England later sent a delegation to the Synod of Dort, which attempted to resolve differences between Calvinists and Arminians in Holland. Until the mid-seventeenth century moderate Calvinism was Anglican orthodoxy and does not serve to distinguish episcopalians from presbyterians within the Church of England.

Scotland, Wales and Ireland

Christianity in Scotland goes back at least to the end of the fourth century and the missionary labours of St Ninian. In the late sixth century St Columba directed a mission from Iona. As the Celtic church declined in England, Roman influence increased north of the border. An episcopally ordered church flourished in the centuries following the Norman conquest of England, and it vigorously asserted its independence of Canterbury and York. Waves of subversive ideas – Lollard, Lutheran and Calvinist – helped to undermine the Roman obedience in Scotland, and in 1560 the reformed Church of Scotland was established under the leadership of John Knox, and presbyterianism was progressively introduced. James VI of Scotland became James I of England in 1603, uniting the kingdoms, and attempted to impose episcopacy and related practices on Scotland.

In Wales, the Christian presence stems from late Roman times, and in the Celtic church, the rule of abbots evolved into the rule of bishops. The Normans extended Roman Christianity into Wales, and to varying degrees the Welsh church was assimilated to the English. Reforming ideas made little impact, but the political moves of dissolution of the monasteries and the break with Rome were absorbed. Elizabeth appointed energetic, resident, Welsh-speaking bishops who imposed the settlement of 1559, but the linguistic divide grew, and Anglicanism became identified with the ruling, propertied class and the clergy.

In Ireland, similarly, a Celtic church was overrun by the Normans reinforcing the Roman connection, but the Irish church retained its distinctiveness, and the Reformation was carried out in a half-hearted manner under both Henry and Elizabeth. Ireland was not permitted a liturgy in the vernacular. Puritan influences began to establish themselves in Ulster from the end of the sixteenth century.

Liturgical changes

Before the Reformation there were regional rites for the Mass (of which the Sarum rite is the best known), and daily prayer was organized on the monastic pattern of frequent services throughout the day and night. Regional variations did not suit Henry's and Elizabeth's policy of uniformity in religion and unity in the nation. Monastic offices were uncongenial to the aspirations of lay people in the workaday world. Lay piety was serviced by a plethora of primers or books of prayers and other devotions. The Mass was not only theologically unacceptable to the Reformers (because of transubstantiation and the propitiatory sacrifice for the living and the dead), but linguistically offensive, because Latin was the mark as well as the means of Roman uniformity.

Thus there were political as well as theological reasons behind the reform of the English liturgy and its appearance in the vernacular (a language 'understanded of the people') together with the English Bible. The comprehending participation of the laity became a hallmark of Anglicanism. Cranmer reduced the monastic offices to Morning and Evening Prayer, in which the laity were invited to pray for the king, for God's protection against national enemies, and for their own docility and obedience. In spite of resistance and occasional rebellion, Henry and Elizabeth had calculated correctly that the spiritual emancipation of the laity would strengthen their own power-base too.

After some piecemeal liturgical changes, Cranmer produced the first English reformed Prayer Book in 1549 and the second in 1552, both under Edward VI. As the logic of reformation proceeded, during the reign of the sickly boy-king, liturgical consequences followed. While the first book provided for the communicant to unite him- or herself to

Christ's once-for-all oblation to the Father in the sacramental action and to believe that he or she was truly receiving Christ in the sacrament, the second book was blatantly Protestant in its abolition of the eucharistic sacrifice (propitiatory sacrifice had been removed in the first book) and its avoidance of the lingering language of real presence.

Defending the Reformation

The scholars of the Church of England (who were usually also the bishops) had to defend the English Reformation and the position of the reformed English church on two fronts – against Rome and against radical Protestants. On the first front, against Rome, they insisted that they had not created a new church but had simply reformed and renewed the old. They had not departed from the catholic Church but only from Roman jurisdiction. They had not separated from the Western church but merely from the papacy. Though the breach had been made for political reasons by Henry VIII, the apologists were able to claim that they were continuing the aspirations of the earlier conciliar movement which had aimed to reform the Church, expunge heresy and curb the powers of the papacy by mobilizing the bishops, scholars and 'secular' rulers of Christendom and bringing them together in councils where the pope had only constitutional power.

The appeal of the reformed English church was to the Bible in the original Hebrew and Greek (and without the Apocrypha as a source of doctrine) and to the primitive Church – its fathers and its councils. Their notion of tradition was restricted to that period, close to the apostles, when (they believed) there was no papacy, no purgatory, no cult of the Virgin Mary and the saints, and no separate estate of religious orders.

The two most successful Anglican apologists were Jewel and Hooker. Jewel defended the English Reformation against Rome; Hooker defended the Elizabethan settlement of religion against those presbyterians within the Church of England (Cartwright and Travers) who argued that while the Church of England maintained episcopacy and a liturgy with 'popish' remnants, it was only half-reformed. Jewel took his stand broadly on Scripture and the primitive Church, Hooker on tradition more widely interpreted and on reason. Jewel is devastatingly polemical; Hooker's argument moves at a more elevated level of appeal to first principles, studied moderation and heartfelt charity, but modern scholars detect in him the astute deployment of special pleading, caricature and sleight of hand. Even allowing for that, Hooker's great treatise on *Ecclesiastical Polity* remains a charter document of Anglicanism and a source of renewal for Anglican theology.

The formulation of doctrine

The centre of gravity in the formulation of doctrine shifted during the Reformation from tradition and the living voice of the Church (magisterium), as in medieval Catholicism, to the Bible as interpreted by scholarly bishops in the light of the primitive Church. Parliament had authority in doctrine and worship. In reality, the crown was the decisive theological influence.

The Thirty-nine Articles of Religion (to be found at the back of the Book of Common Prayer 1662) are the nearest thing to an Anglican summary of Christian doctrine, but as such they appear extremely meagre. They are derived from a series of doctrinal statements put out during the reign of Henry VIII in order to regulate the progress of reform. They reflect the influence of the Lutheran Augsburg Confession of 1530. The Forty-two Articles appeared in 1553 under Edward VI, and these were reduced to thirty-nine ten years later under Elizabeth. The Articles in their present (Church of England) form were issued in 1571. The Articles were an attempt to contain controversy and played their part in creating a context of comprehension for the national church. They make a number of central, positive affirmations and rule out a number of unacceptable deviations. Their targets are (a) speculative heterodoxy in the form of anti-trinitarianism, which flourished on one radical wing of the Reformation; (b) Roman Catholicism, which was the enemy of the state; (c) radical Protestants, labelled Anabaptists, who rejected the union of church and state and advocated gathered communities of more perfect, rebaptized Christians; (d) a more extreme form of Calvinism than was regarded as acceptable in the Church of England.

Origins of comprehensiveness

The origins of Anglican comprehensiveness can be found in the Elizabethan 'settlement' of religion of 1559. Elizabeth refused, as she said, to make windows into men's hearts and minds. There would be no inquisition into the orthodoxy of the clergy; there was no test of orthodoxy for the laity anyway. Outward conformity, expressed by worship at the parish church, combined with loyalty to the throne, was sufficient for a church which attempted to include the whole nation. Religious conflict was subordinated to the security of the realm, and its wounds were at least outwardly healed. The Thirty-nine Articles and the Prayer Book (the Second Prayer Book of Edward VI was reissued with minor changes in 1559) attempted a middle way (*via media*) between Roman Catholicism, which was committed to overthrowing the crown, and militant Protestantism, which demanded that the English Reformation should model itself on Geneva, etc., abolishing bishops and the 'popish' liturgy. The settlement was originally a political device, but it lent itself, in later theological reflection, to a noble ideal of tolerance and comprehension on the basis of the fundamentals of the faith. Whether that ideal was ever fully realized is another question, but at least in the Elizabethan and Jacobean periods, the Church of England became a national as well as an established church.

The major changes

Though the outward structures of parishes, parish churches, parish clergy, cathedrals, dioceses and their bishops continued, there were also visible changes which affected the lives and the worship of the clergy of the Church of England and their parishioners.

Supreme authority on earth was no longer vested in the pope but in the sovereign. The bishops were appointed by him or her and were answerable to the same. The wealth of the English church was no longer siphoned off to Rome but went into the exchequer. The vast properties, lands and endowments of religious houses, guilds and mass-chantries were nationalized by stages, and the numerous 'Religious' had to find other employment. Clergy were allowed to marry, so there was no need for them to have 'housekeepers'. Services were in English, and lay people were offered the cup as well as the bread on the infrequent occasions that they received Holy Communion. Confession to a priest was no longer demanded, but everyone confessed their sins in painless general terms twice every Sunday. The Bible was available to those who could read their native tongue, but the penalties for disputing the official interpretation remained.

The sacred world diminished; it was undoubtedly a smaller, plainer – but less terrifying – place. The communion of saints was being redefined to refer to the gatherings of godly Protestants rather than to the fellowship of prayer between the living and the departed. The saints who presided over every moment and aspect of life in the medieval Church were cut off at a stroke and deleted from the liturgy (with the exception of the Virgin Mary, the twelve apostles, John the Baptist and 'Saint' Michael the Archangel). This impoverishment of the sacred world created a vacuum which, if not actually created by secularization, would steadily be filled by it.

Primary sources

The Parker Society edition of the works of the English Reformers (Cambridge, 1840–).

The Thirty-nine Articles of Religion (printed at the back of The Book of Common Prayer).

G. R. Elton (ed.), 1972. *The Tudor Constitution: Documents and Commentary* (Cambridge: Cambridge University Press).

R. Hooker, [1845] 1977–91. J. Keble (ed.), *Works* (Oxford); new critical edition, W. Speed Hill (ed.), *The Folger Library Edition of the Works of Richard Hooker* (Cambridge, Mass.: Harvard University Press).

Secondary studies

P. Avis, 1989. *Anglicanism and the Christian Church: Theological Resources in Historical Perspective* (Edinburgh: T. & T. Clark; Philadelphia: Fortress Press).

P. Collinson, 1967. *The Elizabethan Puritan Movement* (London: Jonathan Cape).

P. Collinson, 1982. *The Religion of Protestants: The Church in English Society 1559–1625* (Oxford: Clarendon Press).

A. G. Dickens, 1964, 1967. *The English Reformation* (London: Batsford; rev. edn London: Fontana).

E. Duffy, 1992. *The Stripping of the Altars: Traditional Religion in England 1400–1580* (New Haven and London: Yale University Press).

C. Haigh (ed.), 1987. *The English Reformation Revised* (Cambridge: Cambridge University Press).

W. P. Haugaard, 1968. *Elizabeth and the English Reformation* (Cambridge: Cambridge University Press).

P. Lake, 1988. *Anglicans and Puritans: Presbyterian and English Conformist Thought from Whitgift to Hooker* (London: Unwin Hyman).

A. McGrath, 1987. *The Intellectual Origins of the European Reformation* (Oxford: Blackwell).

A. Milton, 1995. *Catholic and Reformed: The Roman and Protestant Churches in English Protestant Thought 1600–1640* (Cambridge: Cambridge University Press).

R. O'Day, 1986. *The Debate on the English Reformation* (London and New York: Methuen).

R. Rex, 1992. *Henry VIII and the English Reformation* (London: Macmillan).

J. J. Scarisbrick, 1984. *The Reformation and the English People* (Oxford: Blackwell).

FROM CIVIL WAR TO THE EVE OF
THE OXFORD MOVEMENT

Was 'Anglicanism' wanted?

In the mid-seventeenth century the Church of England underwent drastic changes and many typical features were abolished. The Archbishop of Canterbury (William Laud) was executed, followed by the King, the highest earthly authority in the church (Charles I). The episcopate was abolished and the bishops were forced to forsake their palaces for humble rural retreats or exile abroad. The Prayer Book was proscribed (including the Christian Year with its feasts and fasts, the former being the more missed), and the Westminster Assembly's 'Directory of Public Worship' was substituted. Although about three quarters of the parochial clergy were left in possession of their benefices, they were required to solemnly abjure the twin pillars of the Church of England's polity: episcopacy and monarchy. Under the protection of a presbyterian regime, independency (congregationalism) mushroomed and there was a modest influx of independent ministers into the parochial ministry of the national church. The Prayer Book was used in private and there were young scholars who sought covert ordination from the ejected bishops. Possibly the Prayer Book was often used for rites of passage. Episcopalians (as we should call them at this stage) were traumatized: the beheading of Charles I was compared to the crucifixion. It seemed, they said, that God had 'spat in their faces'.

In 1660, at the Restoration, the monarchy, episcopate and liturgy swept back again with a vengeance. So was Anglicanism wanted or not? A considerable industry is concerned with the socio-economic causes of the Civil War. But there were also theological and ecclesiastical causes. The moderate Calvinist orthodoxy of the Elizabethan and Jacobean church had given ground before the Arminian challenge located in the higher echelons of the church. High claims for the authority of bishops and a programme of ceremonial changes were allied to this theology that stressed human response, progressive sanctification, the sacraments as means of grace, the beauty of holiness in worship, the duty of obedience to authority and the danger of presumption. In the trial of strength between Charles I and Parliament, the bishops were allied with the King. Ever higher claims for the royal prerogative were matched by escalating claims for episcopacy. James I had warned, 'No bishop, no king', and now the sacred hierarchy of bishop and king would sink or swim together.

However, the local structures of the Church of England, that had persisted through the upheavals of the political schism under Henry, the

13

more radical reform under Edward VI, the Counter-Reformation under Mary and the politically motivated settlement of Elizabeth, showed its durability and strength. The church was identified with the parish and its sacred place – the parish church and churchyard – and its sacred person – the parish priest or parson who had the cure of souls. It spanned the generations, united the living and the departed and breathed with the rhythms of the agricultural year. This foundation was still in place at the end of Civil War and Commonwealth. A secular 'Protector' could not fill the vacuum left by the Lord's anointed sovereign. And of course it was nice to keep Christmas and the other feasts of the Christian Year again! Under Charles II, England would now be 'Merry' once more.

Church and state

From 1625 Charles I, through personal intervention, undermined the Jacobean consensus, alienating many who might have been accommodated within the national church and radicalizing the more extreme puritans. He destroyed the established working relationship between crown, parliament and church by promoting controversial ecclesiastical measures without parliamentary support. Charles's wilful and provocative policy was aided and abetted by Archbishop Laud. Ceremonies, which in a reformed polity might have been accommodated as 'things indifferent', were imposed; ecclesiastical discipline was more rigorously applied in the provinces; conformity was enforced in Scotland, Wales and Ireland; and altogether there took place a creeping clericalization of the Church of England. The violent reaction that followed brought the destruction of crown and church together.

In 1660 Parliament saw that the Church of England – catholic and reformed, with its bishops and its liturgy – was wanted. But Parliament also laid down the conditions on which it was acceptable. The days of untrammelled royal power were over. James II would discover this to his cost when he began to initiate moves to admit Roman Catholics to civic life on equal terms with Anglicans. Never again would the crown, in alliance with the church, be allowed to split the nation into two warring factions. From the late seventeenth century until the eve of the Oxford movement in the late 1820s there was a progressive undermining of Anglican exclusiveness and Anglican civil privileges. Anglicanism was wanted, but not to the exclusion of Nonconformists and law-abiding Roman Catholics.

The Anglican squirarchy and hierarchy consistently resisted proposals for comprehension – for a truly national church with an episcopate that was not monarchical but shared oversight with the presbyters, and a liturgy to which the more protestant sort could accommodate themselves. In 1689 Anglicans settled decisively for *toleration* instead of *comprehension*. Widening the terms of communion would have meant widening access to civil office, but a toleration would simply permit freedom of worship while keeping political power in the right hands. As Spurr suggests, the Church of England ceased to be a national church and became merely an established church (1991, 103f.).

The coronation oath of William and Mary in 1688 was an open-ended commitment to uphold the favoured position of the Church of England, its bishops and clergy, under the constitution as determined by Parliament: 'Will you to the utmost of your power maintain the laws of God, the true profession of the Gospel, and the Protestant Reformed Religion established by law? And will you preserve unto the bishops and clergy of this realm, and to the churches committed to their charge, all such rights and privileges as by law do or shall appertain unto them, or any of them?' The fact that the sovereign is still bound to do this has not prevented the progressive erosion of the Church of England's privileges, over against the other churches, and the emergence of a religiously pluralist society, during the past three centuries.

The Church of England was singularly unfortunate with its Supreme Governors during this period. Charles I failed to defend and preserve the church and contrived to have his head cut off. Charles II was a Roman Catholic fellow-traveller and could not be trusted to safeguard the rights of the Church of England. James II was an outright papist and hoped to bring in the Roman Catholic Church on the same terms as the Church of England. He was deprived of the throne. William of Orange, who accepted the vacancy, was a Calvinist; and the Hanoverians, to whom the throne passed on the death of Queen Anne, were Lutherans (the first George could not speak English) at a time when Anglicans were growing increasingly cool about their continental sister churches of the Reformation. The later outworking of this theme belongs to the next period of Anglican history.

Bishops and Anglican identity

During the interregnum (Commonwealth), while the dispossessed church leadership at home tended to feebleness and despondency, Anglicans abroad (in communion with the French Protestants near Paris as it happens) planned a come-back. Theirs was a never-again mentality. When Anglicanism was restored, it would be rigorous, uncompromising and distinct. Loopholes that had occasionally permitted non-episcopally ordained clergy to minister would be closed. From this point onwards there is a strengthening of the divine right of bishops rather than of

15

kings – an insistence on the threefold ministry of bishops, priests and deacons in historic succession. The Book of Common Prayer of 1662 was bold to say, in the Preface to the Ordinal (as the ordinals of 1549 and 1552 had said before it), that the threefold ministry had existed since the apostles and was clear in the pages of the New Testament. But 1662 added that to have received episcopal ordination or consecration was an inflexible condition of anyone being taken to be a bishop, priest or deacon.

The shift of the centre of gravity from king to bishop (from an Erastian to an apostolic model of ecclesial identity: Avis, 1989) had important implications for Anglicanism generally and for the national church in England. First, it enabled Anglicanism to spread under the leadership of missionary bishops to almost all parts of the globe. The particular churches of the British Empire could eventually coalesce into a worldwide communion under the presidency of the Archbishop of Canterbury. Thus it was possible for autonomous indigenous churches to join in a fellowship that was – at least in theory – independent of political issues.

Second, the move from the Erastian to the apostolic paradigm made space for the emergence of religious pluralism. 'If the Church of England was the territorial church of a godly prince then her claim to be the national church was well-founded; but if the Church of England was constituted by her bishops, why should she be coterminous with the realm of England?' (Spurr 1991, 106).

The Church of England and other churches

During this period Rome continued to be regarded as the enemy and Anglican apologists – however 'high' like Archbishop Laud – engaged in voluminous controversy with Roman claims – especially those of infallibility and universal jurisdiction. The Laudians, however, ceased to regard Rome as Antichrist: she was a sister church, through erring. In the early eighteenth century Archbishop William Wake had friendly contact with the Gallican church (the Roman Catholic church in France), which he hoped to prise from Roman jurisdiction and into an alliance with the Church of England, and with the Reformed in Geneva. With regard to Rome, Wake stated: 'we do confess the Church of Rome to be a part of the true church, tho [sic] indeed we think her one of the worst . . . we do with all our hearts desire a union with her; and in effect do show it as far as we are able, by retaining whatever we can of the same doctrines and practices with her.' With regard to foreign Protestants, Wake began from the fundamentals of the faith held in common and from an assessment of protestant ministries abroad as authentic but incomplete.

Consensus and schism

Looking back on the seventeenth century, an observer commented that the Church of England had been crucified between two thieves – papists and puritans. Between them these rival forces had almost made an end of the Church of England. Both threats were dealt with in 1660–89. The papal threat was removed by the flight of James II, the invitation to the Protestant William of Orange and the securing of the Protestant succession thereafter. The puritan threat was resolved in two stages, first by the Restoration of crown and church in 1660 and then by the Act of Uniformity of 1662 in which up to two thousand clergy who could not accept the Book of Common Prayer were removed in 'the great ejection', thus radically changing the nature of English Nonconformity. Alongside the Independents, the Baptists and the Quakers, there now stood a substantial body of moderate, scholarly, responsible and often extremely able ministers and their congregations. The Church of England was narrowing its definition and impoverishing its life.

Naturally it was now a good deal easier for Anglicans to agree among themselves! It is broadly true that (with one important exception) there was a general consensus as to the nature of Anglicanism until the 1840s and the emergence of the radical wing of the Oxford Movement. Milton finds a unified 'Anglican' position in the high Elizabethan period; Davies in the Jacobean church; Spurr in the Restoration theology of the 1660s. Then, claims Spurr, the Church of England knew where it stood vis-à-vis both Rome and foreign Protestants, and it had a secure status at home, defined by twin loyalties to the bishop and the king (1991: 107, 399). Walsh and Taylor have pointed to 'the existence of massive Anglican consensus and solidarity in the eighteenth century church':

> On the eve of the Oxford Movement the centripetal forces within the Church were still vastly more powerful than the centrifugal. At the parochial level, Anglicanism drew on a massive, unreflecting attachment to the established Church as the Church of the nation, rooted in English history. Its intelligentsia was seldom riven into rival factions. Under George II and George III the Church of England may or may not have been a Latitudinarian Church, but it was certainly a broad Church . . . the forces making for consensus greatly outweighed those making for conflict. (Walsh and Taylor in Walsh, Haydon and Taylor (eds.) 1993, 51f.)

According to this broad consensus which extended from the end of the sixteenth to the middle of the nineteenth century, the Church of England was both Catholic and Reformed. The Bible was the paramount standard of doctrine, though early tradition was valued and reason and the moral sense had their part to play. The threefold ministry in historic succession was upheld, though it was not regarded as necessary to the existence of a church (of the *esse*). The Church of England was the Christian, catholic church in the land – the only one. Though we can identify groupings of churchmen and theologians to whom we give the anachronistic labels of 'liberal Protestant', 'liberal Catholic' and 'High Church', they did not as a rule see themselves as rival power-centres of the church. The network of influence, friendship and collaboration transcended such differences of emphasis. The distinct 'parties' of nineteenth- and twentieth-century Anglicanism existed only in a very embryonic sense, if at all. Members of the Church of England, especially the bishops and parish clergy, owed implicit allegiance to their lawful sovereign who remained Supreme Governor of the church and appointed the bishops and other dignitaries. But during the seventeenth century royal dynasties changed with bewildering regularity. Churchmen as a whole were fairly pragmatic about adapting from one regime to another.

The exception was the Nonjurors. Bound by their oath of allegiance and obedience to King James II, they could not compose their consciences to accepting William of Orange in 1688–9. The Archbishop of Canterbury, Sancroft, eight other bishops and 400 clergy went into the wilderness, being deprived by statute. Since this had been performed without proper ecclesiastical process, the more scrupulous conforming clergy refused to occupy the vacant sees and other offices. The Nonjurors constitute a High-Church ejection parallel to the nonconforming ejection of 1662. In isolation, the Nonjurors tended towards more extreme ecclesiology and liturgical practices. Though they consecrated their own continuing episcopate, in contact with the exiled James II, the Nonjuring schism had virtually disappeared by the end of the eighteenth century, through absorption back into the Established Church where it strengthened the High Church tradition.

In spite of the overarching consensus, the origins of ecclesiastical 'parties' of rival 'churchmanship' can be detected in this period. The High Churchmen exalted bishops, apostolic succession and the grace of sacraments to fill the vacuum created by loss of the grace of monarchy. The Broad Churchmen drew on the Platonic tradition in philosophy in the first part of this period and were receptive to the outlook of the Enlightenment in the second half, stressing reason, morality and good sense. In the eighteenth century a further strand was added to the Anglican spectrum – the evangelicals, divided between the Methodists, who eventually moved outside the Church of England, and the evangelical Anglicans, who remained within her structures, though finding greater scope for their missionary and charitable activities in the numerous voluntary societies that began to burgeon in this period. Evangelicals combined loyalty to the Reformation heritage (justification by faith, the priesthood of all believers and the primacy of Scripture) with a new stress on subjectivity (conversion as an emotional experience and sanctification as a purifying of the religious affections).

Scotland, Wales and Ireland

Archbishop Laud's attempts to impose the Prayer Book turned Scotland decisively against Charles I and Anglicanism, and in 1638 episcopacy was abolished in Scotland. The standards of doctrine and worship produced by the Westminster Assembly, which were intended for the whole of Britain, were applied in Scotland. There was an Anglican interlude between the Restoration in 1660 and the Revolution, when the Church of Scotland became presbyterian for good (1690).

The Welsh church suffered from neglect, poverty and the rival attractions of nonconformity throughout this period, reaching its lowest ebb early in the nineteenth century – though this was countered by Methodist influence which was contained within Anglicanism until the nineteenth century. Anglicanism in Ireland was distinguished by such prelates as Archbishop Bramhall and Bishop Jeremy Taylor but remained a minority allegiance with vastly disproportionate privileges.

Primary sources

The Book of Common Prayer 1662.

The Library of Anglo-Catholic Theology (Oxford: Parker, 1840s).

J. P. Kenyon, 1966. *The Stuart Constitution 1603–1688: Documents and Commentary* (Cambridge: Cambridge University Press).

P. E. More and F. L. Cross (eds.), 1935. *Anglicanism: The Thought and Practice of the Church of England Illustrated from the Religious Literature of the Seventeenth Century* (London: SPCK).

Secondary studies

P. Avis, 1989. *Anglicanism and the Christian Church: Theological Resources in Historical Perspective* (Edinburgh: T. & T. Clark; Philadelphia: Fortress Press), part 2.

G. R. Cragg, 1960. *The Church and the Age of Reason 1648–1789* (Harmondsworth: Penguin).

J. Davies, 1992. *The Caroline Captivity of the Church: Charles I and the Re-moulding of Anglicanism 1625–1641* (Oxford: Clarendon Press).

K. Fincham (ed.), 1993. *The Early Stuart Church* (London: Macmillan).

H. R. McAdoo, 1965. *The Spirit of Anglicanism: A Survey of Anglican Theological Method in the Seventeenth Century* (London: Black).

J. Spurr, 1991. *The Restoration Church of England 1646–1689* (New Haven and London: Yale University Press).

J. Walsh, C. Haydon and S. Taylor (eds.), 1993. *The Church of England c. 1689–c. 1833: From Toleration to Tractarianism* (Cambridge: Cambridge University Press).

FROM THE OXFORD MOVEMENT TO THE PRESENT

The character of Tractarianism

The Oxford Movement began in a blaze of indignation as the reforming Whig government of the late 1820s and early 1830s abolished the civil disabilities of Nonconformists and Roman Catholics and proceeded to liquidate some superfluous bishoprics of the Irish church. Like Cromwell's martyrdom of King Charles, the Whigs were laying profane hands on the Lord's anointed. The Tractarians appealed in vain for William IV to honour his coronation oath and defend the Irish church. As we have seen, there is a consistent pattern running through these two centuries: the failure of the monarch and the consequent turn to the bishop as the sacred symbol of Anglicanism. The progressive distancing of crown and church, which had been fundamental to the existence of a free and reformed church in England, proved traumatic for Anglicanism.

In 1833, despairing of the crown and Parliament, Keble preached on national apostasy while Newman, in the first of the *Tracts for the Times*, called upon the bishops to 'magnify their office' and to lay down their lives, if necessary, for the salvation of the Church. In Tract 4 Keble denied ordination to all Nonconformist ministries and asserted that only in the Church of England, within these shores, could salvation be securely found. The successors of Keble and Newman, the Anglo-Catholics of the late nineteenth and early twentieth centuries, were notorious for combining an uncompromising insistence on 'apostolic succession' with a tendency to indulge in canonical disobedience towards their own bishops. Then as now, they exalted episcopacy but were selective about which bishops they chose to follow.

The Oxford Movement is clearly a watershed in modern Anglicanism and has left an indelible impression on all parts of the Church of England. Tractarianism was a fusion of reactionary traditionalism, in continuity with the old High Church position – hostility towards Nonconformity,

Roman Catholicism, democracy, biblical criticism and the aspirations of the laity – with the intense subjectivity of the Romantic movement, principally in literature. But the Oxford Movement was far from monolithic and contained a range of positions defined by a felt affinity or antipathy towards the Reformation and the Roman Catholic Church respectively. Conversions to Rome and an interest in religious ceremonial, especially vestments, are often assumed to be typical of Tractarianism. In fact a steady continuance in Prayer Book services and pastoral ministry, a sense of affinity with the early Fathers of the Church, and an implacable aversion to Rome and to theological and political liberalism were more characteristic. Keble, not Newman, is the archetypal Tractarian. Fascination with matters of ritual, especially of a baroque Latin variety, came with Anglo-Catholicism in the last quarter of the nineteenth century, whose attitude towards Rome (in spite of – or perhaps because of – the dogmas of the Immaculate Conception and Papal Infallibility) was much more ambivalent than that of the majority of Tractarians themselves.

The more militant wing of the Oxford Movement vowed to 'unprotestantize' the Church of England. In the second half of the sixteenth century and the first quarter of the seventeenth the Church of England was one Protestant church among others. From the Restoration onwards there was agreement that she was a reformed Catholic church, though marked off from most Lutherans and the Reformed by her threefold ministry in historic succession. The Oxford Movement distanced the church from continental Protestants who lacked the historic episcopate; privileged tradition over Scripture ('The Church to teach, the Bible to prove'); and (on the whole) took a jaundiced view of the Reformation.

The Oxford Movement and its aftermath, the Catholic revival, saw the greatest release of consecrated spiritual energy since the Wesleys and Whitefield led the religious revival of the mid-eighteenth century. It carried Anglicanism, as an apostolic, missionary church, rather than as an arm of the church by law established, to the far corners of the earth. It achieved all this, however, at the expense of damaging relations with the free churches in England and widening the gap between Anglicanism and the great world Protestant communions.

The Anglican Communion

By the mid-nineteenth century the Church of England had become the mother church of a family of autonomous churches throughout the Empire. In 1867 the Archbishop of Canterbury invited the bishops of those churches to take counsel with him at Lambeth Palace – the decennial Lambeth Conferences were born. The Conference of 1888

21

made a permanent contribution to Anglican identity when it approved an adapted version of the Chicago Quadrilateral which the (then Protestant) Episcopal Church of the USA had produced two years earlier. The Lambeth Quadrilateral laid down four conditions for the reunion of the churches: the Bible, the Apostles' and Niceno-Constantinopolitan Creeds, the two dominical sacraments, and the historic episcopate, locally adapted to varying circumstances. The Conference of 1920 further promoted unity by issuing its 'Appeal to All Christian People', which significantly described all those who had undergone trinitarian baptism as members of the Christian Church. In the conjunction of the Quadrilateral and the Appeal we see the distinction, so important to Anglican ecumenism, between the conditions necessary to mutual recognition of churches (essentially the ministry of word and sacrament, with agreement in faith implied) and the further conditions necessary to visible unity (the historic episcopate in some form leading to unified episcopal oversight). Finally, Lambeth 1948 gave a classical definition of the Anglican understanding of authority as dispersed and distributed rather than centralized, as 'moral and spiritual, resting on the truth of the Gospel, and a charity which is patient and willing to defer to the common mind'.

Scotland, Wales and Ireland

The Episcopal Church in Scotland derives from those who held on to episcopacy in 1690. It is a minority church and is not established. The Primus presides among its bishops. Approaches to unity between the Episcopal Church and the Church of Scotland have so far proved abortive. In Wales, Nonconformists comprised three-quarters of the church-going population by the mid-nineteenth century, but Anglicanism strengthened its position somewhat after that. The Welsh church was finally disestablished and disendowed in 1920 and has since become more indigenous. Its six dioceses are presided over by the Archbishop of Wales. The Irish church, reduced to two provinces in 1833, was disestablished in 1869. The Anglican churches of the British Isles are of course all member churches of the Anglican Communion and are increasingly cooperating together, especially in ecumenical matters.

Ecumenical perspectives

The Second Vatican Council (1962–5) for the first time encouraged Roman Catholics to participate fully in the ecumenical movement for the reunion of the churches. Archbishop Michael Ramsey immediately sought to capitalize on this change of attitude and, together with Pope Paul VI, set up the Anglican–Roman Catholic International Commission which published the fruits of its first phase of work in 1982. Ramsey also attempted to lead a reunion of the Church of England and the Methodist Church, but was thwarted by resistance among the Anglican clergy.

Ecumenical efforts in the 1980s and 90s presuppose a broader concept of apostolicity than that traditionally defended by Anglo-Catholics. Following the Lima Statement of the World Council of Churches in 1982, *Baptism, Eucharist and Ministry*, apostolicity is defined as a steadfast intention to remain faithful through all historical vicissitudes to the apostolic foundation of the Church, rather than as a tactile succession of the laying on of hands from one bishop to another in an unbroken sequence of consecrations and ordinations going back, as it is supposed, to the apostles themselves. The first fruit of this ecumenical theology was seen in the approval of the Porvoo Declaration by the General Synod in 1995, bringing the Church of England (together with the other British Anglican churches) into communion and visible unity with the Nordic and Baltic Lutheran episcopal churches as and when they also approve it. In 1995–6 fresh approaches were being initiated between the Church of England and the Methodist and United Reformed Churches separately.

Theological changes

Radical, heterodox theology had flourished in the eighteenth century, drawing upon Socinianism and the deism and secularism of the Enlightenment. It had reared its head within the established church but had been firmly rebutted. A new receptivity to progressive theological ideas, and in particular to biblical criticism, was signalled by *Essays and Reviews* in 1860. It gradually became respectable after the thoroughly orthodox and conventional contributors to the Anglo-Catholic symposium *Lux Mundi* in 1889, led by Charles Gore, accepted the theory of evolution, German biblical scholarship and German idealist philosophy. As a result, Gore and his company abandoned biblical inerrancy and the traditional understanding of the incarnation which had left Jesus in possession of the divine attribute of omniscience. As Liddon, the heir of the leading Tractarian Pusey, lamented, the floodgates of criticism were now open, and who knew where the process of questioning traditional assumptions would lead?

In fact the line of enquiry, opened up with an entirely orthodox intention by Gore and his colleagues, was taken further in the symposium *Foundations* (1912), to which the young William Temple was a contributor, and in *Essays Catholic and Critical* (1926). A more radical challenge to orthodoxy was mounted by the Modernist movement (not to be confused with Roman Catholic Modernism at the beginning of the century) which came to a head in 1920. In Gore and company, the doctrine of divine immanence had been balanced by that of divine transcendence, but the Modernists, led by H. D. A. Major, Bethune Baker and Hastings Rashdall, advocated a radical immanentism which postulated no qualitative difference between divinity and humanity, creator and creation. Both Gore and Temple, who had been regarded as dangerously radical young men, now emerged as guardians of orthodoxy. Following the 1920 clash between Gore and Rashdall, the archbishops set up a representative commission on Christian doctrine which reported in 1938. Though essentially orthodox, it reveals a remarkable hospitality to symbolic interpretations. The chairman's introduction by William Temple (then at York) is of particular interest.

Later episodes were tame by comparison, though the alarmist response suggested that the church and its leaders had very short memories. In 1963 John Robinson, Suffragan Bishop of Woolwich, published *Honest to God*, which caused a sensation and became a best-seller. Robinson concocted a jejune mixture of misappropriated Bonhoeffer and boiled-down Tillich in order to challenge childish images of God. The report of the Doctrine Commission in 1976, *Christian Believing* is a useful compendium of the liberal consensus in Anglican theology at the time. (In 1978 the calculated challenge to orthodoxy *The Myth of God Incarnate* was not peculiar to Anglicanism, being edited by the Reformed theologian John Hick, though distinguished Anglican theologians contributed.) In 1984 the new Bishop of Durham, David Jenkins, was wrong-footed by the media into discussing the doctrines of the creed as though he were conducting a seminar with rather raw undergraduates who needed to be shocked into thinking for themselves. However, both Robinson and Jenkins found an appreciative audience well beyond regular Anglican church-goers and succeeded in getting Christian beliefs discussed wherever two or three agnostics were gathered together.

World War and secularization

In the twentieth century the Church of England has lost ground to secularization. Attendance at the parish church is now down to a few percent of the population. The utterances of bishops are seldom thought newsworthy, and only the two archbishops can still be sure of a hearing in the nation. The parish clergy, though usually enjoying respect and affection in their communities, are stereotyped figures of fun in the media. Blunders by the church and its leaders are exposed mercilessly (though so also are those of politicians, show-business 'personalities' and royalty). However, common religion remains strong (except perhaps in the inner cities), central Christian beliefs are held by two-thirds of the population, and the Church of England promotes its mission by offering its ministry to all who will receive it. The occasional offices (baptism, confirmation, marriage and funerals), together with special religious festivals (such as Remembrance Sunday, Harvest Festival and Christmas carol services and so-called Midnight Mass) bring many who are not regular worshippers into contact with the Church and its gospel. The pastoral and educational work of the Church of England is strong in church schools, colleges and universities, the independent preparatory and public schools, hospitals, prisons and the armed services.

Both world wars tended to discredit the church. The immense sufferings of humanity demanded a profound and sophisticated theodicy (i.e. justification of the goodness of God in the face of evil) which, in the absence of serious attention to systematic theology in its theological education, the Church of England lacked. The church's attitude towards the First World War was tainted by jingoism. In the Second, the Church of England briefly enjoyed the leadership of William Temple and was able to make a notable contribution to the reconstruction of the social fabric, the international order and the ecumenical movement. The religious revivals that attended the wars and their immediate aftermath were not sustained. The patriarchal and paternalistic ethos and structures of English Anglicanism soon seemed to belong to a bygone age.

Liturgical changes

The Book of Common Prayer of 1662 had proved inadequate to the needs of the church for half a century before the 1928 revision, rejected by Parliament but approved by church authority, offered some alternatives and in the matter of Holy Communion moved full circle to something not very different to Cranmer's 1549 book. Decades of experiment in the 1960s and 70s led to the *Alternative Service Book 1980*, which introduced multiple choices and an attempt at a modern linguistic idiom into the church's liturgy. Before the ASB had been in use for very long, its sexist language began to jar as the more moderate insights of feminist theology made their impact. For the year 2000 the church proposes a core liturgy with greater uniformity in essentials and more imaginative language.

After more than twenty years of argument and debate the ordination of women priests was approved by the General Synod in 1992, and the first ordinations followed in 1994. This measure only obtained the necessary two-thirds majority in each House voting separately because it had attached to it an Act of Synod, permitting a sort of internal schism for those who could not in conscience accept women priests, and which was reluctantly accepted by the Synod as the lesser of two evils.

In the 1990s, financial stringency and falling numbers of ordinands (except for Evangelical candidates) began to put a severe strain on the time-honoured parochial system that enabled the church to offer its ministry to the whole nation.

Internal distinctions

In the middle of the twentieth century Evangelicals became marginalized for lack of scholarship and statesmanship until the 1980s, while Anglo-Catholicism reached its peak of influence and confidence in the great scholarly Congresses between the wars. Anglican Catholics, split over the ordination of women, have been further weakened by secessions to Rome. The liberal-ecumenical strand of the Church of England reached its highest point with the primacies of William Temple at York and then Canterbury. In the 1960s theological liberalism began to become critical and iconoclastic, and it no longer exists as a distinct position in the church. This is no doubt because the liberal contribution has been absorbed into the other strands, making for liberal Catholicism (Gore, Temple, Ramsey) and liberal Evangelicalism (S. Neill, Coggan, Carey). One of the most important achievements of liberalism may have been its championing of women's ordination and its success in persuading non-liberals to accept this.

It is arguable that each of the great internal traditions of English Anglicanism – Catholic, Evangelical and liberal – has had its distinctive contribution accepted into the mainstream. Catholic sacramentalism, asceticism, insistence on the historic episcopate and regard for tradition; Evangelical emphasis on the centrality of Scripture, justification by faith and the royal priesthood of all believers; liberal openness to scholarly enquiry into the title deeds of the Church (the Bible, the Fathers and the creeds), acceptance of biblical criticism, receptiveness to secular insights, and the ecumenical outlook – all these have ceased to be identified with one strand of churchmanship and have become the common heritage of Anglicans, not just in England but worldwide, though there are sizeable pockets of die-hard Anglo-Catholicism, conservative Evangelicalism and old-fashioned liberalism that stand apart from the growing consensus.

Primary sources

Anglican–Roman Catholic International Commission, 1982. *The Final Report* (London: CTS/SPCK).

O. Chadwick (ed.), 1960. *The Mind of the Oxford Movement* (London: Black).

R. Coleman (ed.), 1992. *Resolutions of the Twelve Lambeth Conferences 1867–1988* (Toronto: Anglican Book Centre).

Commission on Christian Doctrine Appointed by the Archbishops of Canterbury and York in 1922, 1938. *Doctrine in the Church of England* (London: SPCK).

Doctrine Commission of the Church of England, 1976. *Christian Believing: The Nature of the Christian Faith and its Expression in Holy Scripture and the Creeds* (London: SPCK).

Together in Mission and Ministry: The Porvoo Common Statement with Essays on Church and Ministry in Northern Europe, 1993. (London: Church House Publishing).

Secondary studies

P. Avis, 1989. *Anglicanism and the Christian Church: Theological Resources in Historical Perspective* (Edinburgh: T. & T. Clark; Philadelphia: Fortress Press), part 3.

O. Chadwick, 1970. *The Victorian Church*, 2 vols. (Cambridge: Cambridge University Press).

K. W. Clements, 1988. *Lovers of Discord: Twentieth Century Theological Controversies in England* (London: SPCK).

I. Clutterbuck, 1993. *Marginal Catholics* (Leominster: Gracewing).

G. Davie, 1994. *Religion in Britain since 1945: Believing without Belonging* (Oxford: Blackwell).

A. Hastings, 1986. *A History of English Christianity 1920–1985* (London: Collins).

P. B. Nockles, 1994. *The Oxford Movement in Context: Anglican High Churchmanship 1760–1857* (Cambridge: Cambridge University Press).

A. M. Ramsey, 1960. *From Gore to Temple* (London: Longmans).

G. Rowell, 1983. *The Vision Glorious: Themes and Personalities of the Catholic Revival in Anglicanism* (Oxford: Oxford University Press).

J. H. L. Rowlands, 1989. *Church, State and Society: The Attitudes of J. Keble, R. H. Froude and J. H. Newman 1827–1845* (Worthing: Churchman).

W. Sachs, 1993. *The Transformation of Anglicanism: From State Church to Global Communion* (Cambridge: Cambridge University Press).

A. M. G. Stephenson, 1978. *Anglicanism and the Lambeth Conferences* (London: SPCK).

A. Vidler, 1961. *The Church in an Age of Revolution* (Harmondsworth: Penguin).

A. Wilkinson, 1978. *The Church of England and the First World War* (London: SPCK).

UNITED STATES OF AMERICA

R. William Franklin

The origins of the Episcopal Church in the United States of America lie in a convulsion of church history, the Age of Revolution, the period from the American Revolution to the war of 1812. In retrospect, the late seventeenth century and the early eighteenth century had been a placid age of American Anglicanism, not unlike the later period from 1945 to 1965, a time of growth, prosperity and peace.

An Anglican church establishment had been settled in the Virginia colony from 1607, and in due course similar Anglican establishments would be erected in the colonies of Maryland, the Carolinas, New York and Georgia. By 1720 there were forty-four parishes in the twenty-nine counties of Virginia, each with a church and some of the larger ones with chapels of ease, so that the total number of Anglican places of worship in the colony was about seventy. A Virginia parish was some-times 60 miles long, with little spiritual coherence for the isolated priest who was charged with care of the disparate Anglican population. There was a relaxed Southern piety evident here, without the disciplinary power of the Puritan institutions which dominated the New England colonies to the north in Massachusetts and Connecticut.

The earliest American Anglican theological work of substance was directed against this Southern situation. It was Alexander Whitaker's *Good Newes from Virginia* published in 1613. Virginia's greatest early theologian, who had prepared Pocahontas for baptism, was the son of William Whitaker, Master of Saint John's College and Regius Professor of Divinity at the University of Cambridge, one of England's most out-spoken predestinarians. This is also the theological position of *Good Newes*: the leaders of the Virginia Company are declared to be 'miserable covetous men', while the colonists themselves were said to be drawn 'from the dregs of society'. Too many, Whitaker said, 'had not been reconciled to God nor approved of by Him'. For reasons not difficult to imagine, neither this theology nor the Church of England had a hold on the wild, sparsely settled and ill-governed expanses of early Virginia or the other Southern colonies.

However, the Anglican constituency in Puritan New England was growing in the late seventeenth and the early eighteenth centuries. In Boston in 1723, Christ Church was opened for worship, the famous 'North Church' of Paul Revere's ride. Trinity Church was built in Boston in 1735 on a still larger scale, and these parishes, along with King's Chapel, founded in the Puritan capital in 1686, showed considerable theological vitality until they were disrupted by the Revolutionary War and the departure of Loyalist Tories for Canada to the north. The Church of England – with its broad and liberal rationalism, its freedom from a strict moral code and narrow discipline, and with its dignified liturgical worship and music – became an attractive haven from Puritanism to Americans of the northern colonies.

Such attitudes lay behind the 'great apostasy' of 1722 in Connecticut, in which a group of Yale College graduates, who had been reading Anglican divinity in works given to the Yale library by English patrons, began to have serious doubts about the validity of their presbyteral ordination at the hands of the American Puritans, and they proceeded to England for ordination by Church of England bishops. They returned to New England in 1723 and formed the core of Society for the Propagation of the Gospel (SPG) missionaries to the region, the SPG founded by Parliament in 1649 for the purpose of planting Christian missions in the English colonies. By 1742 there were fourteen Anglican churches and seven priests in the Connecticut colony; by 1760, thirty parishes and fourteen clergy. Though these Yale-educated priests were to contribute significantly to the creation of the Protestant Episcopal Church in the United States, they were committed primarily to the High Church cause in the American colonies, and its attitudes about what the Church should be: the importance of the historic episcopate and the necessity of episcopal ordination for valid ministry, and the centrality of the sacraments to the life of faith, baptismal regeneration and the real presence of Christ in the holy eucharist, with some emphasis also on the sacrificial dimension of the eucharist.

Among these Yale converts to Anglicanism was Samuel Seabury, who became an SPG missionary in New London, Connecticut. His son, Samuel Seabury, Jr, also became an SPG missionary in New York, and after the American Revolution, he was elected the first Anglican bishop in the former colonies at a convocation of the clergy of Connecticut, and dispatched to seek consecration in the line of the historic episcopate in England or Scotland. Rebuffed in England, Seabury was eventually consecrated by bishops of the Episcopal Church of Scotland on 14 November 1784, and he returned soon after as the first Anglican bishop in the United States, fulfilling now a persistent goal of the Society for the Propagation of the Gospel in the American colonies since the seventeenth century: to secure episcopacy for the vast unsettled continent.

But now in the last two decades of the eighteenth century the reversal of Anglican fortunes on the American continent was to be unprecedented in Christian history, and perhaps no church, until the Russian Revolution, would suffer as extensive deprivations in the aftermath of social and political upheaval as did the Church of England in America – stripped by war of clergy, schools, finances and prestige. In the South the American revolutionaries disestablished the church, and in Virginia the government seized most of its property. Anglicanism, with its hierarchical ministry, its formal services and prescribed liturgy, seemed to reflect a fading European image of a vanished era, destined, like warfare, to disappear with the last of the eighteenth-century generation and the dawn of a new era of American enlightenment.

In New England the most influential Anglican church – King's Chapel in Boston – moved toward a liberal faith that would abandon the corruptions of European Christianity and dramatically recast Anglicanism in a radical American form that would embrace the toleration and the enterprise of the American citizenry. But despite these bright hopes, the Unitarianism of King's Chapel after 1785 would remain essentially the religion of one region and one class, so much so that the Unitarian was said to believe, at most, in 'the Fatherhood of God, the Brotherhood of Man, and the Neighborhood of Boston'.

In the former colonies of the South by 1784 the Evangelical Revival had led to the formation of the separate Methodist denomination. But despite its later quickening influence elsewhere, American Evangelicalism never really receded as a regional expression of Christianity in the South, to the point that during the last days of the American Civil War, a Mississippi Methodist preacher could exhort his compatriots on the identity of the Southern character with the Evangelical cause: 'If we cannot gain our political freedom from the North, let us at least continue to establish our mental and our spiritual independence in our Evangelical way.'

In this revolutionary period, then, the unique contribution of those Anglicans who cast their lot with the Protestant Episcopal Church – at a meeting of the clergy of Maryland in 1783 the Protestant Episcopal Church in the United States of America was declared to exist – was to create a religious body comprehensive enough to encompass an entire nation: North and South, black and white, saints and sinners, beginners and mature Christians. By 1792 the Episcopal Church had quickly created a series of institutions that successfully transferred to the American continent the old English ideal of the church as an entire nation on its knees. These were:

(1) a united episcopate which joined in one the historic lines of episcopal succession from Scotland and England;

(2) an American version of the Book of Common Prayer which was capable of balancing the varied needs of local congregations with the aims of a new national community;

(3) a federal system of church government that in a remarkable way adapted episcopacy to a democratic society in two ways:
    (a) each state a diocese presided over by a bishop corresponding to the secular state governor, and
    (b) a General Convention corresponding to the national Congress.

This great achievement – historic episcopate and prayer-book liturgy adapted to the spirit of American democracy – was essentially the work of one man, William White, 1748–1836, first citizen of Philadelphia after Benjamin Franklin, first Bishop of Pennsylvania, the central figure in the Episcopal Church in its first half century. William White had an immense capacity for work, friendship and toleration. He developed a practical model of episcopacy, and of the office of Presiding Bishop, of which he was the first distinguished occupant, which allowed him to retain the good will and even the affection of those with whom he disagreed, and as Presiding Bishop, White provided the founding apologetic for the Protestant Episcopal Church in the United States: that despite the preservation of the apostolic understanding and authority of the historic episcopate, the government of this branch of Anglicanism was actually rooted in democratic principles and for that reason is perfectly compatible to American society. Bishop White was thus able to convince Americans that the principles of the English sixteenth-century theologians who really created the interior world of Anglicanism could be legitimately transferred to a new shore and to a new national character, despite the breach with Great Britain brought about by the American Revolution: the primary authority of Scripture interpreted within the historical teaching and public practice of the on-going Church by a General Convention made up of representatives of each order of the Church, including the laity, the Church possessed of some kind of fidelity and rightness in discerning Christian truth when it meets as the General Convention, which leads out through the exercise of the gift of reason and in the light of new developments in knowledge to a deeper understanding of the truths of the gospel.

As a response to the American Revolution William White published in 1782 at the age of thirty-four his *The Case for the Episcopal Church in the United States Considered*, which became the blueprint of the organization of the infant Protestant Episcopal Church at the first two General Conventions of 1785 and 1789. Prior to this, White had written no other work for publication, and he was little known outside of his native Philadelphia. He defined in this one brief essay what he conceived to be the true conception of the Church catholic, the complete development of the Anglican ecclesiastical idea as it had emerged by the eighteenth century, and the essential elements of the identity which he hoped would continue to characterize the Episcopal Church into the nineteenth century.

The significance of William White's plan outlined in 1782 and achieved by 1792 was that he developed both a theological and a practical model of Christianity that could keep in tension, keep in balance, two polarities: the Catholic structure and authority of a historic faith and Christian liberty. What Bishop White intended to do was to hold together a particular tension:

(1) in which the primary authority of Scripture could be recognized;
(2) but always as that was interpreted within
   (a) the historical teaching, and
   (b) the public practice of the on-going Church.

But as a man of the eighteenth century, as a child of the English Reformation and of its first great theologian, Richard Hooker, there was also an important place for reason in White's *The Case for the Episcopal Church*. The function of reason was to determine how Scripture and the Catholic tradition have authority for us, and here White gave us two 'nots':

(1) not to use Scripture and tradition as proof-texts; but
(2) not to dismiss them altogether.

Some things in Scripture and tradition have authority for us, and some do not. This determination is made through reasonable dialogue in the community of faith, the community of faith defined as the General Convention of the Episcopal Church, whose political structures bring bishops, priests and laity into a graced conversation where the future parameters of the Christian life are determined.

By the year 1811, however, the American church began clearly to divide into two parties, one Evangelical and the other High Church. In that year Alexander Griswold (1776–1843) was consecrated bishop of the 'Eastern District', which included all of New England, except Connecticut. Bishop Griswold experienced something like a conversion at the time of his consecration, and he became a dynamic preacher of experiential Christianity all along the upper Eastern Seaboard. This same message of conversion and moral renewal was carried into the interior of the continent by Bishop Philander Chase (1775–1852), Bishop of Ohio and later Bishop of Illinois. The Dioceses of Virginia, Ohio, Rhode Island and Tennessee became the core of an American Anglican Evangelical axis.

These nineteenth-century Anglicans shared much with Evangelicals of other Protestant denominations: justification by faith, the necessity of the experience of regeneration, as well as the primary authority of Scripture, were the keystones of their theology. In practical parochial life confirmation was conjoined to an experience of conversion, revival meetings were encouraged to lead parishioners to the experience of conversion, and extemporaneous prayer within worship and special Wednesday night prayer meetings for devotional exercise were tolerated. The Evangelicals opposed the doctrines of baptismal regeneration, the real presence of Christ in the holy eucharist and the sacrificial dimension of the eucharist, which they believed were all a clear distortion of the Reformation heritage.

It was also in the year 1811 that John Henry Hobart (1775–1830) was elected as Assistant Bishop of New York. The office of bishop in what now was to become America's largest city allowed Hobart quickly to become the leader of the High Church party in the Episcopal Church. Hobart sought a new American Anglican synthesis in which the old-fashioned High Church position of people like Bishop Seabury of Connecticut would be quickened by a passionate evangelistic concern for the Episcopal Church and the special apostolic heritage to which it could lay claim. 'Evangelical Truth and Apostolic Order' were Hobart's famous watchwords, 'Apostolic Faith' perceived in the circumstances of the time by Hobart to be a message of Christian freedom to Evangelical America:

(1) Christians to be freed from the demand to subscribe to an elaborate confessional creed;
(2) Christians to be freed from showing evidence of a conversion experience;
(3) Christians to be freed from following a strict code of rigid social behaviour.

No one can discount the relationship of the articulation of these three freedoms – from confessionalism, from instantaneous conversion, from strict moral code – to the rapid growth of the Episcopal Church in New York City and throughout New York State during the first half of the nineteenth century. The appeal of the Episcopal Church as the only major Protestant non-Evangelical religious body south of Unitarian Massachusetts gave it a great advantage as a socially and theologically acceptable alternative to antebellum Evangelicalism, and for the clarity of the institutional realization of this alternative, in the founding of parishes, the establishment of a national theological seminary in New York City and a new Episcopal college on the western frontier of the diocese, and above all for the practical model of a vigorous American episcopacy in action, we can credit John Henry Hobart.

The reception of the Oxford Movement by the Episcopal Church after 1839 and the impact of the Catholic Revival within Anglicanism on America created a crisis that shattered the unity of the Hobartian vision. Suspicion of Anglican Catholicism and the Tractarian Movement was widespread inside and outside the Episcopal Church. 'Americans believe', in the words of one acid observer in 1844, 'That at some bad place called Oxford, one Pusey . . . and some others, his accomplices, in connection with the Evil one, who is supposed to have had his head-quarters in the Church of England, have been uttering something that Presbyterians, Anabaptists, Unitarians, Universalists and probably Mormons and other "Evangelical Christians" find great difficulty, in their stomachs, in digesting: and that certain abettors of the respectable firm just mentioned, hereabouts, have formed a wicked conspiracy to over-throw and destroy . . . all the religion and liberty of "this our most free, most enlightened, most religious, and most glorious of all nations under heaven".'

Because of bitter division over and suspicion of the teaching of the Oxford Movement in the 1840s, many observers expected a split of the Episcopal Church into separate Catholic and Evangelical denomina-tions. This calamity never happened, but the lives of bishops and priests suffered as they became pawns of the issues and demands of the differ-ent parties in the church as they reacted in a variety of ways to the Anglican Catholic teachings of the Oxford Movement.

The most sensational developments had to do with trials of three of the most important leaders of the early Catholic movement in the Episcopal Church. The General Convention of 1844 accepted the res-ignation of Henry Onderdonk, William White's successor as Bishop of Pennsylvania, and suspended him from the exercise of ministry on moral grounds: Bishop Onderdonk's regular habit of brandy and water had led to occasional instances of public intoxication and indecorous action toward female members of the Diocese of Pennsylvania. In 1852 Bishop George Washington Doane of New Jersey was much harassed in a second trial, though never convicted, for questionable financial dealings in connection with two Episcopal boarding schools he had attempted to found and foster in the diocese.

Most importantly, in 1845 the House of Bishops of the General Convention indefinitely suspended Benjamin Onderdonk, John Henry Hobart's successor as Bishop of New York, on two charges: that he was seen to be publicly 'improperly excited by vinous or spiritous liquors', and that 'at sundry other times he has impurely and unchastely laid his hands upon the bodies of virtuous and respectable ladies of the Diocese of New York'. Because of the vigour with which he had championed the Catholic cause within the Episcopal Church – Bishop Onderdonk was known behind his back as 'the Apostolical Ram' – it was widely suspected that theological faction, not morality, lay behind the suspension.

The atmosphere of harassment and suspicion of all clergy, and the cruel vindictiveness shown to many that followed this incident, dominated the decades through the era of the American Civil War. The tragedy of this time of theological strife, which matched the bitter national division over slavery, was caught in a letter of Bishop Whittingham of Maryland to his wife: 'Never have I so desponded with regard to the Church as I do now . . . What is to become of us who are set as marks for everybody to shoot at, God only knows. Mere innocence can no longer be any man's protection; malice and deceit can break any man down if allowed to work. . . .' A schism finally did disrupt the Episcopal Church in 1873 when Bishop D. G. Cummins of Kentucky led out an Evangelical faction that organized the Reformed Episcopal Church, which held to conservative Evangelical theological positions and specifically rejected the doctrine of baptismal regeneration. More importantly, as the signal of a new post-Civil War era of harmony, was the General Convention's 1874 decision for 'comprehensiveness' precipitated by James DeKoven, an Anglo–Catholic and Ritualist of the Puseyite model, who insisted that he either be tried for heresy for his Catholic teaching and liturgical practices with regard to the holy eucharist, or be left unrestricted by church regulations.

For Episcopalians, the definition of the 'essentials of the one Catholic and Apostolic faith' for purposes of entering into full communion with another Christian body were outlined in 1886 in the Chicago Quadrilateral, subsequently adopted by the entire Anglican Communion at the Lambeth Conference of 1888 and re-stated in a variety of ways by every Lambeth Conference since then.

A central feature of the Episcopal Church as it was understood by

William Reed Huntington (1839–1909), Rector of Grace Church in New York City, the most able theological writer of the liberal Broad Church movement in American Anglicanism after the Civil War, the 'first presbyter of the Church' of his era, and the original proponent of the Quadrilateral in his *The Church Idea* of 1870, was never to act as an exclusive sect, intoxicated, in Huntington's phrase, by 'a fluttering of surplices and the distant vision of church spires, and a somewhat stiff and stately company of deans, prebendaries, and choristers' but rather to act as a branch of the Catholic Church, seeking to bring to ever fuller concreteness the catholicity of the Church and its organic unity. Huntington was inspired by a Catholicism to be completed by what God would do in the future, not a Catholicism imprisoned to past tradition.

Huntington outlined four Catholic essentials necessary to the unity of the Church which God wills: common agreement on Scripture, creeds, and sacraments, and specific achievement of unity on the historic episcopate. Thus the four points of the Quadrilateral proposed by Huntington in 1870, and developed by others through 1886, became:

(1) the Holy Scriptures as the inspired record of God's self-revelation to humanity;

(2) the Apostles' and Nicene Creeds as witnesses to the faith of the Historic Church in its assertion of fundamental Christian truths;

(3) the sacraments of baptism with water, in the name of the Father, and of the Son, and of the Holy Spirit, and the Supper of the Lord, ministered with the unfailing use of Christ's words of institution and the elements ordained by him;

(4) the historic episcopate as fact deeply rooted in Christian history. Acceptance of episcopacy as a basis of reunion meant, for Huntington, accepting it not as a bare fact, but as a fact accompanied by historical meaning.

Huntington defined for the Episcopal Church a twentieth-century mission to the American nation which was to be the gospel imperative of Christian reconciliation on the basis of theological convergence. 'American Christianity', Huntington wrote at the dawn of the new century, 'is languishing today for the lack of a special enthusiasm, the inspiration of a definite purpose. There is certain deadness in the air. . . . But a Church elastic in its methods of work, reverent in its worship, not ambiguous or double-tongued as to its message, but firm in its grasp upon essentials while allowing for the freest play of opinion as to all matters not of the essence of the faith. . . . Such is the Church for which the Republic waits.'

The issue of the role of women in the life of the Church has been the great twentieth-century test of whether or not the Episcopal Church has been 'firm in its grasp upon essentials while allowing for the freest play of opinion as to all matters not of the essence of the faith'. The ordination of women to the priesthood and episcopate of the Episcopal Church has been the culmination of a broadly based twentieth-century movement seeking a representative role for women in the Church. As late as the 1960s, men and women were effectively segregated in their roles of Christian life. Only men could serve in the General Convention – the national church's triennial decision-making body.

In the General Conventions of 1970 and 1973, motions to enable women to be ordained as priest were narrowly defeated. At that point opinion was divided on how next to proceed. A group declared that 'the democratic process, the political dynamics, and the legal guidelines' were 'out of step with the divine imperative which says, now is the time'.

On 29 July 1974, eleven women deacons were ordained to the priesthood of the Episcopal Church in Philadelphia. In a joint statement they answered critics who saw women's ordination as nothing more than an aspect of the women's liberation movement. The women ordained in Philadelphia sought to 'reaffirm and recover the universality of Christ's ministry as symbolized in that order [priesthood]'. Those ordained believed that their action stemmed from their sacramental theology.

Four more women were ordained as priests in Washington, D.C. on 7 September 1975. Then in 1976 the General Convention decided that women could indeed be ordained to the priesthood and episcopate. This ruling, which took effect on 1 January 1977, was a major step in the Episcopal Church's reception of the doctrine that women and men should share equally in all facets of the ordained ministry. By 1987 women made up 39 per cent of the students in the Episcopal seminaries studying for the Master of Divinity degree, the normal academic requirement for ordination in the Episcopal Church.

As women priests became a visible presence among the 2.5 million members of the Episcopal Church, church-goers increasingly asked when they would see the first woman bishop. In September 1985, the House of Bishops passed a resolution expressing its intention not to withhold consent to the election of a bishop on the grounds of gender. Barbara Harris's election on 24 September 1988, as Suffragan Bishop of Massachusetts, was a highly significant sign of increasing acceptance of women's ordination within the Episcopal Church. Election to the episcopate in the Episcopal Church is a long and thorough process. Once the election has taken place in the local diocese, it has to be confirmed by a majority vote in favour by the standing committees and bishops with jurisdiction throughout the Episcopal Church.

Bishop Harris was duly elected by this inclusive process. On 3 January 1989, she received the majority of consents needed from the House of Bishops. She was consecrated on 11 February 1989 as the first woman bishop in the Anglican Communion and the 834th bishop in the episcopal succession brought to the United States by Samuel Seabury from Scotland in 1784.

As the Episcopal Church moved toward these historic actions, from the 1970s its thought was guided by these theological considerations on orders and the place of men and women in the historic ministry of the Church:

(1) the need to take with utmost seriousness the appeal to Scripture and tradition;

(2) the fact that 'the data of Scripture appear divided on the issue' of women in ministry;

(3) that the data of tradition found in the early fathers and the medieval theologians reflect 'biological assumptions about the nature of woman and her relation to man which are considered unacceptable' today; and

(4) that the equality of the sexes demands a presentation of Christian doctrine that would explicitly propose the universality of redemption, the inclusivity of the Church as a priestly body, and women's capacity to represent humanity, the Church, Christ, and God.

Reception of women as bishops and priests is a practice which has become increasingly accepted into the life of the Episcopal Church. Has the ordination of women as bishops and priests been received by the church as a measure of its life in the twentieth century? Certainly not in the four dioceses still extant where the bishop does not ordain women to these orders. Throughout the Anglican Communion the issue still excites considerable and often heated debate. It is difficult, therefore, to claim that the church has received the ordination of women as priests and bishops as a measure of its own life in all parts of the Communion, but we can legitimately claim that the Episcopal Church in the United States is moving in the direction of receiving women's ordination as a legitimate ecclesiological development consistent with a tradition born in a time of revolution and the adjustment of Anglicanism to the new cultural dynamic of democracy.

BIBLIOGRAPHY

Sydney Ahlstrom, 1972. *A Religious History of the American People* (New Haven and London: Yale University Press).

Raymond W. Albright, 1964. *A History of the Protestant Episcopal Church* (New York: Macmillan).

George F. Bragg, 1968. *A History of the Afro-American Group of the Episcopal Church* (New York: Johnson).

Diana Hochstedt Butler, 1995. *Standing Against the Whirlwind: Evangelical Episcopalians in Nineteenth-Century America* (New York and Oxford: Oxford University Press).

E. Clowes Chorley, 1946. *Men and Movements in the American Episcopal Church* (New York: Charles Scribner's Sons).

Arthur Lyon Cross, 1902. *The Anglican Episcopate and the American Colonies* (Cambridge, Mass.: Harvard University Press).

Nathan Hatch, 1989. *The Democratization of American Christianity* (New Haven and London: Yale University Press).

George M. Marsden, 1990. *Religion and American Culture* (San Diego and New York: Harcourt, Brace Jovanovich).

Martin Marty, 1970. *Righteous Empire: The Protestant Experience in America* (New York: Dial).

Robert Bruce Mullin, 1986. *Episcopal Vision/American Reality: High Church Theology and Social Thought in Evangelical America* (New Haven and London: Yale University Press).

Robert W. Prichard, 1991. *A History of the Protestant Episcopal Church* (Wilton, Conn.: Morehouse Barlow).

Robert W. Shoemaker, 1959. *The Origin and Meaning of the Name 'Protestant Episcopal'* (New York: American Church Publications).

David E. Sumner, 1987. *The Episcopal Church's History, 1945–1985* (Wilton, Conn.: Morehouse Barlow).

John F. Woolverton, 1984. *Colonial Anglicanism in North America, 1607–1776* (Detroit: Wayne State University Press).

CANADA

William R. Crockett

Anglicanism took its formative shape in Canada in the colonial period as a British loyalist church. Its first three bishops, Charles Inglis of Nova Scotia, Jacob Mountain of Quebec, and John Strachan of Ontario, dreamt of the establishment of Anglicanism in Canada and played a significant role in the founding of institutions for higher education in their regions. Anglican theology in Canada during the first half of the nineteenth century was a redemptive theology inherited from classical Anglicanism set within an intellectual framework influenced both by eighteenth-century English natural theology and by Scottish 'common sense' philosophy.[1] This outlook is exemplified in the thought of John Strachan, first Bishop of Toronto, and by James Beaven, who was Strachan's choice as professor of divinity at the newly founded King's College opened in Toronto in 1843.

The basic assumption of eighteenth-century natural theology, typified in the writings of William Paley, is that there is an overall design and structure to the natural world as created by God. Strachan united this rational worldview inherited from natural theology with a theology of redemption rooted in the eighteenth-century Anglican High Church tradition before the rise of the Oxford Movement.[2] According to Strachan, reason and nature provide important evidence for the truth of Christian faith, but they are insufficient for the world's redemption. As a result of sin, human nature can be redeemed only by grace. James Beaven in his *Elements of Natural Theology*, published in 1850, argues in similar fashion that revealed truth, as found in the scriptures, is necessary beyond the evidence provided by nature and reason.[3]

Anglican theology during the latter half of the nineteenth century was influenced by the growing secularization of Canadian society, by Darwin's theory of evolution, by the influence of British idealism in philosophy, by continuing conflict between Tractarians and Evangelicals within the church,[4] and by the rise of biblical criticism. Secularization, Darwinism, and Idealism all served to undercut the older natural theology which had formed the basis of Anglican apologetic during the colonial period. Idealism provided a new philosophical framework which replaced both the older natural theology and the Scottish 'common sense' school of philosophy.[5] The English philosopher T. H. Green was the major influence, and his influence was paralleled by the Scottish philosophers John and Edward Caird. British and Scottish Idealism became the dominant philosophical tradition in the Canadian universities from the 1880s to the 1920s. It offered a new philosophical foundation for Christian faith that was compatible both with evolutionary theory and with biblical criticism and provided the philosophical framework for a new role for the Church as an agent in the moral transformation of an increasingly secular and pluralistic society.

This outlook is exemplified in the writings of William Clark, who was appointed in 1883 to teach both philosophy and theology at Trinity College, Toronto. Clark saw no conflict between an Idealist philosophical framework and Darwin's evolutionary theory, and in his Baldwin Lectures,[6] he attempted to work out a defence of the Christian faith in relation to modern thought and culture. The lectures reflect a characteristically Anglican incarnational and redemptive theology interpreted in an Idealist philosophical framework, and provide a theological and philosophical foundation for the formation of moral character and social responsibility. Clark provides a window into the kind of theology which lies behind the Anglican Church's engagement with issues of moral and social reform during the latter part of the nineteenth and the beginning of the twentieth centuries.[7]

Although Bishop John Strachan, the founder of Trinity College in Toronto, was an adherent of the older eighteenth-century Anglican High Church tradition, Trinity College subsequently came under the influence of the Tractarian revival. This led, during the latter half of the nineteenth century, to increasing conflict between Tractarians and Evangelicals and to the establishment in Toronto in 1877 of a rival Evangelical theological school which was subsequently named Wycliffe College.[8] By the end of the first decade of the twentieth century theological colleges were also established on the prairies and in British Columbia. In each case, rival theological colleges were initially set up reflecting the differences between Tractarian and Evangelical traditions.

During the earlier part of the twentieth century, both these streams of Anglican theology and piety as well as the broader stream of Anglicanism in Canada were faced with the new challenges of industrialization, depression, post-war reconstruction and the influence of newer philosophical movements. The Anglican theological response to social change was a theology which emphasized the social implications of the incarnation. This kind of theology is reflected in the work of the Council for Social Service, established in 1915, which was strongly influenced by the thought of William Temple during the 1930s and 1940s. Anglican biblical scholarship during this period reflects the influence of biblical criticism both in Great Britain and on the continent. Liturgical revision of the Prayer Book, begun with the revision of 1918, ultimately led to the revision of 1962, which reflected the work of Archbishop Philip Carrington (historian, and biblical and patristic scholar), Ramsay Armitage (liturgical scholar and Principal of Wycliffe College, Toronto) and Fr Roland Palmer, Superior of the Society of St John the Evangelist.

The experience of two world wars led in Canada as elsewhere to a shaking of the old theological foundations. While the theology of Karl Barth and existential philosophy and theology made their impact on Anglican theology in Canada, the most significant Canadian Anglican systematic theologian during the middle decades of the twentieth century was Eugene Fairweather, Professor of Dogmatic Theology at Trinity College, Toronto. Fairweather stood in the Tractarian tradition and was influenced philosophically by the revival of the philosophy of Thomas Aquinas in Roman Catholic and Anglo-Catholic circles. Fairweather deliberately adopted the Thomist option as an alternative to the radical transcendence of Protestant Neo-orthodoxy on the one hand and the radical immanence of liberal theology on the other.[9]

The 1960s marked the height of the influence of secularization in Canadian society, and secular theology had a limited but significant influence on Canadian Anglicanism. The chief effect of this influence was a new openness of the church to society and the world, leading to greater social involvement by the church in the 1970s and to a reassessment of the church's theology of mission to include development as well as evangelization. This was evident in the establishment of the Primate's World Relief and Development Fund and the emphasis by the national church on World Mission and overseas partnerships.

These developments were influenced, in turn, by the development of political and liberation theology in the 1970s and subsequently by feminist theology. All of these influences are reflected in Canadian Anglican theology in the 1980s and -90s. By the 1970s liturgical revision also moved into a new phase, reflecting both the changes in society and the work of international liturgical scholarship. This culminated in the publication in 1985 of *The Book of Alternative Services* of the Anglican Church of Canada. Paul Gibson (National Liturgical Officer), David

Holeton (Professor of Liturgy at Trinity College, Toronto) and William Crockett (Professor of Systematic Theology, Vancouver School of Theology) played significant roles in this revision.

The 1970s and -80s also brought a revival of Evangelicalism in Canadian Anglicanism, marked institutionally by the founding of Regent College in Vancouver in 1968, which has several Anglicans on its faculty, notably the systematic theologian James I. Packer. Subsequently, Alister McGrath was also appointed as Research Professor of Systematic Theology. More recently, a coalition of Catholic, Evangelical, and charismatic groups held a conference in Montreal in 1995 which issued the *Montreal Declaration of Essentials*, a platform which reflects credal orthodoxy in a Calvinist key and a conservative position on controversial ethical issues, particular in the sphere of human sexuality.[10]

Anglican theology in Canada, with its inheritance of a classical incarnational and redemptive theology and with a capacity for creative adaptation to Canadian culture and society while remaining faithful to the gospel, faces the challenge at the turn of the century of how it can carry forward this heritage in an often conflicted, pluralistic and increasingly post-modern context. This poses new challenges to Anglican theological identity in Canada which will require patient dialogue and constructive theological work.

NOTES

1. For the use of eighteenth-century natural theology and Scottish 'common sense' philosophy in nineteenth-century Canadian Anglican thought, see A. B. McKillop, *A Disciplined Intelligence: Critical Inquiry and Canadian Thought in the Victorian Era* (Montreal: McGill-Queen's University Press, 1979).
2. For Strachan's theology see Mark C. McDermott, *The Theology of Bishop John Strachan: A Study in Anglican Identity* (Ph.D. diss., University of St Michael's College, Toronto, 1983).
3. See McKillop 1979: 65–73.
4. See Curtis Fahey, *In His Name: The Anglican Experience in Upper Canada, 1791–1854* (Ottawa: Carleton University Press, 1991), ch. 8.
5. See McKillop 1979: 171–228.
6. William Clark, *Witnesses to Christ: A Contribution to Christian Apologetics*, The Baldwin Lectures, 1887 (Chicago: A. C. McClurg and Company, 1888).
7. Another important work from the same period is Bishop Kingdon's *God Incarnate* (New York, 1890). Kingdon, a Tractarian, was Bishop of Fredericton, New Brunswick. In this work he develops a theology of the incarnation compatible with evolutionary theory. See Eugene R. Fairweather, 'A Milestone in Canadian Theology: Bishop Kingdon's *God Incarnate*', *Canadian Journal of Theology* 4 (1958): 101–10.
8. See Arnold Edinborough (ed.), *The Enduring Word: A Centennial History of Wycliffe College* (Toronto: University of Toronto Press, 1978).

9. See Eugene R. Fairweather, 'Christianity and the Supernatural', *Canadian Journal of Theology* 9 (1963): 12–19, 95–102.
10. See George Egerton (ed.), *Anglican Essentials: Reclaiming Faith within the Anglican Church of Canada* (Toronto: Anglican Book Centre, 1995).

SELECT BIBLIOGRAPHY

The history of Anglican theology in Canada has yet to be written. The following works provide much of the intellectual background for the history of theology in Canada. However, Methodist, Presbyterian, and United Church of Canada theology is given much fuller treatment in these works than the Anglican tradition.

Leslie Armour and Elizabeth Trott, 1981. *The Faces of Reason: An Essay on Philosophy and Culture in English Canada 1850–1950* (Waterloo, Ontario: Wilfrid Laurier University Press).

Michael Gauvreau, 1991. *The Evangelical Century: College and Creed in English Canada from the Great Revival to the Great Depression* (Montreal and Kingston: McGill-Queen's University Press).

John Webster Grant, 1976. 'Religious and Theological Writings [from 1960]', in Carl F. Klinck (ed.), *Literary History of Canada: Canadian Literature in English*, vol. II, 2nd edn (Toronto: University of Toronto Press).

'Religious and Theological Writings to 1960', in Carl F. Klinck (ed.), *Literary History of Canada: Canadian Literature in English*, vol. II, 2nd edn (Toronto: University of Toronto Press).

A. B. McKillop, 1979. *A Disciplined Intelligence: Critical Inquiry and Canadian Thought in the Victorian Era* (Montreal: McGill-Queen's University Press).

David B. Marshall, 1992. *Secularizing the Faith: Canadian Protestant Clergy and the Crisis of Belief, 1850–1940* (Toronto: University of Toronto Press).

John G. Stackhouse, 1993. *Canadian Evangelicalism in the Twentieth Century: An Introduction to Its Character* (Toronto: University of Toronto Press).

James S. Thomson, 1965. 'Literature of Religion and Theology', in Carl F. Klinck (ed.), *Literary History of Canada: Canadian Literature in English* (Toronto: University of Toronto Press).

William Westfall, 1989. *Two Worlds: The Protestant Culture of Nineteenth-century Ontario* (Kingston and Montreal: McGill-Queen's University Press).

AUSTRALIA

Charles Sherlock

Anglican theology in Australia has much in common with that of other provinces, but also distinctive elements. English theological trends have been followed, especially the Tractarian revival, the rise of science, Parish and People, and the liturgical and charismatic movements. Until 1962 Australian Anglicans looked firmly to England, and only in 1981 did the church's name become 'The Anglican Church of Australia'. Today its theological ethos embraces sharp divisions, especially between dioceses, within a broad orthodoxy. The wider Australian context is one of general acceptance of spirituality, with organized religion suspect, and secular materialism very strong.

Two particular factors shape the background. First, each diocese is formally independent, and many have a distinct theological and ecclesial ethos. The Church of England arrived with European settlement, but through chaplains: this clerical independence began a wider tradition. Australian states derive from colonies with separate constitutions, ethos and traditions: the nation came about in 1900, as a federation. The distinctive cultures of each state, focused in the capitals, are a major factor in the diverse traditions of Australian Anglican life: the Church of England was organized well after initial settlement, with the initial formation of dioceses later still (1847).

Second, it was in Australia that synodical church government first came about: Melbourne in 1854, Newcastle, Sydney, Adelaide and others soon after. Today each diocesan synod is independent, with distinct constitutions, some based on 'consensual compact', others by Acts of (state) parliaments. Only in 1962 did a constitution for the Church of England in Australia as a whole come about, after 40 years' wrangling between the dioceses. Under this each diocese remains independent, some retaining power to withdraw. Canons of the (national) General Synod, which meets each 3–4 years, only come into force locally when a diocese

adopts them. Diocesan independence, and the distinct ethos and isolation of each capital city, have led to largely monochrome patterns of
Anglican tradition. The founding diocese, Sydney, has long identified
itself as Evangelical, and more recently as Reformed. As the largest diocese, its potential national influence is considerable. Apart from the
diocese of Armidale (in northern New South Wales), and one or two
parishes in most capital cities, however, outside its own boundaries
Sydney's influence is small, largely due to closed patterns of clergy training and transfer. On the other hand, the capital city dioceses of Brisbane,
Adelaide and Perth are largely Anglo-Catholic in tradition, as are most
rural dioceses (especially Ballarat, in western Victoria). More mixed
theologically are Melbourne, where diversity is affirmed; Canberra and
Goulburn, in which the national capital is of increasing importance; and
the extra-provincial island diocese of Tasmania, the most English of
Australia's states. It needs to be appreciated that Australian Anglicans
rarely encounter those of different theological perspectives, largely due
to the size and independence of the dioceses.

The Anglican Church of Australia is thus best described as a federation
of dioceses. Its ability to think theologically about national issues in an
Australian context has been limited by this federal character, to the
approval of some and the regret of others. Many argue for theological
perspectives which emphasize the local rather than national church. The
Primate (one of the diocesans) has considerable moral authority, but
none other. Archbishop Keith Rayner has chaired the International
Anglican Theological Commission, and gave firm leadership in theological controversy, as the ordination of women, liturgical change and
lay presidency have been discussed vigorously. The various Commissions
of the General Synod generate most theological thought at national
level, especially the Doctrine, Social Responsibilities, and Missionary and
Ecumenical Commissions, chaired by diocesan bishops. The Liturgical
Commission has been active, especially in producing An Australian
Prayer Book (AAPB) (1978), and A Prayer Book for Australia (1995),
both adopted by General Synod. However, the Commissions have no
funding beyond travel costs, and there are few national officers, though
more emphasis is being given to theology. The Director of the General
Board of Religious Education (GBRE), based in Melbourne, provides a
focus for national reflection on education, rural ministry and catechu-
menal issues. The General Synod Secretary is based in Sydney: the first,
Mr John Denton, a layman, served for some 25 years, and was active in
the Anglican Consultative Council. The second, the Revd Dr Bruce
Kaye, is a priest/theologian whose work *A Church Without Walls* pioneers
reflection on the Australian Anglican scene. *Church Scene* is an independent

national weekly which acts as a national Anglican forum: its founding editor, Mr Gerald Davis, a layman, served for 25 years, and its second editor is the Revd Dr Charles Sherlock, a member of ARCIC-2, the Liturgical Commission, and the Australian College of Theology (ACT).

Until the 1920s, most theological work in Australia was restricted to preparation for ordained ministries, in isolation from the universities, which were constituted on secularist foundations. Most Australian tertiary institutions have no religious faculties, and those that do exist are small: only since the 1970s have local undergraduate degrees in theology been available, and Australian approaches to theology begun.

Today accredited undergraduate and postgraduate programmes are available in capital cities, relationships with universities are growing, Aboriginal theological education is developing (principally through Nungalinya College, Darwin, an ecumenical venture), and a wide range of less formal adult theological education is emerging. Anglican theological education has been the major vehicle through which theology has been done: today its provision is growing but scattered. From 1891 until the mid-1970s it took place in small residential colleges preparing men for ACT external examinations. With changes in Australian education taking place, taught undergraduate degrees could be offered. This required institutions to be accredited: Moore (Sydney's training institution), and Ridley (an independent Melbourne college, of Evangelical tradition) were of sufficient size to gain this, through the ACT. In 1910 the Melbourne College of Divinity was set up, including Anglicans, and continues to be significant. It also began offering an undergraduate degree in theology in the mid-1970s, through Melbourne institutions including the United Faculty of Theology, in which Trinity (a Victorian provincial college of Catholic tradition) participates. The 1980s saw other local Colleges of Divinity form, now existing in Brisbane, Sydney, Adelaide and Perth; Moore (not part of the Sydney one) has been granted the right to offer separate degrees. Each College of Divinity includes an Anglican college: St Francis in Brisbane, St Mark's Canberra in the Sydney College of Divinity, St Barnabas in Adelaide, and the Anglican Institute of Theology in Perth. Good relations exist between local colleges and the ACT, which remains the largest institution, but now includes many non-Anglican colleges, and is today broadly identified with the Evangelical spectrum.

This mixed pattern is now as follows. Moore (Sydney) operates with the largest faculty, library and student body, but independently of others. Ridley (Melbourne) continues within the ACT, while other colleges function as partners in a variety of ecumenical institutions. GBRE offers correspondence education (through the ACT) and sponsors the catechumenate process. Ridley and GBRE offer theological education with an emphasis on lay ministries, St Francis and Ridley include a diaconal focus in their work, and Moore operates a strong extension programme. It should be noted that non-ordinands now represent the majority of students at most institutions. Staff from the various colleges undertake the bulk of formal theological work among Australian Anglicans: they constitute a body of about thirty-five people (about a third with doctorates, and almost half at Moore), with a similar number of former staff now in other ministries. Due to distance, the diversity of traditions and lack of opportunities, however, few encounter one another more than briefly, chiefly through General Synod Commissions.

Moore, the oldest and largest college, had its Reformed ethos shaped by Principals Nathaniel Jones (1897–1911), T. C. Hammond (1936–53, whose writing remains in print), D. B. Knox (1959–85) and Vice-Principal D. W. B. Robinson (later Archbishop of Sydney). A distinctive ecclesiology developed at Moore, centred in an emphasis on the Kingdom of God as a key biblical theme, and an eschatology that regards the 'seeing' of the rule of Christ as exclusively future. Christ is today heard (through words) rather than seen (as in the sacraments or symbols); likewise, the gospel – the powerful proclamation of Christ's right to rule – exists to challenge and change people rather than society. In Knox's view, the Church can be seen only when it meets, and the purpose of such meeting is for 'fellowship'–mutual encouragement and instruction, the task of the ordained ministry, with stress placed on the sovereignty of God and the rational character of divine revelation. Some practical outcomes have resulted: opposition to women exercising authoritative ministry (linked to male 'headship'), little emphasis being placed on liturgy, and a tendency to congregationalism. The distinctive traits of this theological perspective are not appreciated beyond Sydney, and are contested in the diocese, both within and outside the Evangelical tradition.

In Melbourne, Ridley developed a broadly Evangelical approach under Principals Stuart Barton Babbage (1947–63) and Leon Morris (1964–79). Babbage became a major statesman in theological education, especially as Registrar of the ACT during two decades of change (1972–91). Morris is the most prolific Protestant Australian theological author, stressing the centrality of the redemptive love of God shown in the cross of Christ, and influential in setting forward an open approach to biblical exegesis. Trinity College has had a number of theologians associated with it: the Revd Barry Marshall (Ecclesiology), Bishop James Grant (Church History), and the Revd Dr John Gaden, a key theological focus in the ordination of women debate.

In Adelaide, the Society of the Sacred Mission operated St Michael's College, Crafers for many years, until it was burnt down. Gabriel Hebert and Gilbert Sinden (Editor of AAPB) were influential liturgists based there. St Barnabas's is a diocesan college for clergy training, where John Gaden was Principal until his early death.

A number of Anglican bishops have been or are theologians, notably Ernest Burgmann (Social Ethics), Charles Pilcher (Theology), Arthur Garnsey (Church History, Liturgy), Marcus Loane (Church History), Donald Cameron (Ecumenics), David Penman (Islam, Multi-culturalism), Donald Robinson (New Testament and Liturgy), Paul Barnett (New Testament), Bruce Wilson (Sociology), Keith Rayner (Theology, Church History), John Wilson (Old Testament), Antony Nichols (Missiology), Peter Hollingworth (Social Issues), Peter Carnley (Theology and Philosophy) and David Silk (Liturgy). Since the mid-1970s a growing number of women have begun to do theology: the struggle over ordination focused much feminist theological work initially, but its influence is wider. A number of women now teach in the colleges, and form large minorities in student bodies.

A growing concern with theology in and for Australian contexts has begun to emerge since the 1970s. Themes such as land, fate, success and failure, and the desert are typical, reflecting Australian geography and history. Liturgy has been a focus for much of this work, a field in which Australian Anglicans remain pioneers, The sensitive issues in producing the Anglican Communion's first modern-language prayer book, AAPB, in 1978 largely centred around faithfulness to the Book of Common Prayer. Those surrounding the revision of AAPB were more to do with enabling effective worship in Australian cultures, and ecumenical concerns: the result is the first revision of a modern prayer book in the Communion, A Prayer Book for Australia (1995). As regards worship beyond the boundaries of the church, diocesan and national social policy commissions have contributed in some depth to issues such as immigration policy and multi-culturalism, the economics of welfare and tax structures, defence arrangements, housing, education, abortion and genetic engineering.

Theological work among Australian Anglicans has thus made significant progress since the early 1970s, and despite continuing divisions, promises much for the future, especially as the number and quality of those taking part in theological work grows.

BIBLIOGRAPHY

I. Breward, 1988. *Australia: 'The Most Godless Place Under Heaven'?* (Adelaide: Lutheran).

K. Cable and S. Judd, 1987. *Sydney Anglicans* (Sydney: Anglican Information Office).

W. J. Lawton, 1988. *Being Christian, Being Australian* (Sydney: Lancer).

W. J. Lawton, 1990. *The Better Time to Be* (Sydney: University of New South Wales).

M. Porter, 1989. *Women in the Church* (Melbourne: Penguin).

M. Porter, 1990. *Land of the Spirit?* (Geneva: World Council of Churches).

NEW ZEALAND AND POLYNESIA

Brian N. Davies

The Anglican Church in Aotearoa, New Zealand and Polynesia, with its theology, can only be understood in the light of historical factors that have shaped its life. It grew first among the Maori inhabitants of Aotearoa (New Zealand), from 1814, and then among the new settlers from the British Isles, who began arriving in significant numbers after 1840. The church of the Province of New Zealand came into being with the Constitution of 1857. This Constitution was radically revised in 1992 to provide for the one Anglican Church to express its worship and mission within three cultural strands: Maori (or Tikanga), Pakeha (or European), and Polynesian. Polynesia had become an associated missionary diocese in 1925. Each of the three cultural groupings represented in General Synod would also have the power to veto any proposed legislation. This provision was an application to the church of the principle of cultural partnership inherent in the founding treaty (the Treaty of Waitangi of 1840), between the British Crown and the Maori tribes of New Zealand.

The Fundamental Provisions of the first Constitution were retained. The Anglican Church in Aotearoa, New Zealand and Polynesia (the new official name), would continue to 'hold and maintain the Doctrine and Sacraments of CHRIST as the LORD hath commanded in His Holy Word, and as the United Church of England and Ireland hath received and explained the same in the Book of Common Prayer, in the Form and Manner of Making, Ordaining, and Consecrating of Bishops, Priests and Deacons, and the Thirty Nine Articles of Religion'. To this list was also added the New Zealand Prayer Book of 1989.

The Constitution of 1992 begins with a number of theological preambles. The one, holy, catholic and apostolic church is described as 'the body of which Christ is the head and all baptised persons are members, believing that God is one yet revealed as Father, Son and Holy Spirit –

a Holy Trinity'. The Church as the agent of the Kingdom of God is called to offer worship and service to God in the power of the Holy Spirit. The Preambles also describe the mission of the Church in line with the Sixth and Eighth Anglican Consultative Council statements. Mission involves 'proclaiming the Gospel of Christ, teaching, baptising and nurturing new believers within eucharistic communities of faith, responding to human needs by loving service, seeking to transform unjust structures of society, caring for God's creation, and establishing the values of the Kingdom'.

The Anglican Church in Aotearoa, New Zealand and Polynesia has a clear theological definition of its nature and mission. It also recognizes that cultural experiences and perceptions can and do affect the way theology is done and doctrines are expressed, and the new Constitution provides the space for this to develop. It is noted that the church advances its mission, safeguards and develops its doctrines, and orders its affairs within the different cultures of the peoples it seeks to serve and bring into the fullness of Christ.

In addition to the constitutional formulas, the church has a new Prayer Book. It includes significant portions of Maori language, and provides a contemporary and indigenous expression of the theological position of the church. A statement of Anglican beliefs is systematically set out in its Catechism.

Visitors from overseas have often praised New Zealand Anglicans for their adventurousness. They have been at the cutting edge of many of the major changes in Anglican ecclesial practice and these have been subjects for theological study and debate. Christian initiation reform, and the ordination of women are obvious examples. Yet they have sometimes been criticized for a lack of theological rigour. The church has an on-going Doctrine Commission, currently led by Bishop David Coles of Christchurch, and a great deal of theological reflection takes place at all church levels, and involving clergy and laity. However, it is a plain fact that New Zealand Anglicans, up until now, have produced very little substantial theological writing.

The theological colleges have attracted theologians of ability. The most notable have been biblical scholars. Frank Synge, Principal of Christchurch College 1959–63, Raymond Foster, Warden of St John's College 1962–71, Allan Catley, St John's faculty 1948–63, and Francis Foulkes, Warden of St John's College, 1986–90, are examples. George Armstrong, a New Zealander who trained in North America, was lecturer in systematic theology at St John's College 1965–87. His emphasis was on contextual theology, and he radically explored indige-nous issues. His successor is Stephen May, English born and trained

Evangelical scholar. Both Raymond Pelly, English born and trained, who was Warden of St John's College 1977–85, and John Rymer, an Australian by birth, who taught at Christchurch College and then became Dean of Auckland, were notable theological thinkers. Ken Booth and Colin Brown have also contributed to Anglican theological thinking and writing in New Zealand.

The best-known New Zealand Anglican theological writer is an Anglican layman, John Morton, now a retired professor of zoology. He has written several thoughtful books on Christ and science. Merlin Davies, who was Warden at St John's 1974–6, wrote a book published in 1993 on the theology of F. D. Maurice. Beyond these works, apart from some biblical commentaries and various papers and articles, very little substantial theological writing by New Zealand Anglican authors has been achieved.

Among Pakeha New Zealanders, part of the reason for the lack of theological scholarship is the pragmatic attitude which prevails, a legacy of the pioneering years. Within Maori culture oral tradition has tended to remain dominant and up until recently has not provided the necessary impetus for academic writing. New Zealand Anglicans have tended to look beyond their shores for theological direction and expertise, reflecting perhaps a theological inferiority complex. In addition, until very recently Anglican theological institutions have not provided the opportunity or incentives for advanced theological study. Only now has it become possible to do advanced degrees and doctoral studies at St John's, within its Maori and Pakeha colleges. Indigenous theological endeavour is likely to expand in the future for both Maori and Pakeha partners and for the increasing number of Polynesian students.

At least since the 1960s, theological thinking in New Zealand has been dominated by liberalism, and we have not been immune to its more secularized versions. The catholic theological tradition has been weak. In more recent years the Evangelical tradition has been most dynamic and has produced perhaps the most promising New Zealand born Anglican theological scholars. Peter Carrell, Derek Tovey, Tim Meadowcroft and Douglas Campbell are examples of this new generation of theological scholars. An English scholar now living and working in New Zealand, David Kettle, is involved in the gospel and culture movement and is doing creative writing, as is New Zealand born Brian Carrell, an Assistant Bishop in the Diocese of Wellington.

The evangelical *Latimer* journal, which in 1993 became the *Affirm* magazine, has brought together Evangelical and charismatic groupings and provided a useful national outlet for theological writing. In August 1995 *Affirm* held a highly successful theological conference at St John's

College, Auckland, on the theme of orthodoxy. The papers are to be published under the title, 'Contributions to Orthodoxy: Foundations for Faith Today'.

There has been a clear shift away from the more excessively liberal theologies of the 1960s and -70s. At the other end of the spectrum, the influence of the charismatic renewal has been considerable, within the Anglican Church in New Zealand. Though this has tended to encourage uncritical biblicism, the theological climate in the church has not generally been hospitable to fundamentalism. Informed orthodoxy seems to best describe the emerging theological emphasis. A potential field of theological creativity could well come with a renaissance of traditional Maori theology and its impact on cultural modernism and traditional Christian categories of thought. (My book, *The Way Ahead*, 1995, deals at greater length with the contemporary theological scene in New Zealand.)

One of the most encouraging developments in the life of the Anglican Church in New Zealand in recent years has been the growth of lay theological education. More people than ever before are completing a range of available courses in theology and religious studies. As a result lay Anglicans are better informed and are demanding better quality theological teaching from their clergy. Another development has been the entry of women into the theological arena. Janet Crawford, a member of the St John's faculty, and Sue Patterson, a priest associate in Waipawa, are among those making creative contributions to theological reflection in New Zealand. Sue Patterson has become one of New Zealand's most productive theological writers and works within the classical Christian framework.

The major theological achievement of the New Zealand church must be its Prayer Book of 1989. A product of a commission representative of the main theological streams within the church working over a period of 25 years, it has been positively received, is well used within the country and has won wide acclaim internationally. The language of worship has long been considered by Anglicans as the best way to express theology. This book is no exception, and it anchors the Anglican Church in Aotearoa, New Zealand and Polynesia firmly in the tradition of credal orthodoxy.

BIBLIOGRAPHY

Ken Booth, 1976. 'How to Detect Heresy', in Peter David and John Hinchcliff (eds.), *Dialogue on Religion, New Zealand Viewpoints 1977* (Third Colloquium, Auckland University).

Colin Brown, 1975. 'Pentecostalism, Neo Pentecostalism and Naturalistic Explanation', in John Hinchcliff (ed.), *The Religious Dimension* (collection of essays presented at the Colloquium on Religious Studies at the University of Auckland).

Colin Brown, 1976. 'How Significant is the Charismatic Movement', in Peter Davis and John Hinchcliff (eds.), *Dialogue on Religion, New Zealand Viewpoints 1977* (Third Colloquium, Auckland University).

Brian Carrell, 1990. 'Agenda for a Secular Society', *Today's Christian* 15.

Brian Carrell, 1992. 'The Christian Faith in a Post Christian Society', *The Reaper* 73.6.

Brian Carrell, 1993. 'Breaking Through the Barriers of Faith Today', *Latimer* 112.

Brian Carrell, 1994. 'Baby-Boomer Culture and the Church', *Affirm* 2.2.

Janet Crawford, 1987. 'Faith and Feminism', in Douglas Pratt (ed.), *Signposts: Theological Reflections in a New Zealand Context* (University of Waikato Printing).

Allan Davidson (ed.), 1991. *In All Humility and Gentleness* (Auckland: St John's College).

W. Merlin Davies, 1993. *F. D. Maurice, a Prophet for Today* (Auckland: ColCom Press).

Brian Davis, 1995. *The Way Ahead, Anglican Change and Prospect in New Zealand* (Christchurch: Caxton Press).

Francis Foulkes, 1983. *How the Good News Began: Study Guide to Mark's Gospel* (Ghana: African Christian Press).

Francis Foulkes, 1984. *Bible and Ministry: The Griffith Thomas Memorial Lectures* (Auckland College Communications).

Francis Foulkes, 1989a. *The Letter of Paul to the Ephesians: An Introduction and Commentary* (Leicester: Inter-Varsity Press).

Francis Foulkes, 1989b. 'The Challenge of our Cultures', *Latimer* August.

Francis Foulkes, 1989c. 'Evangelism and the Church in a Multi-cultural Society', *Journal of the Christian Brethren Research Fellowship* August.

Francis Foulkes, 1989d. 'Male, Female and God', William Orange Memorial Lecture, *Latimer* December.

Francis Foulkes, 1993. *Christian Thinking about Sexuality* (Homebush

West, NSW: ANZEA Books).

David Kettle, 1993. 'The Battle for Public Truth', *Stimulus* 1.4.

David Kettle, 1994–5. 'Michael Polanyi and Human Identity', *Tradition and Discovery, The Polanyi Society Periodical* 21.3.

David Kettle, 1995. 'The Footprints of God and the Face of Dionysius', *Stimulus* 3.2.

David Kettle and Philip Gendall, 1992–3. 'New Zealand: The Most Secular State in the World?' *Today's Christian* December/January.

Stephen May, 1990. 'Beyond Polarisation: Bi-culturalism and the Gospel', William Orange Memorial Lecture, *Latimer* 112.

John Morton, 1972. *Man, Science and God* (London: Collins).

John Morton, 1975. 'Evolution and Redemption', in John Hinchcliff (ed.), *The Religious Dimension* (collection of essays presented at the Colloquium on Religious Studies at the University of Auckland).

John Morton, 1984. *Redeeming Creation* (Auckland: Zealandia).

John Morton, 1989. *Christ, Creation and the Environment* (Auckland: Anglican Communications).

Sue Patterson, 1992. 'Gratuitous Truth: Metaphor and Revelation', *Colloquium* May.

Sue Patterson, 1993. 'Janet Martin Soskice, Metaphor and a Theology of Grace', *Scottish Journal of Theology* 46.

Sue Patterson, 1994a. 'Theological Geography', in Murray Rae and D. Bruce Hamill (eds.), *Theological Fragments, Essays in Honour of Alan Torrance* (Dunedin: Lada Publications).

Sue Patterson, 1994b. 'Christ at the Centre: The Logic of Biblical Christianity'. *Affirm* December.

Paul Trebilco (ed.), 1995. *Contributions to Orthodoxy: Foundations for Faith Today* (Auckland: ColCom Press).

SOUTH AFRICA

John Suggitt

The earliest work of the Anglican Church in South Africa was performed by colonial chaplains ministering to the garrisons and British residents of the Cape when under British occupation (1795–1803 and 1806). Only after the formal cession of the Cape to Great Britain in 1814 did English chaplains move further afield. The arrival of the 1820 British settlers in the Eastern Cape brought more chaplains. From 1827 the Bishop of Calcutta was given a commission by the Bishop of London to exercise episcopal functions in South Africa.

In 1848 Robert Gray arrived in Cape Town as its first bishop, with oversight over all South Africa under British rule. In 1853 the diocese of Grahamstown and Natal were created, and Orange Free State in 1863.

Partly as a result of the controversy with Colenso, leading to the schism of the Church of England in South Africa, the church in southern Africa became a separate Province in 1870. By 1995 there were twenty-three dioceses, including Swaziland, Namibia, Lesotho, Mozambique, St Helena and the Order of Ethiopia (a partly independent association of black Christians with their own bishop since 1983). Although in 1870 the church was called the Church of the Province of South (later, Southern) Africa (CPSA) it was generally known until the 1950s as the English Church. While free to administer its own affairs, it is constitutionally committed to the formularies of the Church of England.

THEOLOGICAL TRENDS

The theology of the CPSA has been moulded by different emphases on the various factors which have marked Anglican thought – Scripture, tradition, reason and context.

Colenso's teaching on the importance of reason and context, leading to a re-evaluation of Scripture and its place in the life of the church, was generally rejected. Bishop Robert Gray was largely responsible for the predominant ethos of the CPSA, with its stress on the traditional teaching of the church, as influenced especially by the Oxford Movement. There was little fresh theological thought, as the church strove both to minister to English South Africans and to convert and instruct Africans. The 1662 Prayer Book was the church's official liturgy, and even the South African Prayer Book (published as a whole in 1954) was canonically only a permitted alternative. Its aim to recapture some of the Catholic ethos of the church's worship was partly influenced by the English 1928 Prayer Book, and its eucharistic liturgy recalled some of the themes of the 1549 Prayer Book.

Theologically, therefore, the CPSA was generally conservative, and believed that the British way of life and culture best represented God's will for his world. Archbishop Carter (1909–30), influenced as he was, like Colenso before him, by F. D. Maurice, recognized the importance of the church's witness in the sphere of social and economic justice. In spite of this, Geoffrey Clayton, Bishop of Johannesburg (1934–48) disapproved of Michael Scott's participation in passive resistance campaigns.

After the Nationalist victory at the polls in 1948, the CPSA was still not much involved in the struggle against apartheid before the protests of Trevor Huddleston, whose efforts were not always applauded by Archbishop Clayton. Only when the church was *directly* affected did Clayton make a real stand. Huddleston regarded the South African context as determining the theological response demanded by the gospel.

This concern for social and political change was later taken up by Bishop Bill Burnett when secretary of the South African Council of Churches. He had a special hand in producing *A message to the People of South Africa* (1968), to which a response was made in *No Other Gospel* by Anglicans who believed that the church's task was not to interfere in politics. The church's concern for social justice hastened ecumenical cooperation in the struggle against apartheid, and Anglicans shared in the production of *The Kairos Document* in 1985, in which the interpretation of Scripture was greatly influenced by the prevailing context.

The charismatic movement of the 1970s and 80s resulted in a stress on personal experience, with the place of reason and the role of the Church in social and political issues falling more into the background, so that many considered *The Kairos Document* to be a distortion of the gospel. The injustice of the apartheid policy, however, resulted in growing Anglican involvement in the struggle for liberation and social justice, in which Desmond Tutu played a key role both before and after his election in 1986 as Archbishop of Cape Town.

Liturgy and theology hang together, and new forms of experimental liturgies (1969, 1975) led to *An Anglican Prayer Book 1989*, which reflects modern theological understanding of the eucharist, and incorporates eucharistic canons from the English Series II and the Roman Catholic Mass.

In 1976 Provincial Synod asked the bishops to form a Southern African Anglican Theological Commission, which has since regularly met to examine theological issues, with special attention to the theology of relevant worship, the nature and function of the ordained ministry, and church and society. The commission's reports have influenced the bishops in their decisions on liturgy, ethics and doctrine.

The involvement of the CPSA in official ecumenical Conversations from 1960 maarked a change from the earlier position in which the CPSA tended to stay aloof from other churches. Bishops and other Anglican theologians have played a prominent part in the Church Unity Commission (involving Anglicans, Methodists, Presbyterians and Congregationalists) since its formation in 1967. This has necessarily led to a new examination of the teaching of the church, especially with regard to the ordained ministry.

In the new climate of opinion due partly to the charismatic movement, Evangelicals began to play a more influential part in the affairs of the church, shown in the election of Bruce Evans as Bishop of Port Elizabeth in 1975. Greater emphasis now tended to be placed on Scripture, sometimes leading to a somewhat superficial interpretation. The future of theology, especially in the changing South African society, depends on the maintenance of the proper balance between Scripture, the teaching of the church, and the use of reason within the context of the church's life and experience.

Perhaps, therefore, the recognition of the importance of the present context has led to a wide acceptance of the ordination of women to the priesthood. Though some still have reservations, on the grounds either of Scripture or tradition (or both), most have been ready to accept this as a development inspired by the Holy Spirit in the Church. Here too, as elsewhere, the feminist understanding of Scripture and of the church's teaching and practice is being promoted.

An important development is the way in which black theology and liberation theology, arising from the South African context, have impelled Anglicans and others to consider the relation between Christianity and other faiths, with special reference to African traditional beliefs and practices.

BIBLIOGRAPHY

Denise Ackermann, 'Faith and feminism: Women doing theology', in J. de Gruchy and C. Villa-Vicencio (eds.), *Doing Theology in Context* (Maryknoll: Orbis), 197–211.

Sigqibo Dwane, 1982. 'In search of an African contribution to a contemporary confession of Christian faith', *Journal of Theology for Southern Africa* 38 (March): 19–25.

Frank England and Torquil Paterson (eds.), 1989. *Bounty in Bondage: The Anglican Church in Southern Africa* (Johannesburg: Ravan Press).

John de Gruchy, 1979. *The Church Struggle in South Africa* (Grand Rapids: Eerdmans).

Peter Hinchcliff, 1963. *The Anglican Church in South Africa* (London: Darton, Longman & Todd).

Trevor Huddleston, 1957. *Naught for your Comfort* (London: Collins).

The Kairos Document: Challenge to the Church, 2nd edn, 1986. (Braamfontein: Skotaville).

Luke Pato, 1994. 'African theologies', in J. de Gruchy and C. Villa-Vicencio (eds.), *Doing Theology in Context* (Maryknoll: Orbis), 152–61.

Alan Paton, 1973. *Apartheid and the Archbishop* (Cape Town: David Philip).

Barney Pityana, 1994. 'Black theology', in J. de Gruchy and C. Villa-Vicencio (eds.), *Doing Theology in Context* (Maryknoll, Orbis), 173–83.

SOUTH ASIA

Michael Nazir-Ali

There have been Anglicans in the South Asian subcontinent since the seventeenth century.[1] Until the closing years of the eighteenth century, however, much of this presence had to do with ministry to expatriates of British origin. It is true that some of the chaplains took an interest in the concerns of the indigenous population, but this was an exception rather than the rule and, in any case, it was often marginal to their work. Similarly, the work of the earliest missionary societies, such as the Society for the Propagation of the Gospel (now 'the United', USPG), and the Society for Promoting Christian Knowledge (SPCK), was, at the time, focused on the pastoral care of British expatriates.

It was the appointment of chaplains such as Henry Martyn (1781–1812), the great Bible translator, and the formation of the Society for Missions to Africa and the East (now CMS) which changed this situation in a significant way. Martyn's great interest lay in the translation of the Scriptures, and during his brief missionary career he was able to translate the Scriptures into Urdu, Persian and Arabic. Nor was he narrowly focused on linguistic matters: he took great pains to learn about people's habits and thought-forms as he translated the Bible into their language.[2]

Such a primary interest in the ways of people who were not yet Christian came to be typical of the approach of the CMS. Here, at last, was an Anglican society, committed to the Church, but with a primary interest in mission to the non-Christian world. It is paradoxical, therefore, that one of CMS's first engagements in India should be, not with non-Christians, but with the ancient Christians of St Thomas! In 1816, CMS was invited by the Indian Syrian Church to assist it in theological education and liturgical renewal. The missionaries who went at first were courteous and patient and earned the respect of that church's bishops. Later on, the missionaries were not so patient, and relationships became so difficult that the mission had to be terminated – and CMS moved on to continue its work with Muslims and Hindus. The seeds sown by CMS resulted ultimately in the emergence of the Mar Thoma Syrian Church; an oriental church which, nevertheless, bears the mark of Anglican influence and is now in full communion with the churches of the Anglican Communion.[3]

The ancient churches of India, including the Mar Thoma, have had lively interaction with Anglicans in matters of liturgy. On the one hand, the ancient liturgy of the Mar Thoma has been influenced by Anglicanism. On the other, the Anglican and, later on, the united churches in the subcontinent, have been significantly influenced by the oriental liturgical tradition. Successive liturgies have restored the *Maranatha*, instituted oriental features to the wedding service, placed the *epiclesis* in the 'Eastern' position and introduced the now-familiar responsive embolisms in the Eucharistic Prayer. Such Anglican 'reception' of oriental features has become commonplace in the work of liturgical revision throughout the Anglican Communion.[4]

All the ancient churches of India have, from time to time, produced eminent theologians. For our present purposes we need to note a few names from the Mar Thoma Church. M. M. Thomas is the doyen of living theologians in India today. His work has largely been about the Church's involvement in society, but he has also reflected on relations with people of other faiths.[5] E. V. Mathew (sic) is another lay theologian from this tradition. His area of interest has been the relationship between law and Gospel. Saphir Athyal represents a more conservative aspect of this tradition, one that often appeals to traditionalists in the Western churches.

Unsurprisingly, from the earliest years, theologians, both expatriate and Indian, have tried to engage with the diverse religious traditions of the subcontinent. Their engagement covers the whole spectrum of faith in India but, until recently, it has in the main been with some aspect of Vedic Hinduism or with Islam. (We should not, however, forget the work of people like Bishop Lakshman Wickremsinghe, who tried to relate their Christian faith to Buddhism.) Contemporary theologians such as Roger Hooker and Andrew Wingate obviously stand in the tradition of scholars such as W. D. P. Hill.[6] Indian theologians who have contributed significantly to Hindu–Christian dialogue include Herbert Jai Singh (a colleague of M. M. Thomas), Stanley Samartha and Bishop Pritam Santram.[7]

Much of the early work of CMS, for instance, was with Muslims, many of them well-educated in traditional learning. This was to produce a succession of scholars who sought to interpret Islam from a Christian point of view and who attempted to explain the Christian faith to Muslims. Dr Imad-ud-din, Archdeacon Ihsanullah and, in this century, Archdeacon Barkatullah are only a few of the names which come to mind.[8]

Some theologians, like Murray Rogers and Bede Griffiths (an Anglican convert to Roman Catholicism), have tried to promote a dialogue between the mystical traditions.[9] Others, like Sadhu Sundar Singh, have sought to model their mission and ministry in terms of the Indian ascetical tradition.[10]

More recently, many have become conscious that much of the church's mission is with the *Dalit* or casteless people of India. There are, moreover, many people of *Dalit* origin in the Indian churches. The *Dalit* have never had access to the Vedic tradition, and yet their spirituality, aspects of which pre-date Vedic Hinduism, pervades Indian life. Some theologians have, therefore, begun to 'do' theology from a *Dalit* perspective. The present Bishop in Madras, M. Azariah, the former Bishop in Medak, Victor Premsagar, and the General Secretary of ISPCK, James Massey, are all examples of this approach.[11]

Towards the end of the nineteenth century and the beginning of the twentieth, more and more Christians in India and elsewhere began to feel that the divisions among Christians were a notable obstacle to mission. Thus the Edinburgh Missionary Conference of 1910 also became an important watershed in the burgeoning Ecumenical Movement. Bishop Samuel Azariah of Dornakal was one of the few Indians present at Edinburgh, but he became a great advocate of Christian unity in India. He looked forward to the day when both the ancient and newer churches of India could form one Church of India which would retain the diversity of traditions, while bringing Christians of different kinds into fellowship with each other. This vision was partly fulfilled when first the Church of South India (CSI) and then the Church of North India (CNI) were formed. The joint council which consists of the CSI, the CNI and the Mar Thoma Church brings together Christians from the ancient and the newer churches.[12]

There are notable biblical scholars in India, many of them belonging to the CSI, the CNI or the Mar Thoma. Some names that come to mind are Dhyan Chand Carr, Vinay Samuel and Christopher Durai Singh.

Mission-thinking permeates every aspect of theology in the subcontinent, but it has been specially focused in the work of people like Vinay Samuel and Christopher Sugden in India, and Michael Nazir-Ali in Pakistan.[13] There is also considerable emphasis on the importance of the inculturation or contextualization of the faith in relation to the various cultures of the region.[14]

On the one hand, the Anglican tradition in the subcontinent has been subsumed into the United Churches. On the other, it is enabling the United Churches to play a full part in the Anglican Communion, thus challenging the communion to fulfil its ecumenical vocation.

NOTES

1. Stephen Neill, *A History of Christian Missions* (London: Penguin, 1954), 232.
2. J. Sargent, *Memoir of the Rev Henry Martyn*, 8th edn (London, 1825).
3. Alexander Mar Thoma, *The Mar Thoma Church: Heritage and Mission* (Kenda: Tiruvalla, 1985).
4. Michael Nazir-Ali, *From Everywhere to Everywhere: A World View of Christian Mission* (London: Collins, 1990), 57ff.
5. One of his best known works is *The Acknowledged Christ of the Indian Renaissance* (London, 1969). Here he assesses the impact of Christian faith on Hindu social reformers.
6. Roger Hooker and Christopher Lamb, *Love the Stranger: Christian Ministry in Multi-Faith Areas* (London: SPCK, 1986).
7. H.-Jai Singh (ed.), *Inter-Religious Dialogue* (Bangalore, 1967); S. J. Samartha, *The Hindu Response to the Unbound Christ* (Madras: CLS, 1974); P. B. Santram, *Mission of the Church in the Indian Context*, in P. Turner and F. Sugeno, *Crossroads are for Meeting* (Sewanee: SPCK, 1986).
8. These scholars wrote mostly in Persian, Arabic and Urdu. This makes their work inaccessible to those working in European languages. A good example is Barkat Ullah's, *Sahat-i-Kutb-i-Muqadasa* (Integrity of the Books of the Bible) (Lahore: PRBS, 1968).
9. B. Griffiths, *The Marriage of East and West* (London: Collins, 1982).
10. It is interesting to note that Sundar Singh was, at one time, an Anglican ordinand! See further A. J. Appasamy, *Sundar Singh: A Biography* (CLS, 1966), 34ff.
11. The problem is set out in Abraham Ayroo Kuzhiel, *Untouchability: Gandhian Solution on Trial* (ISPCK, 1987).
12. Carol Graham, *Azariah of Dornakal* (London: SCM, 1946). See also W. J. Marshall, *Faith and Order in the North India–Pakistan Unity Plan* (London: Friends of CNI, 1978).
13. M. Nazir-Ali, *Mission and Dialogue: Proclaiming the Gospel Afresh in Every Age* (London: SPCK, 1995).
14. See further Bruce J. Nicholls, *Contextualization: A Theology of Gospel and Culture* (Downers Grove, Ill.: Intervarsity Press, 1979).

EAST AFRICA

Tudor Griffiths

In 1844 Dr Krapf of the Church Missionary Society (CMS) came to Mombasa, signalling the arrival of Anglicanism in East Africa. Under the leadership of Bishop Tozer, the Universities' Mission to Central Africa (UMCA) withdrew from the Shire Highlands near Lake Malawi and established a base in Zanzibar in 1864. The arrival of Christianity in the island was dramatically symbolized by the consecration of a cathedral on the location of the former slave market in Zanzibar. From the two bases of Mombasa and Zanzibar, the evangelization of the interior proceeded. The CMS Uganda Mission began in 1877, and within a decade there were Christian martyrs, both African and European. Under the leadership of Bishop A. R. Tucker, the Anglican Church in Uganda grew at a rate unparalleled within the CMS sphere, and it developed a powerful commitment to evangelization. During the twentieth century Uganda became the centre of evangelization for western Kenya, eastern Zaire, southern Sudan, Rwanda and Burundi.

The Kikuyu controversy of 1913 revealed a division between the Low Church and Evangelical Anglicans of the CMS tradition, who favoured some form of Protestant unity, and the Anglo–Catholics of the UMCA tradition, who were totally opposed to any form of intercommunion with other Protestants.

The East Africa Revival broke out in the early 1930s in Rwanda, and spread rapidly into Uganda and neighbouring countries, where it has had a major influence on the spirituality and theology of the Anglican Church. The 1960s saw the start of political and ecclesiastical independence; so by the mid-1990s there were separate Anglican Provinces in Kenya, Tanzania, Uganda, Sudan, Zaire, Rwanda and Burundi.

Contemporary Anglican theology has been shaped not only by its post-colonial political context, but also by three particular influences: the Anglican traditions of the founding societies, the East Africa Revival tradition and African traditional culture. Although deeply influenced by European Evangelical pietism, the Revival has taken a distinctively East African form. The Revival emphasizes the centrality of the atonement and the cleansing blood of Jesus. A believer's response is one of repentance, signified by open confession in the fellowship of the Revival *brethren* (a term used inclusively in East Africa). The key to spiritual life is personal brokenness before the cross and 'walking in the light' with other brethren. The Revival emphasizes the importance of witnessing and evangelism for all the *Balokole* (the saved ones).

In 1963 J.V. Taylor published *The Primal Vision*, a reflection arising out of his experience as a CMS missionary in Uganda and significant for its treatment of African culture with theological seriousness. The doyen of East African theologians, the Kenyan John Mbiti, has produced much of his work also outside Africa. Mbiti rightly has attained international stature for his writing, which has shown particular interest in the theological implications of the encounter between the Christian gospel and African traditional cultures. Mbiti's significance for Anglican theology in East Africa is threefold. He was the first to treat traditional African philosophy and religion systematically as theological data, such that it constituted a preparation for the gospel. Second, Mbiti has indicated the centrality of Christology to the development of an African Christian theology. Third, Mbiti's international recognition has given confidence to other aspiring theologians in East Africa.

The spirit of Kikuyu lives on in the participation of many Anglicans in various theological fora. The Ecumenical Association of Third-World Theologians (EATWOT) was founded in Dar-es-Salaam in 1976. A number of Anglican Evangelicals contributed to the Africa Theological Fraternity conference in Kenya in 1985, papers from which were published as *The Living God*. Theological educators are brought together under the Association of Theological Institutions of Eastern Africa, which holds an annual Institute. One leading Anglican participant in ecumenical theological ventures has been Professor J. N. K. Mugambi of Nairobi University. In collaboration with the Eastern Africa Ecumenical Theological Symposium, he has been closely involved in the production of an on-going series of books of essays exploring Jesus, the Church, moral and ethical issues, mission and pastoral care in African Christianity. Many of the essays are programmatic, and few achieve sufficient rigour or depth to make an impact on the international theological scene, but they represent a significant step in ecumenical theology within East Africa. Mugambi himself has written prolifically since 1987. In his book *From Liberation to Reconstruction* (1995), he suggests reconstruction as a new paradigm for African theology. Whereas the Exodus motif was particularly significant for liberation, Nehemiah is the central text for reconstruction. This idea is certainly worth further exploration than that given by Mugambi, whose work is frustratingly marred by factual errors and a tendency towards over-generalizations. There is an interest among theologians in a theology of development arising out of a consideration of the holistic nature of salvation throughout East Africa, but little has been written for a wider audience, and more attention is required to what is distinctively *theological* about development.

Significant figures in political theology have included Bishops Kivengere in Uganda and Henry Okullu in Kenya. Kivengere was a man of the Revival who nonetheless challenged its quietist tradition by speaking against Amin's terrors. He remained opposed to any violent resistance, and after Amin's fall in 1979, he led calls for national reconciliation. Okullu sees the Church having a vocation to be the conscience of the State, and he shows awareness of the tensions which may exist between them. He and Bishop David Gitari have been leading critics of the Kenyan government, especially in its perceived failure to deal with institutional corruption and tribalism. In Tanzania Anglicans have been active in speaking out when there have been difficulties with the government, and especially with Christian–Muslim relations. This has usually been in conjunction with other denominations that are members of the Christian Council of Tanzania. The quietist traditions of the Revival have come under stern questioning since the 1994 slaughter in Rwanda.

Liturgically the churches of East Africa have been conservative. Tanzania produced a prayer book to unite the Province in 1995, the main purpose of which was that it could be used by both the Low Church (CMS) and the High Church (UMCA) traditions present. There was no deliberate attempt by the Liturgical Committee to introduce any inculturation. In Uganda the Liturgical Committee has been inactive in recent years, although a couple of dioceses are working at producing liturgies in the vernacular which are more than translations of traditional books. The Church of the Province of Kenya has been the most adventurous in developing a more contextualized liturgy, and the result has been widely admired as a model.

Within East Africa, some dioceses ordain women while others do not. Bishop Kivengere led the way, having been influenced by the Revival tradition that *at the cross the ground is level*, in this case between men and women. Another bishop influenced by the Revival is Yustasi Ruhindi, who has developed Garuka ('Come as you are') theology in western Uganda. This was a response to the continuing polygamy among Christians. Garuka theology does not endorse polygamy as a legitimate option but rejects the tradition that eucharistic discipline is appropriate in this case. This has not met with universal agreement in East Africa.

Oral theology is best represented in the vernacular Christian songs in East Africa. The theme of these songs is frequently a testimony and yearning for heaven; there is clear emphasis on maintaining a close personal relationship with Jesus, who is seen as the Saviour and Healer in spite of all the problems in the world. Testimonies are another form of oral theology. The Revival tradition is found primarily in oral form; traditionally Revival brethren have been suspicious of academic theology.

The form as well as the content of theology is important. The former Anglican and late critic of the Christian faith, Okot P'Bitek set out the chaos caused by the coming of Christianity and colonialism in a traditional poem form, *Song of Prisoner*. In the 1890s the CMS missionary George Pilkington compiled a list of Luganda proverbs scripturally applied. There is room for the development of an East African wisdom tradition. It is significant that the best Western-style academic theology has been written outside Africa yet reflecting experience within. The basic economic and social structures in the region suggest that this pattern is unlikely to change in the near future. However, the continued production of Christian songs in the vernacular stands as a major though unwritten resource and testimony to the vitality of oral theology throughout East Africa.

SELECT BIBLIOGRAPHY

W. B. Anderson, 1977. *The Church in East Africa 1840–1974* (Tanzania: ATIEA).

A. Coomes, 1990. *Festo Kivengere* (Eastbourne: Monarch).

D. M. Gitari and G. P. Benson (eds.), 1986. *The Living God* (Nairobi: Uzima).

J. S. Mbiti, 1969. *African Religions and Philosophy* (London: Heinemann).

J. N. K. Mugambi, 1992. *Critiques of Christianity in African Literature* (Nairobi: East African Educational Publishers).

J. N. K. Mugambi, 1995. *From Liberation to Reconstruction* (Nairobi: EAEP).

J. N. K. Mugambi, and L. Magesa (eds.), 1989. *Jesus in African Christianity* (Nairobi: Initiatives).

J. N. K. Mugambi, and L. Magesa (eds.), 1990. *The Church in African Christianity* (Nairobi: Initiatives).

J. N. K. Mugambi and A. Nasimiyu-Wasike (eds.), 1992. *Moral and Ethical Issues in African Christianity* (Nairobi: Initiatives).

A. Nasimiyu-Wasike and D. Waruta (eds.), 1993. *Mission in African Christianity* (Nairobi: Initiatives).

Z. Nthamburi (ed.), 1991. *From Mission to Church* (Nairobi: Uzima).

J. H. Okulli, 1984. *Church and State in Nation Building and Human Development* (Nairobi: Uzima).

J. V. Taylor, 1963. *The Primal Vision* (London: SCM).

D. Waruta and H. Kinoti, 1993. *Pastoral Care in African Christianity* (Nairobi: Initiatives).

PART TWO

A Survey of Anglican Theologians

Abbott, Edwin Abbott (1838–1926), New Testament scholar, educator, grammarian, biographer and Broad-Church theologian. Though imperfectly appreciated, because of his excellent scholarship and theology, Abbott should be considered a 'Cambridge Fourth' to colleagues Westcott, Hort and Lightfoot. Like them, he swept Firsts in the Theological Tripos, etc., at Cambridge (St Johns). Calling himself a 'scientific' or 'natural' Christian, Abbott was initially influenced by the Christian Socialist circle of his headmaster father Edwin Abbott (1808–82) and J[ohn] Llewelyn Davies (1826–1916), the champion of F. D. Maurice. Improving upon his friend J. R. Seeley's Positivistic and philanthropic *Ecce Homo* (1865), he further advocated emulation of Christ as the 'Son of Humanity'. As Headmaster of the City of London School (1865–89), Abbott wrote *Bible Studies* (1871–2) pioneering Edwardian 'higher criticism' in lower schools. His Hulsean lectures *Through Nature to Christ* (1877) placed Jesus within Comte's pantheon and thus fulfilled Huxley's evolutionary scientism. With the controversial *Kernel and the Husk* (1886), Abbott casuistically supported conscience-stricken clergymen in subscribing to The Thirty-Nine Articles. With Hort's support, Abbott wrote the 'Gospels' for the *Encyclopedia Britannica* (1879); and – with W. G. Rushbrooke – *The Synopticon* (1880) and *Common Tradition of the Gospels* (1884), which made 'Markan priority' dominant in England. *St Thomas of Canterbury* (1898) analysed accounts of Becket's martyrdom as a model for understanding issues relating to the synoptic problem in general, and the propagation of miracle stories in general. Abbott's controversial and penetrating attack, *The Anglican Career of Cardinal Newman* (1892) and vehement *Philomythus* (1891) revived the Kingsley–Newman battle, though it desecrated Newman's memory. After retirement, Abbott devoted himself to his encyclopedic 'Diatessarica' series. It includes the *Johannine Vocabulary* (1905) and *Johannine Grammar* (1906), according to Raymond Brown, 'indispensable starting points for Johannine studies'. *Light on the Gospel from an Ancient Poet* (1912), per James Charlesworth, is a superior commentary on the *Odes of Solomon*. *The Son of Man* (1910), as *the* cornerstone study, also elucidates the Merkabah mysticism underlying Jesus' Danielic allusions. *The Fourfold Gospel* in five volumes (1913–17) exhaustively analyses Gospel interrelationships. Esteemed by mathematicians, *Flatland: A Romance of Many Dimensions* (1884) by 'A Square' interprets the incarnation via 'Fourth Dimensional' geometry, while lightheartedly pressing for human rights. His theological summa, *The Spirit on the Waters* (1897), aphoristically supports non-miraculous Christianity.

Andrewes, Lancelot (1555–1626), was born (the precise date unknown) in Barking. His father was a merchant seaman, from whom he probably inherited a flair for languages – he is reputed to have known at least sixteen in adult life. He was educated at Merchant Taylors School and Pembroke Hall, Cambridge. A serious and studious young man, he met many of the rising tide of Puritans at Cambridge, but his own interests were more and more for the older traditions of Christian thought. He graduated in 1578 and became a Fellow of his college, was ordained four years later, and was given the post of Catechist, which immediately put him in the position for which in later years he was renowned, namely that of preacher. Evidently his sermons attracted some degree of attention, and in 1589 he was made incumbent of St Giles, Cripplegate, which was held with a prebendal stall in St Paul's Cathedral that had associated with it the role of penitentiary. Andrewes did his best to revive this ministry and spent part of each day in Lent walking up and down an aisle of the cathedral making himself available for individual counsel and advice. Eleven years later he preached before the Court on the Sunday after Easter, 1600, on the need for private confession, a sermon that caused something of a storm among those who feared that he was turning the clock back to Catholicism, when all he was doing was to give biblical authority for the practice of private confession as contained in the office for the sick in the Prayer Book. In 1597, he was given a prebendal stall also at Westminster Abbey, by which time he was preaching before Queen Elizabeth. In 1601, although the most junior of the canons, he was still elevated to the Deanery of Westminster, in which capacity he officiated at the funeral of the Queen, and also at the coronation of King James. This latter relationship was to prove of vital importance to his future. He was one of the few people the King listened to intently and in depth. Preferment inevitably followed. He became Bishop of Chichester in 1606, Ely in 1609, and finally Winchester in 1619. As a diocesan bishop, he preached at nearly every major festival and solemn season, Christmas, Lent and Whitsun before King James at Court. He died on 25 September 1626. His four major publications draw various strands of his life together. First, he was closely involved in the production of the Authorized Version of the Bible in 1611. Partly the result of the Hampton Court Conference in 1604, when Puritans met with the new king and other churchmen to air grievances about church matters, this remarkable project was divided into different groups; Andrewes chaired those responsible for translating the first twelve books of the Old Testament, from Genesis to 2 Kings. The intricacy of that task cannot be overestimated, and although William Tyndale's translation of much of the scriptures lies more firmly behind the Authorized Version than many people today are led to believe, Andrewes's sure knowledge of Hebrew – demonstrated in his prayers and sermons – will have equipped him well for this lasting work. Second, he published at King James's suggestion his *Response to Cardinal Bellarmine* in 1610. Robert Bellarmine was a Jesuit and probably the greatest Catholic theologian of his day. Bellarmine had already written a counter-attack on a work by the King himself, at the Pope's instigation, to prove that the Church of England was no church whatever. Andrewes' reply reads like a Bentley car driving along with effortless style, huge amounts of power in reserve, and a faultless engine. The next two main works were both published posthumously. The *96 Sermons* were gathered together at King Charles's instigation by William Laud and John Buckeridge and published in 1629. By that time, Laud was Bishop of London and Buckeridge (who as Bishop of Rochester had preached at Andrewes' funeral) was Bishop of Ely. Reprinted repeatedly in the years following, they express the mind of Andrewes, bulging with ideas, at all times seeing many things, but always whole, and drawing on many different sources, particularly patristic. Finally, there are the *Preces Privatae* (Private Prayers) of Andrewes. These were never intended for publication, since they were, literally, his own private prayers. Andrewes had two copies in his lifetime; one he gave to William Laud, which survives, and another Richard Drake, a Fellow of Pembroke, obtained from Samuel Wright, Andrewes' secretary. The first edition was published in 1675, since which times there have been several, notably that by F. E. Brightman, which was published with copious sources and other material in 1903.

Andrewes is without doubt along with Hooker one of the two giants of the era in which Anglicanism took shape. He was no Anglo-Catholic before his time, nor does he fit into any other convenient mould. He is his own man. And that shines through in his works, for although there are at times sources and hidden (or less hidden!) agendas sufficient to keep a lesser mind happily reeling interminably, Andrewes is always the master of the material, the subject, the sources. The most important aspect of Andrewes for the development of Anglicanism lies in the close integration between his preaching and his praying. In the 1903 edition of the Private Prayers just mentioned, one of the feats performed by Brightman is to give copious short quotations from his sermons in an appendix. The echoes between them are sometimes uncanny. For example, in his prayers for each morning of the week, there is always a short section on 'Faith', which is invariably a quasi-credal prayer. On Fridays he would pray a prayer beginning, 'I believe that thou didst create me: the workmanship of thy hands despise not.' In a sermon on prayer he once uttered the words, 'We are thy workmanship created by

Thee; therefore "despise not the works of thy own hands".' And the same sermon is quoted three further times in this short prayer. It is true that Andrewes actually prayed these devotions in Latin, Greek and Hebrew, which means that there is no 'correct' English version (and modern versions are therefore just as possible as Cranmerian English); nonetheless, the proximity if image and idea is striking.

Another outstanding feature of Andrewes is his conception of authority, which is at once dynamic but also rooted in tradition, at once ready to correct misapprehensions and willing to be open to new insights that the Spirit may show to the Church. In 1617 at Whitsun, preaching at Holyrood Palace Chapel on the occasion of the fiftieth anniversary of the coronation of King James as VI of Scotland, he states that 'we submit our heads in ordination to have hands laid upon them', and refers to the principal criteria for tradition: 'This book chiefly [i.e. the Bible]; but in a good part also, by the books of the ancient Fathers, in whom the scent of this ointment was fresh, and the temper true; on whose writings it lieth thick, and we thence strike it off, and gather it safely.' Here is a man who sees tradition as a living dynamism, to be rediscovered, reappropriated.

A special ingredient in the Andrewes theological repertoire is the notion of sharing in the divine nature (2 Peter 1.4). A favourite theme in the Eastern Fathers, Andrewes will have been aware of the sensitivity with which it had been handled in the West. Preaching the sermon on absolution on the Sunday after Easter in 1600 while still a priest, he approaches the matter circumspectly, as if defining his terms: 'Christ, to whom alone this commission [i.e. John 20.22f.] was originally granted, having ordained Himself a body, would work by bodily means, and having taken the nature of a man upon Him, would honour the nature He had so taken.' Here is the embodiment of the Christian faith, the natural theology that has run through Anglican theology in various ways, with its starting-point in the human person, taken, honoured, redeemed. There are times when he is more direct, using a favourite device, contrast, as at Christmas 1609: 'We made the sons of God, as He is the Son of Man; we made partakers of His divine, as he of our human nature.'

In his sermons, too, there are a number of tricks which he uses that have inspired Anglican (and other) writers in the period since. One is the emphasis on the Trinity. The Prayer Book Collect for Trinity Sunday, itself written originally by Alcuin of York (c.735–804) is couched in the Augustinian phraseology such as 'in the power of the divine majesty to worship the unity'. Andrewes, following in part Hooker in his *Laws of Ecclesiastical Polity*, V, sets out to write of the Trinity in more dynamic terms. In the same absolution sermon, he draws the Trinity from his text (John 20.23): 'To the service and ministry of which divine work a commission is here granted to the Apostles. And first, they have their sending from God the Father, their inspiring from God the Holy Ghost, their commission from God the Son.' And yet more directly in an iconographic brushstroke at Whitsun in 1612, when speaking of the baptism of Christ, that very Eastern epiphany of the Trinity, 'The Father in the voice, the Son in the flood, the Holy Ghost in the shape of a dove.'

Finally, Andrewes' theology is thoroughly sacramental and eschatological. One of his styles is to conclude his sermons with a call to receive the eucharist and to look forward to the end of all things. The sheer cumulative effect of this is to bounce the eucharist off whatever text he has chosen for the occasion and to set all Christian life, in all its complexities and difficulties, in the context of eternity. Preachers since have emulated one or other of these traits, but seldom both, and seldom with such uncontrived success. Preaching at Christmas 1616 on the meeting of the virtues (Ps. 85.11, 12), he ends by calling the Church to the eucharistic 'meeting':

> The sooner and the better to procure this meeting, the Church meets us . . . with bread and wine . . . Where truth from the earth may look up to heaven and confess; and righteousness from heaven may look down and pardon; where we may shew mercy, in giving where need is; and offer peace, in forgiving where cause is. . . . And even so them let there be. So, may our end be as the end of the first verse, in peace; and as the end of the second, in heaven. . . . So we may then meet in a perfect man, in the measure of the fulness of the age of Christ.

All these strands, and much more, converge in Andrewes' theology, as has been demonstrated by various studies, including the seminal work by Nicholas Lossky, a Russian Orthodox lay theologian in France. For what stands out most prominently is Andrewes' ecumenical vision, all the more surprising in a man who (as far as we know) never set foot outside Britain. And much of it served up with a lavish use of vivid language. It is no surprise that the Tractarians rediscovered him and edited his works in the Library of Anglo-Catholic Theology series, nor yet that T. S. Eliot (whose 'Journey of the Magi' was inspired by his Christmas 1622 sermon) should have written so decisively in an essay published in 1928. Andrewes, it would seem, keeps coming back, not so much on concepts as a man playing lovingly with the things of God.

The works of Andrewes were collected and edited by J. P. Wilson and J. Bliss as *The Works of Lancelot Andrewes*, 11 volumes, (London: Parker, 1841–54). In addition, there are the sermons and lectures delivered while at St Giles' Cripplegate, and published as *Apospasmatia Sacra: or a collection of posthumous and orphan Lectures: delivered at St Pauls and St Giles his Church* (London: Hodgkinson, 1657).

The seminal edition of the Private Prayers is *The Preces Privatae of Lancelot Andrewes*, translated with an introduction and notes by F. E. Brightman (London: Methuen, 1903).

For a biography, see Paul Welsby, *Lancelot Andrewes 1555–1626* (London: SPCK, 1958). For a study of his theology, see Nicholas Lossky, *Lancelot Andrewes the Preacher (1555–1626): The Origins of the Mystical Theology of the Church of England* (Oxford: Clarendon Press, 1991). See also T. S. Eliot, *For Lancelot Andrewes: Essays on Style and Order* (London: Faber, 1928, reprinted 1970), 11–26. A. M. Allchin, *Participation in God: A Forgotten Strand in Anglican Tradition* (London: Darton, Longman and Todd, 1988), 7–23. Kenneth Stevenson, *Covenant of Grace Renewed: A Vision of the Eucharist in the Seventeenth Century* (London: Darton, Longman and Todd, 1994) 39–66; Kenneth Stevenson, 'Human Nature Honoured: Absolution in Lancelot Andrewes', in Martin Dudley (ed.), *Like a Two-Edged Sword: The Word of God in Liturgy and History* (Norwich: Canterbury Press, 1995) 113–37; and Kenneth Stevenson, *Handing On: Borderlands of Worship and Tradition* (London: Darton, Longman, and Todd, 1996).

See also Marianne Dorman (ed.), *The Sermons of Lancelot Andrewes*, vol. I, *Nativity, Lenten and Passion*; vol. II, *Paschal and Pentecostal* (Edinburgh, Cambridge, Durham: The Pentland Press, 1992, 1993). P. E. Hewison, *Lancelot Andrewes: Selected Writings* (Manchester: Carcanet Press, 1995). (KS)

Arnold, Thomas (1795–1842), scholar, liberal theologian, and Head Master of Rugby School. Educated in classics, he obtained a fellowship at Oriel in 1815. Remarkably he was appointed Headmaster of Rugby in 1828 at the young age of thirty-three without applying or interviewing for the post. At Rugby he gained a reputation as one of England's great educators. Believing in the essential unity of church and state, he tried to educate his students with a high sense of duty and public service based upon religious principles pertaining to personal character. In 1841 he was appointed Regius Professor of Modern History at Oxford but prematurely died the following year. Although disinterested in the philosophical theology of Germany, he was captivated by historical criticism in the biblical study of Neander. His *Sermons* (1829–34) are a persuasive demonstration of how in the context of faith historical criticism can support and complement Scripture rather than weaken it. Concerning the progressive revelation of God in Scripture and man's development in understanding it, Arnold addressed himself in his 'Essay on the Right Interpretation and Understanding of Scripture' which is found in his second volume of *Sermons*. The spiritual meaning of Scripture is for him distinct from the literal meaning, without any denial of the historicity of the text. Believing that bishops served only a legal function in ordinations, together with his views on the unity of church and state, 'the State in its highest perfection becomes the Church', brought him into serious conflict with the Tractarians. His article in the *Edinburgh Review* in 1836, 'The Oxford Malignants' was written in defence of Dr Hampden and ensured the enduring antagonism of Newman. Perhaps his greatest influence was upon the large number of boys who passed through Rugby School and who went on to play significant roles both in Britain and in the British Empire.

Oxford Dictionary of The Christian Church, 93.
M. G. Reardon, 1973. *From Coleridge to Gore* (London: Longman Group Limited).
T. Walrond in *Dictionary of National Biography*, II, 113–17.

Barnes, Robert (1495-1540), Protestant divine and martyr. An Augustinian friar, he joined the convent of Austin friars at Cambridge which he later served as prior of the house. After returning from study in Louvain, he was involved with a revival of learning at Cambridge and was made D.D. in 1523. After exposure to the writings of Luther he embraced his views. Brought up on heresy charges for preaching against the special observance of great festivals, in a sermon preached 25 December 1525 he was convicted and sentenced to recant or burn. Choosing to recant he spent three years in prison before faking death by drowning and escaping to Germany. At this time he became a friend of Luther and his circle and wrote a treatise in defence of Lutheran views in 1531. This same year he was invited back to England by Cromwell, who wanted to use Barnes's knowledge of Luther's Protestant arguments to secure Henry VIII's divorce against Roman Catholic opposition. From 1534 to 1536 he was sent by the King on various trips to Germany to generate support for his position. He lost favour with the King after his negotiations in Germany for the acceptance of the marriage of the King to Ann of Cleves did not succeed. By preaching stridently against the Bishop of Winchester, Gardiner, who had attacked the Lutheran view of justification by faith, he further endangered his weakened position with the King. After being forced to sign a retraction, he once again went back to his Lutheran views and preached them in a sermon with Gardiner present. On 30 July, 1540 he was sent to the Tower and burned. His major works include *Furnemlich Artickelder Christlichen Kirchen*; *A Supplication unto the most gracious prince Henry VIII* (London: 1534); *Vitae Romanorum Pontificum* (Basle: 1535); *Various Tracts on Faith and Justification*; and *What the Church is and who bee thereof*. His confession of faith at the time of his death was published the same year in Germany.

J. G. in *Dictionary of National Biography*, XXIX, 253–6.

Baxter, Richard (1615–91). Pastor, evangelist, theologian and church-man, Baxter presented himself as a conforming Puritan Anglican till 1645, a non-partisan Puritan while Anglicanism was outlawed, and a nonconforming Puritan Anglican after 1662. Largely self-educated, he was ordained in 1638. After a year as a preaching schoolmaster and another as a pastoral assistant, he fulfilled at Kidderminster a fourteen-year ministry (1641–60, with 1642–7 away as an army chaplain) that transformed the town and, with his writings, made him perhaps England's best-known clergyman. Under Cromwell's congregationalist church establishment he created the Worcestershire Association, an informal quasi-presbytery of pastors committed to parish discipline and family catechizing, and this was widely imitated. Acknowledged as a leader, Baxter shared in the Sion College discussions of 1660 and the Savoy Conference of 1661 on how episcopacy and liturgical uniformity should be reinstated. Having declined a bishopric and found the terms of continued Anglican ministry under the 1662 Act of Uniformity unac-ceptable, he thereafter lived near London, attending his parish church, preaching as opportunity allowed, and writing constantly (he ended up the most voluminous English theologian ever). Though tagged a Presbyterian, as nonconforming clergy generally were after 1662, he remained a Protestant episcopal Erastian national churchman, identifying himself as a 'mere Christian' and 'mere nonconformist', championing the parochial system and pleading for an enlarged comprehensiveness that would embrace clergy ejected in 1662. Christian and church unity, both at home and abroad, was for 40 years his constant concern.

Baxter's practical writings include at least four stellar achievements: *The Saints' Everlasting Rest* (1650), a sprawling, electrifying meditation on how the hope of heaven should impact life on earth; *The Reformed Pastor* (1656), a searching plea to clergy to take their teaching and con-verting ministry seriously – 'the best manual of the clergyman's duty in the language' (H. Hensley Henson, 1925); *A Call to the Unconverted* (1657), in Baxter's phrase a 'wakening persuasive' of landmark status; and *A Christian Directory* (1673), the fullest compendium of Puritan lore on the Christian life that was ever produced. It is as a practical and devotional writer that Baxter is deservedly remembered, though his extraordinary powers of logical analysis and rhetorical articulation mark all his works. But his learned doctrinal folios, *Richard Baxter's Catholick Theology* (1675), an ecumenical *tour de force* seeking to square Reformed, Lutheran, Arminian and Roman Catholic systems with each other, and the Latin *Methodus Theologiae* (1681), an attempt to break into the world of inter-national Protestant theology with a rejigged Ramism (trichotomizing instead of dichotomizing), were stillborn; so, it seems, were his brilliant apologetic treatises, *Reasons of the Christian Religion* (1667) and *More Reasons for the Christian Religion* (1672); and his many polemics against papal imperialism, apologias for nonconformity, and pleas for an establishment that would embrace the presbyterally ordained and others rejected in 1662, were tracts for the times that in a post-Erastian age have only historical interest.

Marginalized by the Restoration Church, Baxter is often not seen as an Anglican theologian at all. He was, however, a mainstream exponent of the reformed Augustinianism that united Anglicans for two generations following the Elizabethan settlement. Its focus was God bringing lost sinners to faith and regenerate life in Christ through the sovereign agency of the Holy Spirit, according to his electing decree. From this centre sprang defence of the Trinitarian gospel of atonement and justification; exploration of the life of conscious confident communion with God in faith, love, hope and holiness that the converted are privileged to enjoy; and affirmation against Roman Catholicism of the catholic visible church as essentially a faithful fellowship, locally manifested, that lives by the New Testament gospel and orders its liturgy, ministry and sacraments in a way which shows dependence on, and appreciation of, God's life-giving grace. In tackling all these theological and pastoral issues Baxter occupied familiar Anglican ground, except in his formulation of justification by faith.

Viewing justification (correctly) as a Kingdom blessing, and conceiving God's Kingdom (less correctly) in seventeenth-century political terms as analogous to a European monarchy, Baxter explained Christ's death as an act of universal redemption, in virtue of which God has made a new law offering amnesty to breakers of his old law who now repent and submit to Christ as Lord. Repentance and faith, being obedience to the new law, thus become the personal righteousness that qualifies us for that law's benefits. This conception was constantly and understandably criticized by Baxter's peers as a doctrine of justification by works; they called it Neonomianism.

Baxter's life spanned a transitional era in which the analytical-polemical theological style in which he excelled was superseded by the reactionary Latitudinarian rationalism, moralistic but inexact, that marked Hanoverian Anglicanism throughout. In this new era Baxter's fair-mindedness, moderation, precision and pacific purpose in polemics went for nothing, while the intricacies of his argumentation repelled. His *Practical Works* (four folios, 1707) lived; his other publications died.

Baxter tenaciously championed Archbishop Usher's *Reduction of Episcopacy unto the form of Synodical Government received in the Ancient Church* (1641), where each chief pastor is viewed as bishop of his congregation, and diocesans chair clerical gatherings as first among equals. In this, as in his pastoral idealism and devotional authenticity, Baxter might yet be thought a prophet for our time.

Richard Baxter, *Practical Works*, 4 vols. (Ligonier, Penn.: Soli Deo Gloria, 1990–1).
Richard Baxter, *A Holy Commonwealth*, ed. William Lamont (Cambridge: Cambridge University Press, 1994).
The Autobiography of Richard Baxter, abridged J. M. Lloyd Thomas, ed. N. H. Keeble, 1974. (London: Everyman's University Library).
N. H. Keeble and Geoffrey F. Nuttall, 1991. *Calendar of the Correspondence of Richard Baxter* (Oxford: Clarendon Press).
F. J. Powicke, 1924, 1927. *A Life of the Reverend Richard Baxter 1615–1691* and *The Reverend Richard Baxter Under the Cross* (1662–91) (London: Jonathan Cape).
Geoffrey F. Nuttall, 1965. *Richard Baxter* (London: Thomas Nelson).
N. H. Keeble, 1982. *Richard Baxter Puritan Man of Letters* (Oxford: Clarendon Press).
Hans Boersma, 1993. *A Hot Peppercorn: Richard Baxter's Doctrine of Justification* (Zoetermeer: Boekencentrum). (JIP)

Bell, George Kennedy Allen (1883–1958), Anglican bishop and ecumenical statesman. Educated at Oxford, Bell served a curacy in Leeds before becoming in 1914 a domestic chaplain to the then Archbishop of Canterbury, Randall Davidson, under whom he established himself as both administrator and skilful diplomat. From 1924 to 1929 he was Dean of Canterbury; thereafter, until shortly before his death, he was Bishop of Chichester. In his role as bishop he is remembered not only as a diocesan pastor and a weighty voice in public affairs, but also as encourager of the arts.

Bell's contribution to the life of the Western church was primarily practical rather than theological. He was one of the major architects of the early ecumenical movement, and chaired both the *Life and Work* movement in the 1930s and the World Council of Churches from its inception in 1948. In its formative years between the two world wars, the ecumenical movement owed a great deal not only to his tireless committee work and his skills in organization and the cultivation of contacts, but also to his consistent promotion of a vision of the worldwide church as a society in which human fellowship is restored through the gospel. This vision (expressed, for example, in his semi-popular works *Christian Unity: The Anglican Position, Christianity and World Order*, and *The Kingship of Christ*) was neither theoretical nor sentimental. Not only did it drive a life devoted to fostering ecumenical relations, it also lay behind his advocacy for Jewish and other refugees, internees and prisoners of war during the Second World War. In a courageous series of prophetic speeches in the House of Lords (collected in *The Church and Humanity*) Bell called into question the moral and spiritual propriety of aspects of the Government's conduct of the war, such as obliteration bombing. Moreover, both before and during the war, Bell (almost alone among English church leaders) retained contacts with members of the Confessing Church in Germany, with many of whom (such as Bonhoeffer) he had established friendships through his ecumenical work. Though Bell's abhorrence of the Nazi regime was made plain, his refusal to identify the German nation as a whole with Nazism occasioned much misunderstanding from church and political leaders, and may have led to his being passed over as successor to William Temple as Archbishop of Canterbury.

Apart from his writings on ecumenical and church issues intended for a general audience, Bell's chief literary legacy is his life of Randall Davidson (Bell's intimate acquaintance with the subject makes this a major source for Anglican history in the late nineteenth and early twentieth centuries), and his edition of the *Documents on Christian Unity*. But Bell's primary gift to contemporary Anglicanism is the example of his life and work. Though his vision of the Church is less dominant in modern ecumenism, which is theologically and culturally more diverse, he is of singular significance as a Christian leader of unparalleled spiritual integrity, consistency of moral vision and undeflected application to the pursuit of ideals.

Randall Davidson, 2 vols. (Oxford: Oxford University Press, 1935).
Christianity and World Order (Harmondsworth: Penguin, 1941).
The Church and Humanity, 1939–46 (London: Longman, Green, 1946).
Christian Unity: The Anglican Position (London: Hodder and Stoughton, 1948).
The Kingship of Christ. The Story of the World Council of Churches (Harmondsworth: Penguin, 1954).
Documents on Christian Unity, 4 vols. (Oxford: Oxford University Press, 1924–58).
R. C. D. Jasper, 1967. *George Bell: Bishop of Chichester* (Oxford: Oxford University Press).
E. H. Robertson, 1995. *Unshakeable Friend. George Bell and the German Churches* (London: Council of Churches for Britain and Ireland). (JW)

Blair, James (1655–1743), Scottish clergyman, Anglican commissary, founder and first president of the College of William and Mary, Virginia. Graduated from the University of Edinburgh in 1673, he was ordained in 1679. Forced to resign his position as a minister for refusing to submit to the test oath acknowledging James II, a Roman Catholic, heir to the British throne, Blair went to the colony of Virginia as a missionary. In 1689 he was designated the first colonial commissary to the Bishop of London, under whose jurisdiction the American colonies were. With no previous model to follow, Blair was at first determined to structure the colonial church along traditional lines, attempting to establish ecclesiastical courts and bolster and stabilize colonial clergy salaries. But his efforts came up against a colonial temperament that was at least as determined in its sense of independence and strong local autonomy, particularly as the latter was embodied in the power enjoyed by parish vestries. Blair learned quickly that the success of his mission lay more in his ability to persuade than in any perceived authority of his office. In this respect he was moderately successful, especially in fostering solidarity among his clergy, and in proving himself a formidable advocate when church prerogatives were at stake; the latter demonstrated in his securing the dismissals of two colonial governors. Blair's crowning achievement was the founding of the College of William and Mary in 1693, where he served as the first President. Despite persistent opposition, both colonial and hierarchical indifference, and a devastating fire, he managed to see the college firmly established before his death in 1743.

Dictionary of Christianity in America.
J. F. Woolverton, 1984. *Colonial Anglicanism in North America* (Detroit: Wayne State University Press).

Bliss, William Dwight Porter (1856–1926) Episcopal clergyman and Christian socialist. Educated at Amherst College (B.A., 1878), and Hartford Theological Seminary (B.D., 1882), he served as a Congregational minister for three years prior to his ordination in the Episcopal Church in 1887. Bliss served as Rector of Grace Church, Boston until 1890. Attracted by Christian Socialism he was influenced by F. D. Maurice, Charles Kingsley, and Henry George. Bliss became the primary impetus behind the Christian Socialist Movement in the United States when he founded the Society of Christian Socialists in 1889, the first organization of its kind. He was publisher of their periodical *The Dawn* until 1896. The president of the National Reform Union, he co-founded the Church Association for the Advancement of the Interests of Labor (1899) and the American Institute of Social Services (1909). Though more activist than scholar, he did edit a few works including *The Communion of John Ruskin* (1891), his own collected essays entitled *Handbook of Socialism* (1895), and the *Encyclopaedia of Social Reform* (1897). Generally regarded as a liberal evangelical, Bliss was originally attracted to the Episcopal Church because of its sacramental character and catholicity. These otherwise disparate theological strands, combined with his inexhaustible energy and social consciousness, produced in Bliss a unique, and somewhat enigmatic theology of social regeneration. Basing all lasting social solutions on the redemptive work of Christ, he was able to distinguish his own perception of the Kingdom of God from the popular socialist utopianism of his day. Thus social regeneration

84

necessarily began with individual regeneration, but true regeneration necessarily bears fruit in social consciousness. In practice Bliss's Christo-centric theology embodied the best emphases of both evangelicalism (repentance, faith) and catholicity (the sacraments).

Dictionary of American Biography, I.
Dictionary of American Religious Biography.
Dictionary of Christianity in America.
R. B. Dressner, 1978. 'William Dwight Porter Bliss' Christian Socialism', *Church History* 47:66–82.
C. L. Webber, 1959. 'William Dwight Porter Bliss (1856–1926): Priest and Socialist', *Historical Magazine of the PEC* 28:9–39.

Bennett, Dennis Joseph (1917–91) Episcopal clergyman, popular author and pioneer of the charismatic movement. Born in England, the son of a Congregational minister, he moved to the United States in 1927. Ordained into the ministry of the Congregational Church in 1949, he served congregations in San Diego for a brief period before being appointed lay vicar of St Paul's Episcopal Church in Lancaster, California. Ordained deacon in 1952, and priest later that same year, he was called to be rector of St Mark's Church in Van Nuys, California in 1953. In 1959 Bennett publicly announced to the parish that he and many of the members had received the baptism of the Holy Spirit. Feeling pressure to defend his new beliefs he resigned voluntarily for reflection. In 1960 he accepted a call to a small mission parish on the verge of closing in Seattle, Washington. Under his ministry St Luke's Church quickly became one of the strongest parishes in the Diocese of Olympia, and a major centre of influence for the charismatic movement, which was now spreading throughout other mainline denominations as well his own. His personal testimony of Spirit Baptism was given in his first book *Nine o'clock in the Morning* (1970). Bennett's first wife, Elberta, died in 1963. Three years later he married Rita Marie Reed, a leading figure in the charismatic movement in her own right. Together they formed Christian Renewal Association, and co-authored several books including the best-selling *The Holy Spirit and You* (1971). Leaving pastoral ministry in 1981 to pursue writing, speaking and conducting seminars with his wife, he was designated an honorary canon of his diocese for his work in the charismatic renewal.

D. Bennett, 1974. *Nine O'clock in the Morning* (London: Coverdale House).
D. and R. Bennett, 1974. *The Holy Spirit and You* (London: Coverdale House).
S. M. Burgess and G. B. McGee, 1989. *Dictionary of Pentecostal and Charismatic Movements* (Grand Rapids: Zondervan).

Booty, John Everitt (1925–) Episcopal priest and Anglican historian. Educated at Wayne University (B.A., 1952), Virginia Theological Seminary (B.D., 1953), and Princeton University (M.A., 1957, Ph.D., 1960), he was ordained to the priesthood in 1954. After serving various churches he held academic posts including: Assistant Professor of Church History (1958–64) and Associate Professor (1964–7) Virginia Theological Seminary; Professor of Church History at Episcopal Divinity School, Cambridge, Massachusetts (1967–82); Dean of the School of Theology (1982–5), and Professor of Anglican Studies (1984–90), University of the South, Sewanee, Tennessee. One of the foremost Anglican historians of the twentieth century, Booty's particular expertise is the Elizabethan church and the sixteenth-century Anglican Divines, John Jewel and Richard Hooker. A prolific author of many books and articles, his most important books are *John Jewel as Apologist of the Church of England* (1963), *The Godly Kingdom of Tudor England* (1981), and *The Book of Common Prayer in the Life of the Episcopal Church* (1990). Several of his important articles include: 'Hooker and Anglicanism' in W. S. Hill (ed.), *Studies in Richard Hooker*; 'The Bishop Confronts the Queen: John Jewel and the Failure of the English Reformation' in F. Church and T. George (eds.) *Continuity and Discontinuity in Church History*; 'Richard Hooker' in W. J. Wolf (ed.) *The Spirit of Anglicanism* (1979); and 'The Judicious Mr. Hooker and Authority in the Elizabethan Church' in *Authority in the Anglican Communion*. S. W. Sykes (ed.) (1987). Booty has also edited a number of important scholarly works including John Jewel's *Apology of the Church of England* (1963), *The Book of Common Prayer 1559: The Elizabethan Prayer Book* (1976), Volume IV of the Folger Shakespeare Library Edition of Richard Hooker's *Works* (1982), and, with English scholar Stephen Sykes, *The Study of Anglicanism* (1988).

J. E. Booty, 1963. *John Jewel as Apologist of the Church of England* (London: SPCK).
Episcopal Church, USA. *The Clerical Directory* (1995).
R. Hooker, *Works*, vol. IV, Folger Shakespeare Library Edition. (Cambridge: Harvard University Press 1982).
S. W. Sykes, 1987. *Authority in the Anglican Communion* (Toronto: Anglican Book Centre).
S. W. Sykes and J. E. Booty, 1988. *The Study of Anglicanism* (London: SPCK).

Bramhall, John (1594–1663) Bishop of Derry, 1634; Archbishop of Armagh, 1661. Theologian, man of affairs and administrator, Bramhall was a leader of moral and physical courage in troubled circumstances which drew on all his Yorkshire resilience. The pastor who refused to desert his flock in Ripon 'in a time of most contagious and destructive pestilence' was the same who, ejected from his diocese, refused 'to serve the times' and was driven into a 12-year exile on the Continent. Earlier imprisoned in Ireland (to which he courageously returned in 1648), he had two narrow escapes from being captured, and Vesey records that Cromwell 'declared that he would have given a good sum of money for that Irish Canterbury'. Astoundingly during those twelve years of banishment among his fellow-exiles 'whose minds are more intent on what they should eat tomorrow, than what they should write', Bramhall in his poverty wrote seven books setting out a robust and unapologetic Anglicanism. In old age at the Restoration he was to be the instrument of renewal, consecrating twelve bishops in St Patrick's Cathedral, Dublin, when Jeremy Taylor was the preacher. Two years later he would preach Bramhall's funeral sermon: 'In him were visible the great lines of Hooker's judiciousness, of Jewel's learning, of the acuteness of bishop Andrews' (Taylor, *Works*, VI, 445).

What was the nature of Bramhall's theology? His books, written in a difficult situation, are all in the nature of replies, as to the Puritans in his *A Fair Warning* (1649), to Roman Catholicism in his *Answer to de la Milletière* (1653), in his *Just Vindication of the Church of England* (1654) and in other works. There was also his forceful reply to Thomas Hobbes's determinism. Strikingly, what emerges is not a self-conscious negative theology but a positive, solid and reasoned Anglicanism. Bramhall records how as a student Samuel Ward had advised him that only a deep knowledge of the Fathers and of the Schoolmen would illuminate contemporary controversies (*Works*, 1676 edn: 636). It was on this basis that he asserted the continuity of Anglicanism with the Early Church – no new faith, no new Orders, no new Church – describing the apostolic succession both of persons and of faith as 'the very nerves and sinews' of that continuing unity and communion (*Works*: 62, 101, 625). We meet in his work what *The Malta Report* (1968) calls 'the Anglican distinction of fundamentals from non-fundamentals', and the classical threefold appeal to Scripture, tradition and reason is thematic for his theology. The clear demarcation of fundamentals, the *hapax*, allows for liberality in secondary questions. This is evident in his writings and is underlined by his critical approval of Grotius (*Works*: 494, 611). His eucharistic theology is elaborated in the *Answer to de la Milletière* in which he affirms 'A true Real Presence, which no genuine son of the Church of England did ever deny . . . Christ said not, after this or that manner, *neque con, neque sub, neque trans*. Therefore we place it (i.e. the manner of the presence) among the opinions of the schools, not among the Articles of our Faith.'

Works (Folio edition 1676); Library of Anglo-Catholic Theology edn, 5 vols. (Oxford, 1847).

Athanasius Hibernicus, a *Life* by his contemporary, Thomas Vesey.
W. J. Sparrow Simpson, 1927. *Archbishop Bramhall* (London).
H. R. McAdoo, 1964. *John Bramhall and Anglicanism* (Dublin).
H. R. McAdoo, 1965. *The Spirit of Anglicanism* (London and New York), 368–85. (HM)

Bray, Thomas (1658–1730), Anglican clergyman, commissary, and founder of the SPCK and the SPG. Born of a humble Shropshire family, he received a B.A. degree at All Soul's, Oxford (1678), and later B.D. and D.D. degrees at Magdalen College. Ordained priest in 1682, he served as rector of Sheldon from 1690 to 1695. Appointed in 1695 by the Bishop of London, as commissary for the struggling Anglican presence in the colony of Maryland, Bray set to work on securing a qualified clergy for the vacant parishes of Maryland. Realizing that only poorer clergy would respond to his invitation, he conditioned his acceptance upon the bishops' approval for the provision of colonial libraries. With enthusiastic support for his plan, he set out to raise the needed funds and produced a comprehensive volume of the ideal clerical library entitled *Bibliotheca Parochialis* (1697). A born teacher, with a clear, orderly mind, the selection of works which Bray included in *Bibliotheca Parochialis* also reveals a range of scholarship that few in his day, or since, could rival. His passion for Christian education had already been established by the publication in 1696 of his four-volume commentary on the Catechism of the Church. Bray believed that the neglect and decay of Christian teaching was the source of all societal evil and wantonness, and that the revival of Christian knowledge was the only true remedy. Realizing that the needs of the colonies could not be met by voluntary efforts alone, he set out a plan to establish a chartered body to hold and administer funds for overseas work. The result in 1698 was the establishing of the Society for Promoting Christian Knowledge (SPCK), and in 1701 the Society for the Propagation of the Gospel (SPG), the latter to supply the want of 'learned and orthodox ministers' in the plantations, and colonies overseas. These agencies came to embody Bray's real genius and vision in understanding that the frontier problem could only be addressed by assuaging intellectual poverty.

S. Sykes and J. Booty (eds.), 1988. *The Study of Anglicanism* (London: SPCK).
H. P. Thompson, 1954. *Thomas Bray* (London: SPCK).

Brent, Charles Henry (1862–1929), bishop and ecumenist, was born 24 April 1862 in Newcastle, Ontario, the child of Henry Brent, who was an Anglican clergyman, and his wife Sophia Frances Cummings. He received his education at Trinity College School, Port Hope, which he entered in 1880, and Trinity College, Toronto, which he entered in 1882 and from which he graduated with honours in classics in 1884. After two years of private study he was ordained a deacon (1886) and priest (1887).

Brent's early ministry was characterized by a scrappy Anglo-Catholicism. Unable to find a parish position in the Diocese of Toronto, in which there was party strife between Evangelical supporters of Wycliffe College and the High-Church supporters of Trinity College, Brent crossed the border to the United States and accepted a position as an organist and curate at St John's Church in Buffalo, New York. After a year he moved to St Andrew's Mission in Buffalo, but left soon, after a dispute. Brent favoured the use of altar candles; Bishop Arthur Cleveland Coxe objected to their use and insisted that as bishop he had final say about worship in missions of his diocese. Brent moved to Boston, where he became a novice of the Society of St John the Evangelist (Cowley Fathers) and a missioner at the society's St Augustine's Mission for Negroes. In 1891 Brent was involved in another dispute. The English superior of the order recalled the head of the community in Boston because he had not campaigned with sufficient energy against the election of Phillips Brooks as Bishop of Massachusetts. Brent went to England to complain directly to the superior and then resigned from the order. While he would never again be affiliated with a monastic order, Brent's early experience with the Cowley Fathers influenced him for the remainder of his ministry. He never married and would always place a high premium on the value of prayer.

On his return to the United States, Brent accepted a position as an assistant to the rector of St Stephen's, a parish in the impoverished South End of Boston. The rector, Henry Martyn Torbert, had, like Brent, recently resigned from the Cowley Fathers because of the recall of the community's head. The two men would work together until 1901, when Brent would succeed Torbert as rector.

In October of 1901 the General Convention selected Brent as the Episcopal Church's first missionary bishop for the Philippines. Brent was consecrated in December of the same year. During his episcopate he focused his efforts in three directions: toward the American diplomatic, business and military community; to the non-Christian Igorot and Moro peoples; and against the international opium trade. Although criticized for his decision, he chose not to direct Evangelical efforts toward the large nominally Roman Catholic population of the colony, even discouraging former Roman Catholics who took the initiative and asked for his assistance.

Prior to the Spanish-American War, Spanish authorities had allowed the sale of opium in the Philippines, but had limited the quantities available, thereby keeping both the prices and the profits for opium traders high. This situation changed when the Americans took control of the colony. Drug traders took an initial American decision not to renew the monopolies granted by the Spanish as an invitation for an open market. The number of people engaged in the drug trade, the quantities of opium and the attendant social problems increased rapidly. The colonial government responded with a plan to re-establish the Spanish quotas, but this aroused so much opposition in the United States that President Theodore Roosevelt vetoed the plan. The colonial government then attempted to suppress the opium trade, but with little success because of the support given the trade by other colonial powers. Bishop Brent came to see the problem as an international one and played an active role in seeking a solution. He served in a variety of organizations opposing the trade both before and after World War I. He was the president of the International Opium Commission (1908–9), the chair of the US delegation to the International Opium Conference of 1911, the president of that conference in 1912, a member of the League of Nations' advisory board on narcotic drugs, and a delegate to the Second Opium Conference in Geneva (1924).

Brent was elected Bishop of Western New York in October 1917, but delayed beginning his episcopate there in order to serve as senior chaplain to the American Expeditionary Force in Europe during the First World War. He took up his responsibilities in Western New York in 1919 and continued to serve in that position until his death on 27 March 1929. From 1926 to 1928 he was also responsible for the American congregations in Europe.

Brent is best known for his ecumenical activities. Following the World Missionary Conference held in Edinburgh in 1910, he became a committed advocate of ecumenical involvement. He convinced the General Convention that met in the same year to establish a commission to promote a world conference on faith and order. With the cooperation of others, including Episcopal layman Robert Hallowell Gardiner (d. 1924) and Peter Ainslee of the Disciples of Christ, he laid the groundwork for the first World Conference on Faith and Order, which was held at Lausanne, Switzerland in 1927. The body later joined with the Universal Conference on Life and Work (first conference 1925) in forming the World Council of Churches (1948).

Brent was not a systematic thinker. There was, nevertheless, consistency to his thought. He constantly returned to three interrelated themes: mission, ecumenism and the Church's responsibility in the international arena.

(1) Mission. From the time of his early work among the poor in

Boston, Brent saw the need for a unified approach to missions. He rejected any separation between ministering to physical and spiritual needs or between domestic and foreign missions. For Brent, body and soul were so closely related that whatever happened to one affected the other. As he explained in *Splendor of the Human Body* (1904), 'the body is intended by God to be the sole instrument by which the soul acts and through which it receives impressions' so that 'there must be such intimacy between the outer and inner that the health of the soul will find some expression in terms of the body'. (1912 edn: 42)

It was not only those who worked with the poor, however, who needed to keep in mind the relationship of body and soul. *Splendor of the Human Body* was dedicated to the students of Groton School, an exclusive secondary school in Massachusetts. He explained to them the dangers of both sensuality and extreme asceticism.

> In our day, [he cautioned] the pendulum has swung too far, and the moderation of renaissance times has given place to a widespread sense-worship. The cure lies not in a reversion to the moral fierceness of asceticism, nor in Puritan casuistry, but in insistence upon the perfection of the human mechanism and its capacity for noble uses. Men must be inspired from a worship which desecrates to a reverence which exalts and saves, until they know the body as the 'basement for the soul's emprise,' and rejoice in it. (13–14)

Similarly, Brent believed in the essential relationship between domestic and foreign missions. As he explained in 1899, 'the only way to have power and to serve abroad is to live a deep full life at home, and . . . the only way to have large power and to serve at home is to cast the eye far abroad and wind the interests of a whole world around the heart'. (*With God in the World*, 1908 edn: 117). The domestic church received as well as gave in its relationship with foreign missions. He explained,

> not only does the uttermost part of the earth need Christianity, but . . . Christianity needs the uttermost part of the earth. We cannot fully know Christ until all the nations have seen and believed and told their vision. The Church of God is poor, in that it lacks the contribution which the un-Christianized nations can alone give by being evangelized. Just as the speculative East needed in the first days the practical West to balance its concept of the Gospel, and *vice versa*, so it is now. Before we can see the full glory of the Incarnation, representatives of all nations must blend their vision with that which has already been granted. Every separate stone

must be set before the temple reaches its final splendour. Foreign missions are as much for the Church's sake as for the heathen's, as much for the eternal profit of those who are sent as for those to whom they go. (*With God in the World*, 1908 edn: 121)

The expression of such sentiments and the popularity of the book in which they appeared, which was reprinted at least fives times between 1900 and 1920, explain how a priest who spent most of his ministry as an assistant in a parish in a poor section of Boston was elected a bishop in a foreign mission field.

(2) Ecumenism. As he worked in missions, both in the USA and the Philippines, Brent inevitably noticed that other denominations laboured alongside him at a similar task. This led him to two convictions: an unwillingness to dismiss the efforts of others and a strong desire to unite for more effective action.

He came to see a measure of legitimacy and a measure of weakness in every church. 'Neither the Roman, the Greek, any of the Protestant churches with which I am familiar, nor our own, exhibits a superior "Christian *ēthos*". Each has its own distinctive type of righteousness and its individual disposition' (*The Mind of Christ Jesus*: 30–1).

For Brent, the most effective Christian cooperation drew on the distinctive strengths of the various denominations. He also believed that Christians could make strides toward unity by considering their differences, rather than ignoring them. This approach formed the basis for Brent's work with the World Conference on Faith and Order.

(3) His acquaintance with Governor (and later President) William Howard Taft and other American officials in the Philippines gave him an appreciation of the importance of acting not only on a local, but also on an international level. He provided leadership in the international arena in two areas: in the campaign against the international opium trade and during the First World War.

He visited Canadian troops in Europe even before the United States entered the fighting and then returned to visit Americans at the request of the American YMCA. General Pershing, whom he had known from the Philippines, asked Brent to organize the chaplains for the Expeditionary Force. He did so, establishing an interdenominational executive committee.

Brent's internationalism, ecumenism and interest in mission have made him a popular figure for twentieth-century Episcopalians. Historians of the Episcopal Church link his name with those of William Augustus Muhlenberg and William Reed Huntington (the author of the Chicago–Lambeth Quadrilateral) as the Episcopal Church's major contributors to the ecumenical movement. Frederick Ward Kates's edition of three brief works by Brent – *Things that Matter* (1949), *Walking with God* (1956), and *No Other Wealth* (1965) – have kept his thought before the church. Brent is included in the calendar of the 1979 American *Book of Common Prayer*.

Brent's written works are collections of sermons, occasional papers, devotional talks, and what he subtitled in one of his books as 'musings'. The earliest was *With God in the World* (1899), a set of devotional talks on mission delivered while he was in Boston. *The Consolations of the Cross* (1904), *Liberty* (1906), *With God in Prayer* (1907), and *Prisoners of Hope* (1915) were volumes of sermons. *Adventure for God* (1905), *Leadership* (1908), and *The Commonwealth* (ed. R. B. Ogilby, 1930) were lectures. *The Mind of Christ Jesus* (1908) and *Understanding* (1925) focused on ecumenism. *The Sixth Sense* (1912) and *Presence* (1915) reflected upon personal religious experience, and *The Splendor of the Human Body* (1904) on a Christian understanding of the body. *The Conquest of Trouble* (1916) was a meditation on the Psalter. *The Mount of Vision* (1918) contained his reflections upon the First World War. *The Inspiration of Responsibility* (1915) and *The Revelation of Discovery* (1915) were collections of essays. Brent's *A Master Builder* (1916) was a biography of Bishop Henry Satterlee of Washington.
There are two biographies of Brent: Eleanor Slater's *Charles Henry Brent: Everybody's Bishop* (Milwaukee: Morehouse Publishing Co., 1932) and Alexander C. Zabriskie's *Bishop Brent: Crusader for Christian Unity* (Philadelphia: Westminster Press, 1948). A 1969 dissertation focused on his effect upon foreign policy: Emma J. Portuondo, 'The Impact of Bishop Charles Henry Brent upon American Colonial and Foreign Policy, 1901–1917' (Ph.D. diss., The Catholic University of America, 1969). Roy J. Honeywell's *Chaplains of the United States Army* (Washington: Office of the Chief of Chaplains, Department of the Army, 1958) deals briefly with Brent's work with the chaplaincy corps during World War I. (RP)

Brooks, Phillips (1835–93), Episcopal bishop, noted preacher and author was the son of William Gray Brooks and Mary Ann Phillips of Boston. Both parents were the children of New England patrician families. The Brooks family was active and successful in business. The Phillips family was active in education and the church; members of the family participated in the founding of Phillips Exeter Academy, Phillips Andover Academy, and Andover Theological Seminary. Although both families had played important roles in the Congregational Church, they became active in St Paul's Episcopal Church in Boston, during Phillips Brooks's early childhood.

Phillips Brooks attended the Boston Latin School and Harvard University, which he entered in 1851. Upon graduation in 1855 he returned to the Boston Latin School for a brief unsuccessful career as a teacher. The following year he made the decision to enrol in the Virginia Theological Seminary in Alexandria, Virginia, in order to prepare for the ordained ministry of the Episcopal Church. His first year of studies there was not particularly enjoyable; while impressed by the personal piety of the evangelical students and faculty, he found the level of instruction unchallenging and few of the students equipped with the grounding in the classics that he had gained at Boston Latin School and Harvard. He persevered, however, and, thanks to a growing personal friendship with the professor of divinity, William Sparrow, an appointment to teach in the school's preparatory department, and permission to pursue many of his studies at his own pace, his appreciation of the institution increased.

He was ordained a deacon in July of 1859, following the completion of his studies at Virginia. He served in Philadelphia at the Church of the Advent (1859–61) and as rector of Holy Trinity Church (1862–9), before returning to Boston to become the rector of Trinity Church in 1869.

From the very beginning of his ministry, Brooks was recognized as a skilful preacher. In 1877 he delivered a series of lectures at Yale Divinity School on preaching. In 1878 he published the first of what would eventually be seven collections of sermons. A much sought after preacher and lecturer, he was invited to speak or preach in Philadelphia (1879 Bohlen lectures), Westminster Abbey (1880), and Trinity Church, New York (Lent of 1890). In 1880 he was offered and declined the position as Preacher to Harvard University and professor of Christian ethics.

Brooks was twice elected to the episcopate: by the Diocese of Pennsylvania in 1886 and by the Diocese of Massachusetts in 1891. He declined the first election, but accepted the second. His episcopate would prove to be short, however. He was consecrated in October of 1891 and died in January of 1893. He had never married.

Theologically, Brooks was part of a generation of Episcopalians who moved gradually from Evangelical convictions to Broad Church attitudes. John Woolverton suggested in *The Education of Phillips Brooks* (1995) that, in the case of Brooks, college and seminary reading of Romantic poetry, and Platonic, middle Platonic, and neo-Platonic philosophy was a contributing factor for the shift. Brooks

> came to look . . . toward God . . . as the Ideal One. His moral philosophy led him to seek the absolute good rather than to strive to find in humans an intuitive moral faculty. Brooks searched for that absolute good in his heroes, in certain characteristics of his Puritan ancestors, and finally and preeminently in the person of Jesus Christ. (82)

Brooks was the target of occasional criticism, but generally not because of his theological views. When, for example, Bishop George F. Seymour objected to his election to the episcopate, he simply raised a time-worn High-Church complaint against Evangelicals: Brooks had engaged in joint worship services with other Protestants.

Brooks was largely able to avoid theological criticism because of his ability to know what not to say. While other Broad Church figures openly attacked such doctrines as that of the Virgin Birth, Brooks generally did not. He simply ceased using such concepts literally, interpreting what had been fixed truths for the Evangelicals as metaphors for responsible social action or for the growth of the human spirit. His general approach was already evident in his well-known hymn 'O Little Town of Bethlehem', which was first performed in Philadelphia in 1868. The fourth verse, which was not included in most hymnals prior to 1940, declared that 'where misery cries out to thee,/Son of the mother mild/Where charity stands watching/And faith holds wide the door,/ The dark night wakes, the glory breaks,/and Christmas comes once more.' The incarnation had become a metaphor for charitable activity toward the poor.

In 1870 Brooks resigned from the Evangelical Education Society, in which he had been active, because of the organization's requirement that recipients of educational grants answer a series of doctrinal questions. Brooks objected, saying that 'these are times in which all men truly Evangelical ought to stand firmly together', and that he was 'sure that the way to bring that to pass is not to narrow their standing ground' by asking such questions (*Life and Letters*, 2: 199). In his 1873 lecture on Heresy, which was later included in *Essays and Addresses*, Brooks pushed for similar latitude on the question as to what constituted heresy. He rejected what he called the 'ecclesiastical' and 'dogmatic' ideas of heresy in favour of what he called the 'moral' idea. The later view defined heresy as an individual's 'wilful adherence to some view which God makes known to him'. Only this 'wilfully shutting [one's] eyes to light' was for him properly understood as heretical.

The titles of the individual lectures given at the Bohlen lectureship of 1879 – 'The influence of Jesus on the moral life of man', '. . . on the social life of man', '. . . on the emotional life of man', and '. . . on the intellectual life of man' provided further indication of the direction in which his thought was moving. As he explained in the introduction to the published form of the lectures,

I have been led, then, to think of Christianity, and to speak of it, – at least in these lectures, – not as a system of doctrine, but as a personal force, behind which and in which there lies one great

inspiriting idea. . . . The personal force is the nature of Jesus. . . .
The inspiring idea is the fatherhood of God, and the childhood of
every man to Him.

As Brooks explained in an address to the Young Men's Christian
Association in 1889, the personal force of Jesus could not only transform individuals, it could change institutions as well.

The Life of Christ . . . represents [and] . . . declares, the perpetual
union between God and man, the way in which God is forever
uttering Himself in love, and man may forever utter himself in obedience. Every institution may represent this. . . . No . . . institution
has any genuine life that is not a representation of the life of
man, or God, or the Christhead. So every religious institution, and
every institution which is in its highest view capable of being
called a religious institution, is the true manifestation of this perpetual life, of man's life, and of the God-life, and the Christ-life,
that is filling the whole world from the beginning to the end.
(*Essays and Addresses*: 172)

Brooks may have worked out the details of his thoughts in the meetings
of a series of clubs for progressive clergy. He formed the first such group
in Philadelphia in 1868. In 1874 he and other clergy who were involved
in similar groups formed the Church Congress, taking the name in imitation of a similar English group. Members of the congress gathered in
years in which the Episcopal Church's triennial General Convention did
not meet. Sessions were devoted to such issues as labour conditions or
biblical scholarship. Although speakers representing a variety of perspectives were invited to participate, there was no question about the
attitude of the leadership. As Brooks explained in a letter to a friend, the
organizers of the congresses were 'all . . . broad churchman, [who want
to see] what can be done to keep or make the Church liberal and free'.
  Brooks's contemporaries saw him as the model Broad Churchman.
He had the ability to disagree with others without offending, and to
incorporate new scholarship and ideas without directly challenging
traditional convictions. His writing was extremely popular up to the
time of the First World War, and enjoyed a renaissance in interest after
the end of the Second, particularly among Episcopalians interested in
social action. Bishop William Scarlet prepared an edition of *Selected
Sermons* by Brooks in 1949, and Brooks's lectures on preaching were
reissued in 1954 and 1959. The second of these editions was prepared by
Bishop John Moorman. When the Episcopal Church adopted a calendar

of lesser feasts and fasts in the 1960s, an entry was included for Brooks on January 23.

Most of Brooks's published works were sermons. Numerous individual sermons were published, and there were at least nine collections. The first, which was simply titled *Sermons*, appeared in 1878. Brooks followed this with four other volumes, which were issued at roughly three-year intervals: *The Candle of the Lord* (1881), *Sermons Preached in English Churches* (1883), *Twenty Sermons* (1886), and *The Light of the World* (1890). There were, in addition, four posthumous volumes: *The Battle of Life* (c. 1893), *The Mystery of Iniquity* (1894), *New Starts in Life* (1896) and *The Law of Growth* (1902). As the number of volumes would indicate, Brooks was easily the most popular Episcopal preacher at the end of the nineteenth century. His sensitivity about what not to say made him attractive to a wide variety of readers.

Brooks published his Yale and Bohlen lectures as *Yale Lectures on Preaching* (1877) and *The Influence of Jesus* (1879). Numerous collections of his essays and lectures appeared after his death; most were simply titled *Addresses*. The most comprehensive of these collections was *Essays and Addresses* (1892).

Brooks was the author of a number of poems, some of which appeared in *Phillips Brooks's Poems* (1886). Letters that he had written during his travels in Europe were published posthumously as *Letters of Travel* (1894).

Excerpts from Brooks's writings were incorporated in numerous devotional books, particularly in the years immediately after his death. The books include *Brilliants: selected from the Writings of the Rt. Rev. Phillips Brooks* (1893), *Daily Thoughts from Phillips Brooks* (c.1893), *Phillips Brooks Year Book* (1893), *Good Cheer for a Year: Selections from the Writings of the Rt. Rev. Phillips Brooks* (1896), and *Helps to the Holy Communion from the Writings of Phillips Brooks* (1903).

Much of Brooks's personal correspondence was published in Alexander V. G. Allen's *Life and Letters of Phillips Brooks*. It was published in two volumes by the Knickerbocker Press of New York in 1900, and reprinted the following year in the same city in three volumes by E. P. Dutton, 1901. Allen also produced the one-volume *Phillips Brooks, 1835–1893* (New York: E. P. Dutton, 1907). William Lawrence, who followed Brooks as Bishop of Massachusetts, wrote the *Life of Phillips Brooks* (New York: Harper and Brothers, 1930). John Woolverton's *The Education of Phillips Brooks* (Urbana: University of Illinois Press, 1995) deals with Brooks's youth and formation. The final chapter of Diana H. Butler's *Standing against the Whirlwind* (New York: Oxford, 1995) provides an excellent summary of the process by which the generation of Episcopal Evangelicals who came of age in the 1850s gradually moved from Evangelical to Broad Church convictions. Richard M. Spielmann wrote about the work of Brooks and other Broad Churchmen in the Church Congress movement in 'The Episcopal Church Congress, 1874–1934' in *Anglican and Episcopal History* 58 (March 1989). (RP)

Brown, William Montgomery (1855–1937), bishop. Brown is remembered by many as the 'atheist bishop' and for being the first American bishop to be deposed for heresy. After his ordination as deacon in 1883 and priest in 1884, he served as special lecturer of the theological seminary of Bexley Hall. Early publications include: *The Church for Americans* (1896); *The Crucial Race Question* (1907); and *The Level Plan for Church Union* (1910). In 1898 he was appointed as bishop coadjutor

in Arkansas before becoming diocesan bishop of Arkansas from
1899–1912. His election to the episcopate was overshadowed by charges
of fraud and strong opposition. Due to poor health Brown retired as
bishop in 1912 but soon became strongly influenced by the writings of
Marx and Darwin. The result of his interest in socialism was his book
*Communism and Christianism Analyzed and Contrasted from the Marxian
and Darwinian Points of View* (1920). The focus of the book was an attempt
to promote Marxism, remove the 'blight' of theism and capitalism, and
freedom of truth. Communism was portrayed as synonymous with
morality, religion and Christianity. In short, Marxism was hailed as a
greater gospel for humanity than that which came from Jesus Christ. In
1922 the Diocese of Arkansas requested the General Convention to try
Brown for heresy. The trial was delayed until May 1924 and was marked
by Brown's aggression in trying to test the doctrines of Anglicanism
rather than defend his orthodoxy or lack thereof. The sentencing of
Brown came in October 1925, the presiding bishop passed sentence
and formally deposed Brown for heresy. Brown had already become
a consecrated bishop in the Old Catholic Church in North America.
It was later learned that he had also contributed money to a group of
Communists in Michigan who had plotted to overthrow the United
States Government. He spent his final days contributing towards the
spread of Marxism and condemning the Episcopal Church.

Stowe's Clerical Directory of the American Church, 1920–1.
John L. Kyser, 'The Deposed Bishop', *Louisiana History*, 8(1) (Winter 1967).

Bull, George (1634–1710). In many ways a prototype of the learned
Anglican country clergy who were regarded as *stupor mundi*, Bull, who
paradoxically never took his primary degree because of his refusal when
at Oxford to take the oath to the Commonwealth, was over a period of
forty-seven years rector first of Suddington and afterwards of Avening.
During this time he produced five major and memorable works which
made their impact abroad as well as at home although their author
described himself 'to the Reader' of his *Defensio Fidei Nicaenae* (1685) as
'a man of mean parts and learning, the master of a small study, often
indispos'd, involv'd in domestic cares, ty'd down to a country cure, far
remov'd from the conversation of learned men'. Bull is also an illustration
of the successful working of Hammond's scheme for active Anglican
propaganda between 1650 and 1660. When, on leaving Oxford in 1649,
he went into Somerset he came under the influence of one Samuel
Thomas, who turned Bull's attention to the writings of Taylor, Hooker
and Hammond, with the consequence that, like hundreds of others

during the Commonwealth, he sought and received episcopal ordination from the ejected bishop of Oxford, Skinner. Many of those so ordained received their Orders from three Irish bishops (Tilson, Maxwell and Fulwer) then living in England, though bishops Hall, Duppa and Brownrigg among others were similarly engaged. It was not until 1704–5 that Bull himself became a bishop, being consecrated to the see of St David's when the great champion of orthodoxy was aged and infirm and where he served for only four years until his death. His first book, *Harmonia Apostolica* (1670), immediately produced controversy, its theme being that 'a faith which has good works united with it, more-over, which neither is, nor can be, without good works, is the true and justifying faith' (ch. 6). Tully and Gataker among others passed many strictures on this exercise in theological sanity, and Bull had to reply in 1675 with his *Examen Censurae* and his *Apologia pro Harmonia*, in which he defended his book which he hoped would be 'a timely antidote to this Solifidianism' – ('To the Reader'). The then customary smear of Socinianism was made, resulting in Bull's greatest work, *Defensio Fidei Nicaenae* (1685), in which he also rejected the ideas on 'development' set out by the Jesuit Petavius. The book, published at the expense of Fell, bishop of Oxford, became the standard treatment of the subject, and Bull was praised by Bossuet and congratulated by 'the whole clergy of France' for proving 'that all the approv'd Fathers and Doctors of the Church . . . from the days of the Apostles, taught the very same thing . . . which the Nicene Fathers determin'd concerning the Son's Divinity' ('To the Reader'). Both his *Judicium Ecclesiae Catholicae* (1694) and his *Primitiva et Apostolica Traditio* (1710) may be regarded as a follow-up to the *Defensio* which had caused Bossuet to enquire why Bull did not accept Roman Catholic claims. Bull told him why in his *The Corruptions of the Church of Rome*, which quickly went into a number of editions. Bull's *Life* by his pupil the lay-theologian Robert Nelson, was published in 1710. The works of this outstanding Anglican exponent of credal orthodoxy appeared in a Clarendon Press edition by Burton in 1827 and there is a Library of Anglo-Catholic Theology edition of 1842/55. (HM)

Butler, Joseph (1692–1752). It was while studying at the dissenting academy at Tewkesbury that Butler, like his fellow pupil, Thomas Secker (the future Archbishop of Canterbury) abandoned the Presbyterianism of his parents. This made possible his admission to Oriel College, Oxford in 1714 (where he thought poorly of the education) and his ordination four years later. Until 1726 he was preacher at the Rolls Chapel in London (demolished in the nineteenth century). Thereafter, though from a family of modest means (his father was a linen draper), his friendship with the Talbots secured for him the wealthy living of Stanhope in County Durham. On her deathbed in 1737 Queen Caroline recommended him for a bishopric, but Butler only accepted with reluctance, as George II offered Bristol, the poorest in the country. However, this was supplemented two years later by the deanery of St Paul's. Finally, in 1750 he was translated to the wealthy see of Durham. From the little of a more personal nature that has survived, we can glean that he was conscientious in his duties, generous, and particularly concerned for the poor. He disliked Wesley's enthusiasm and demanded that he leave his diocese immediately. On the other hand, his introduction of a cross into his private chapel and other forms of devotion were sufficient to generate absurd rumours after his death of his secret conversion to Rome.

His two principal works are *Sermons preached at the Rolls Chapel* (1726) and *The Analogy of Religion* (1736). Both are concerned to assert the key role of natural theology in religion. In the case of the former a defence of Christian morality is developed which sees it rooted in the nature given to us by God, upon which the commands of Scripture then build, rather than acting in a vacuum or even against a hostile nature. Implicitly arguing against the egoism of Hobbes and the intellectual intuitionism of Clarke, he identifies three key factors in human nature (self-love, benevolence and conscience) which together with the cultivation of specific virtues will enable the individual to flourish and lead a fulfilled life. Thus expressed, his argument can be seen to have much in common with Aristotle, though with the significant addition of the key role for conscience (derived ultimately on his own admission from Stoicism). While willing to concede that it might be appropriate for God to be a utilitarian and so for him to make general calculations of benefit and harm, he insists that the appropriate conduct for human beings is quite different: this should reflect our particular dispositional commitments and loyalties, with conscience exercising final sway overall.

The Analogy was intended as a response to the deism of writers such as Tindal and Toland, the view that the only religion we require is one based on natural theology. Revealed religion, it was maintained, merely introduced irrational, unnecessary additional beliefs and the irrationality of arbitrary divine action, whether in miracle or other special acts of grace that favoured one individual but not another for no obvious reason. Butler's response is to draw an analogy between natural and revealed religion, and argue that the difficulties attaching to the latter are no greater than those attaching to the former. So, for example, the notion of the resurrection of the body is no more startling than the transformation of caterpillar into butterfly, while the gifts of nature are no less arbitrarily distributed: what matters is not equality but our appropriate stewardship of them, however derived. In this work, as in its predecessor, there is much stress on arguments from probability, as in his famous declaration that 'probability is the very guide of life'. That stress is another mark of the Aristotelian or empirical character of his approach, and so should be contrasted with the more Platonic or Idealist philosophical influences on Anglicanism which come from elsewhere.

Butler's Aristotelianism is very prominent in the writings of John Henry Newman, in both his Anglican and Roman Catholic periods, as can be seen from his *University Sermons* of 1843 and his *Grammar of Assent* of 1870; and in fact Newman labelled Butler 'the greatest name in the Anglican church'. Gladstone produced the definitive edition of his works in 1896, combined with his own (even by then) rather dated defence. Though that alliance with the more Catholic side of the Church was to produce explicit hostility from some (notably Mark Pattison and Benjamin Jowett), for J. B. Lightfoot the *Analogy* was 'the greatest work of English theology', while in the twentieth century Butler has continued to exercise influence. The moral theory of the two Anglicans, Hastings Rashdall and A. E. Taylor, bears clear marks of Butler, and though J. S. Mill's *Utilitarianism* is now by far the most commonly used text to introduce students to issues in moral philosophy, Butler's *Sermons* continue to be widely used as a way of broaching the issue of conscience. It is often claimed that Freud with his notion of the superego undermined the viability of any such idea, but, as Piaget's *Moral Judgment of the Child* of 1932 well illustrates, it is still possible to argue that certain general moral ideas will inevitably arise, provided the child has a normal upbringing. Indeed, the failure to develop an other-regarding perspective is in English law regarded as a type of illness and the person known as a psychopath.

In the case of the *Analogy*, a decline in influence was inevitable once the debate moved away from the precise form of divine action to the more basic question, of divine existence as such. Nonetheless, a continuing influence is detectable, particularly in the more informal types of justification now given for religious belief. A good example of this is the Anglican Basil Mitchell's *Justification of Religious Belief* of 1973, which talks of a 'cumulative case' for theism, and draws parallels with how argument proceeds by probabilities in other areas as well.

Also of continued influence has been his short dissertation 'Of Personal Identity', where he argues that consciousness of our identity cannot be analysed into any more fundamental notion such as connectedness of memories or bodily continuity. There are, for instance, repeated references to Butler in the debate between Sydney Shoemaker and Richard Swinburne in their *Personal Identity* of 1984.

Christopher Cunliffe (ed.), 1992. *Joseph Butler's Moral and Religious Thought* (Oxford: Clarendon).

Austin Duncan-Jones, 1952. *Butler's Moral Philosophy* (Harmondsworth: Penguin).

W. E. Gladstone, 1896. *Studies Subsidiary to the Works of Bishop Butler* (Oxford: Clarendon).

E. C. Mossner, 1936. *Bishop Butler and the Age of Reason* (New York: Blom).

Terence Penelhum, 1985. *Butler* (London: Routledge & Kegan Paul).

W. A. Spooner, 1901. *Bishop Butler* (London: Methuen). (DB)

Chillingworth, William (1602–1644), Fellow of Trinity College, Oxford, 1628, became a Roman Catholic in 1629 under the influence of Fisher and went to the Jesuit College at Douai, whence he returned to the Church of England in 1631; Chancellor of Salisbury, 1638. He supported the Royalist cause, acting as engineer (he was also a mathematician) at the siege of Arundel Castle, captured by Waller in 1643. Chillingworth was taken ill and removed to Chichester, where he died. Drawn into the war of books between the Jesuit, Knott, and Potter, Provost of Queen's College, Oxford, Chillingworth, then resident at Lord Falkland's house at Great Tew, prepared an answer to Knott's second book, *Charity Maintained by Catholics* (1634), and this was his widely valued *The Religion of Protestants, a Safe Way to Salvation* (1638). The mark of the Tew Circle was what A. R. Vidler (*Essays in Liberality* (1957); 21–8) called liberality, a quality of flexibility and vitality, the opposite not of conservatism but of intransigence. Chillingworth's plea for Christian liberty and toleration was part of this: 'Restore Christians to their just and full liberty of captivating their understanding to Scripture only' and 'Take away this persecuting . . . damning of men for not subscribing to the words of men as to the words of God.' Inevitably, like many moderates of the time, he was misrepresented as a Socinian, although he affirmed a strict orthodoxy on the Trinity, the atonement and the person of Christ. Equally, he was misrepresented then and later as a literalist by reason of a simplistic understanding of his famous claim that 'the Bible and the Bible only' is the religion of Protestants. In fact, he insisted on the individual's right to interpret the authority of Scripture in the light of reason. What is 'plainly set down in Scripture', this is 'necessary truth' and in this regard he insists on the relevance and need for 'the distinction of points, fundamental and not fundamental'. This is a constant element in Anglican understanding of the faith. It was asserted by Wake in his correspondence with the Gallicans, by Gore at the Malines Conversations and is so affirmed in the *Malta Report* (1968),

I(6). Chillingworth defended episcopacy as 'acknowledged to have been universally received in the church, presently after the apostles' time'; and as to the eucharist he holds 'the sacrament after consecration, to be bread and wine, as well as Christ's body and blood'. One could say of Chillingworth that his was a mind *in via*, questing and open and, as he said himself, 'desiring, not that I, or my side, but that truth might overcome, on which side so ever it was'. He sets a headline, still valid, for the exercise of liberality within the parameters of revealed truth. (All quotations are from *The Religion of Protestants*, 12th edn, 1840.)

For the Tew Circle and Chillingworth, see H. J. McLachlan, 1951, *Socinianism in Seventeenth Century England* (Oxford) 63–89; H. R. McAdoo, 1965, *The Spirit of Anglicanism* (London and New York) 12–23; B. H. G. Wormald, 1951, *Clarendon* (Cambridge) 240–82. (HM)

Colenso, John William (1814–83). Consecrated Bishop of Natal in 1853, he came to the new diocese imbued with missionary zeal. His theology had been moulded by his mathematical studies and especially by the influence of F. D. Maurice. Stressing the importance of reason, he considered orthopraxis to be the true evidence of Christian faith. He believed in the presence of God in all people and their common humanity now redeemed by the death and resurrection of Christ, and found this reflected in the Zulu name for God, *Nkulunkulu*. This stress on the love and mercy of God towards everyone sharply challenged the conventional missionary preaching with its aim to save souls from damnation.

Because of these views, Colenso was ready to accept certain African customs, including polygamy, along the lines later suggested by the Lambeth Conference of 1988, but then vigorously opposed. His belief in the importance of the scriptures led him to translate them into Zulu and to prepare a Zulu grammar and other aids for missionaries. But in expounding them to intelligent Zulus, he recognized that the stories in Genesis and elsewhere could not be treated as factual accounts. He was therefore accused of denying the authority of Scripture. Much of his theology was summed up in his commentary on Romans (1861) 'newly translated, and explained from a missionary point of view', in which he rejected the penal substitution theory of the atonement, and the belief that the sacraments were necessary for salvation. Such views earned condemnation from traditional Anglicans and others. Colenso saw the missionary endeavour as being to convince people that the gospel displayed the true value and dignity of human beings, who he believed (in common with other Englishmen) should find fulfilment in the context of British culture.

In his desire to convert Zululand as a whole he planned to have a string of mission stations across Zululand centred on Ekukanyeni. In 1863 he was convicted of heresy by the court of the metropolitan, Robert Gray, and was formally excommunicated in 1866. But owing to legal principles involved, Colenso was able to remain as the titular bishop of Natal until his death. In 1867 W. K. Macrorie was consecrated as Bishop of Maritzburg, which helped to lead later to the schism between the Church of the Province of South Africa and the Church of England in South Africa. The conflict occasioned the calling of the first Lambeth Conference in 1867.

In the last years of his life (1866–83), Colenso fought for a just treatment of the African, especially in the cases of Langalibalele and Cetshwayo.

Though Colenso was neither a biblical scholar nor a theologian, his teaching anticipated ideas of the twentieth century, and in 1985 Provincial Synod formally recognized his 'courageous leadership' in 'biblical scholarship, cross-cultural mission and the pursuit of social justice'.

Jeff Guy, 1983. *The Heretic: A Study of the Life of John William Colenso 1814–1883* (Johannesburg: Ravan Press).
Peter Hinchliff, 1964. *John William Colenso: Bishop of Natal* (London: Nelson). (JS)

Coleridge, Samuel Taylor (1772–1834), poet, theologian, philosopher, never was ordained or held a university lectureship. The unity of polarities in philosophy and theology through faith and imagination, 'the esemplastic sense' constitute Coleridge's life, mind and art. Fourteenth child of a priest, he left Cambridge without his degree, intending to help build a pantisocracy in Pennsylvania. Only his unsatisfactory marriage to Sarah Fricker (1794) came of it. However, Coleridge gained political insights expressed in *On the Constitution of the Church and State* (1830), which strongly influenced T. S. Eliot's *The Idea of a Christian Society* (1939). His addiction to opium, first prescribed as medication, frustrated the completion of many projects he planned.

Coleridge's poetic metaphors of religion and nature, which reflect his refusal to separate natural from supernatural, invite continuous debate. His greatness as a seminal poet rests on several contributions: 'Fears in Solitude' exemplifies his new genre, the 'conversation poem', a type of blank verse; 'Kubla Khan', a Romantic lyric, poses special problems of form and meaning; 'Christabel' introduces a metric principle of counting accents instead of the syllables of a line; 'Rime of the Ancient Mariner', another masterpiece, presents a complex parable of sin and redemption.

Omnivorous reading and unceasing conversation fired Coleridge's imagination. Like his contemporary, Schleiermacher, Coleridge made of friendship a construct essential for self-realization. His periodical, *The Friend*, included essays on the meaning of existence. He inspired profound friendships in Wordsworth, Lamb, and the Wedgwoods. He disregarded Kant's pure and practical reason, to define Reason the faculty of perception, and Understanding the faculty of arranging the data of experience. *Biographia Literaria* rejects materialism and mechanism to champion imagination. Coleridge elaborates this in *Aids to Reflection* and emphasizes prudence and morality in cultivating personal religion. Many young priests, Bushnell, the Transcendentalists, and Broad Church Anglicanism appropriated his continuously provocative philosophy.

Complexities of the self consumed Coleridge. Sixty Notebooks written over forty years (1796–1834) distil the essence of his evolving self. They constitute his *magnum opus*. They reveal an incomparable diarist, evaluations of great thinkers, outlines of books and poems, notes on theology, science and art, to present a challenge to religious psychology and theology today. *Confessions of an Inquiring Spirit* expands the argument of *The Statesman's Manual* (1816), for reading Scripture as symbol. Studying the relationship of God and creation led Coleridge away from inchoate pantheism and Unitarianism to the Trinity doctrine which occupied the last decade of his life. His trinity, constructed on a Pythagorean concept, the 'Tetractys', became his paradigm of unity in diversity, foundation of his epistemology, and the criterion of every scholarly endeavour. It remains highly suggestive for Anglicans studying the Trinity, *logos*, and the *filioque* clause of the Creed.

J. Robert Barth, 1969. *Coleridge and Christian Doctrine* (Cambridge, Mass.: Harvard University Press).
S. T. Coleridge, *Collected Works*, L. Patton and Peter Mann (eds.), 1971. (Princeton, N.J.: Princeton University Press).
S. T. Coleridge, *Notebooks,* Kathleen Coburn (ed.), 1957. (Princeton, N.J.: Princeton University Press).
R. R. Niebuhr, 1983. *Streams of Grace* (Kyoto: Doshisha University Press).
I. A. Richards, 1935. *Coleridge on Imagination* (New York: Harcourt). (WE)

Cosin, John (1594–1672), Bishop of Durham. Educated at Caius College, Cambridge, he was elected fellow before his appointment as Bishop Overall's secretary and librarian. After holding a variety of positions he became Archdeacon of East Riding in Yorkshire. At this time difficulties with the Puritans began, due to publication in 1627 of his *Collection of Private Devotions*, and his Laudian views, including the use of vestments, altar lights, and eastward position of the celebrant during Holy Communion. In 1634 he was elected to the Mastership of Peterhouse, Cambridge and immediately set up the chapel according to his High Church principles before being made Dean of Peterborough by King Charles I, in 1640. After being deprived of all his offices by the Long Parliament for support of Charles I, he moved to Paris to serve as chaplain to the Household of Queen Henrietta Maria. While in France he made many friends with the Huguenots, because he distinguished between those who were not ordained by bishops by no fault of their own and those who had rejected it by choice. At the Restoration in 1660 he regained his position as Dean and boldly went back to his High Church practices before being made the Bishop of Durham that same year. At the Savoy Conference in 1661 he tried unsuccessfully to reconcile the Presbyterians and the Church of England to no avail. Of particular importance are his polemical writings against the Roman Catholics including: *Historia Transubstantiationis Papalis* (1675), written against the doctrine of Transubstantiation; and *A Scholastical History of the Canon of Holy Scripture* (1657), in which he argued against the inclusion of the Apocrypha in the scriptures. A model of the High Church position in the seventeenth century, his anti-Romanism on the one hand and anti-Puritanism on the other makes him a key figure in the search for an historic identity of later High Churchmen and Anglo-Catholics.

Oxford Dictionary of the Christian Church, 350.
Geoffrey Cuming, 1975. *The Anglicanism of John Cosin* (Durham: Dean and Chapter of Durham).
John Overton in *Dictionary of National Biography*, XII, 264–71.

Cranmer, Thomas (1489–1556). While the debate concerning the nature and origins of the English Reformation continues to rage unabated, there is little doubt that Thomas Cranmer played a critical role in the institutionalization of Protestantism in England. It would not be unfair to suggest that Cranmer's grasp of the importance of liturgy as a means of mediating both piety and theological correctness gave considerable impetus to the development of the distinctively Anglican ethos which was to emerge during the Elizabethan Settlement.

Cranmer was born in the village of Aslacton, in the English East Midlands. He was educated at Jesus College, Cambridge. Initially, he appeared destined for a scholarly life. However, he was drawn into the growing debate concerning the propriety of Henry VIII's divorce of Catherine of Aragon. Pleased by Cranmer's advice to consult European universities on the issue, Henry gradually advanced him, eventually appointing him Archbishop of Canterbury in 1532, apparently on the advice of the Boleyn family. Cranmer found himself with relatively little theological or liturgical freedom under Henry VIII, and was often put in the position of retaining traditional Catholic practices and beliefs which were increasingly in tension with his growing commitment to Lutheranism. In 1532, Cranmer secretly married the niece of the leading German Lutheran theologian Andreas Osiander, despite Henry's known views on the matter. In other matters, however, Cranmer judged it wise to remain discreet in relation to issues touching on 'the old religion', which Henry was known to favour. One such sensitive matter was that of the revision of the Latin text of the Mass and other rites.

The impetus for such revisions dates from late in Henry's reign. Alarmed that intense rain in August might damage crops, Henry demanded that there should be 'general rogations and processions' to counter the threat. The resulting English Litany of 1544 was more than a translation of the Latin original; it was a significant revision, foreshadowing the greater works which would be forthcoming during the following reign. Cranmer justified his revisions to Henry by arguing that stylistic alteration was necessary on account of the 'barren' nature of the Latin originals. Cranmer invited Henry to improve on his English style, but shrewdly avoided mentioning any theological alterations resulting from his revisions.

It was in the reign of Edward VI that Cranmer was able to introduce the decisive liturgical reforms he felt were essential to the shaping of the reformed English church. Informed by the theological debates of the Reformation, Cranmer undertook a revision of the text of the mass, in which the English language and the theology of the Reformation were substituted for the Latin original. The revisions of 1549 and 1552 show a considerable degree of theological variation, reflecting at one point an affinity with the eucharistic theology of the Zurich reformers, such as Zwingli, and at others with Luther. Nevertheless, the fundamental principle to emerge was that liturgy was a means of expressing and enforcing theological orthodoxy. The old patristic tag *lex orandi lex credendi* found new vitality in Cranmer's liturgical experiments of the period.

Cranmer's wish to use liturgy as a means of communicating theology remains of major importance to Anglicanism; indeed, it can be pointed out that, for much of its history, Anglicanism has been defined with reference to the 1662 Book of Common Prayer. Cranmer's masterly appreciation of the role of liturgy in offering theological stability to the Church remains an insight of defining importance for Anglicanism. Yet alongside this must be placed Cranmer's grasp of a related principle, derived from the Reformers, of the importance of a 'tongue under-standed by the people' for public worship and preaching. Cranmer affirmed that:

> By God's laws, all Christian people are bounden diligently to learn his word, that they may know how to believe and live accordingly ... to give themselves wholly to know and serve God. Therefore God's will and commandment is, that when the people be gathered together, ministers should use such language as the people may understand and take profit thereby, or else hold their peace.

Important though Cranmer's concerns were in the sixteenth century, they remain important today, as the issue of the effective communication of the Christian gospel continues to be of critical significance. Cranmer's insistence that the important things of faith be discussed, celebrated and proclaimed in a language understood by the people remains as important as ever.

Cranmer's liturgical programme thus integrated the regular reading of Scripture within the context of worship. While early English congregations were allowed access to a limited range of sermons, as defined by the *Book of Homilies* (some written by Cranmer, often incorporating Melanchthon's theology), it is clear that the general principle of the interrelatedness of Word and worship was firmly enshrined in Cranmer's approach.

Cranmer was executed in Oxford during the reign of Mary Tudor. Many of his basic themes can, however, be seen in the emerging theology of the Elizabethan Settlement, which placed particular emphasis upon the importance of liturgy as a means of conveying theology, maintaining consensus and ensuring uniformity. Cranmer may not have been an original theologian; nevertheless, he realized the enormous importance of public worship as a means of communicating and safeguarding theology. Perhaps it is fair to regard him as one of the most significant architects of the Anglican ethos, with its distinctive emphasis on the importance of this point.

Miscellaneous Writings and Letters of Thomas Cranmer (Cambridge: Parker Society, 1846).
Peter Newman Brooks, 1989. *Cranmer in Context* (Cambridge: Lutterworth Press).
Peter Newman Brooks, 1992. *Thomas Cranmer's Doctrine of the Eucharist*, 2nd edn (London: Macmillan).
Diarmaid MacCulloch, 1996. *Thomas Cranmer: A Life* (New Haven: Yale University Press).
Jasper Ridley, 1962. *Thomas Cranmer* (Oxford: Clarendon Press). (AM)

Cutler, Timothy (1684–1765), Congregational and Episcopal clergyman. Born in Massachusetts, he was educated at Harvard College, receiving his B.A. in 1701. Appointed Rector of Yale College (1719–22), he had served as a Congregational minister for the previous nine years. Ordained to episcopal orders in England, he received an honorary doctorate from Oxford in 1723. On his return to the colonies he became the rector of Christ Church, Boston, where he served until his death. From his study of seventeenth-century Anglican Divines, Cutler became convinced that both Presbyterian ordination and Congregational polity were invalid. In a move which would be dubbed 'the Great Yale Apostasy', Cutler, along with colleagues Samuel Johnson and Daniel Brown, shocked the Congregational establishment by defecting to Anglicanism in 1722. A formidable and outspoken polemicist, he quickly established himself both as a leading spokesman for Anglican prerogatives in Congregational New England, and as an ardent opponent of the Great Awakening. Cutler's theology and mission were guided by both High Church ecclesiology and Arminian rationalism, no doubt accounting for his hostility towards the itinerant revivalism of fellow churchman, George Whitefield. His sermons also reflect a large debt to Lockean epistemology and Newtonian cosmology. However, his greatest contribution to American Episcopalianism was his encouragement of the missionary activities of the SPG in New England, through which Anglicanism gained a small but formidable foothold, especially in Connecticut. As much the embodiment of Cutler's ecclesiological convictions as his sense of divine mission, New England High Church Anglicanism would one day exert an influence disproportionate to its size on the shape and character of the Episcopal Church in the United States.

Dictionary of Christianity in America.
Dictionary of American Biography, III.
Dictionary of American Religious Biography.
R. E. Daggy, 1971. 'Education, church and state: Timothy Cutler and the Yale Apostasy of 1772', *Journal of Church and State* 13: 43–69.
D. Huber, 1975. 'Timothy Cutler: the convert and controversialist', *Historical Magazine of the PEC* 44: 489–96.

DeKoven, James (1831–1879) Episcopal clergyman, educator and defender of ritualism. Born in Connecticut, he was educated at Columbia College in 1851, and General Theological Seminary in 1854. In this same year he was appointed tutor at Nashotah House Seminary, Wisconsin, and upon ordination to the priesthood the following year he became Rector of the Church of St John Chrysostom in Delafield,

Wisconsin. In 1855 he founded St John's Hall, a preparatory school for postulants to the ministry, which in 1859 merged with Racine College. DeKoven was foremost an educator who was renowned for his sharp mind, precise method, learning and oration, but he also gained respect and affection from his students as a man of great piety and devotion. That his holiness was widely acknowledged even during his own life-time is attested by his commemoration in the present calendar of the Episcopal Church. Nevertheless, he was unable to avoid controversy, and the anti-ritualist movement during the post-Civil War era spurred him to raise a formidable defence for the cause of ritualism and Anglo-Catholic eucharistic devotion, in which he enunciated the case for Anglican comprehensiveness in doctrine and worship. His defence of ritualism climaxed in his opposition to attempts to legislate ritual uniformity at the volatile General Conventions of 1871 and 1874. Despite both threatened and actual departures of substantial numbers of Evan-gelical churchmen, his case for comprehensiveness eventually won the day. However, his views kept him from the office of bishop, to which he was nominated five times, elected once, but failed to be confirmed. As warden of Racine College since 1859, DeKoven was content to devote himself to the cause of Christian education until his death in 1879.

Dictionary of Christianity in America.
Dictionary of American Biography, III.
T. C. Reeves (ed.), 1979. *James DeKoven, Anglican Saint.*

Dillistone, Frederick William (1903–93), studied mathematics and theology at Oxford, and, after pastoral work in England, was Professor of Systematic Theology at Wycliffe College, Toronto, 1938–45. After a brief spell as Vice-Principal of London College of Divinity, he returned to North America to teach at Episcopal Theological School, in Cam-bridge, Massachusetts. From 1952 to 1963 he was Chancellor and then Dean of Liverpool Cathedral, moving to Oxford in 1964 as Fellow and Chaplain of Oriel, and retiring in 1970. He was awarded an Oxford D.D. in 1951, and was Bampton Lecturer in 1968.

He was a renowned preacher and classroom teacher, as well as a pro-lific author. His published work demonstrates an unusually broad range of religious and intellectual interests. His earlier writings around the period of the Second World War (such as *The Significance of the Cross* and *Revelation and Evangelism*) identify him with traditional Evangelical emphases on the atoning work of Christ and the Church's missionary vocation. The theology of salvation remained a preoccupation throughout his writing, and his most significant account of the topic is to be found in what is probably his most widely studied work, *The Christian Understanding of Atonement*. From the late 1940s, his interests expanded to embrace the worlds of culture, art, religious experience and symbolism. Both in the USA and in England, he wrote a considerable number of works devoted to exploring the ways in which religious experience can be expressed through cultural and symbolic forms – most notably in his Bampton lectures, *Traditional Symbols and the Contemporary World*. In this area, Tillich was a powerful influence on his thinking. He also produced three significant works of biography, the subjects of which (C. H. Dodd, Charles Raven and Max Warren) once again indicate the diversity of his interests.

His work was more suggestive than systematic, synthetic rather than critical. For his conversation partners, he turned more readily to the worlds of religious experience and art than to the classical texts of the Western Christian or philosophical traditions. He did not follow a characteristic modern Anglican procedure of expounding Christian doctrine by exegesis of biblical or patristic materials, or by critical analysis of dogma, especially incarnational dogma. Despite Protestant roots, he was not seriously impacted by the renewal of Reformation theology on the continent. The heart of Dillistone's mature theology lay in a conviction that humanity's 'highest and most constructive characteristic' is the 'symbol-forming capacity' (*The Christian Faith*: 187), a capacity supremely embodied in the symbols of Christian faith (the Gospels, epistles, creeds and sacraments) and continued in the 'inspired' works of thinkers and artists. This orientation to the aesthetic and imaginative dimensions of Christian faith set him apart, and he remains rather marginal to contemporary Anglicanism, whose ecumenical, ethical or ecclesiological concerns do not feature in his work.

The Significance of the Cross (London: Lutterworth, 1945).
Revelation and Evangelism (London: Lutterworth, 1948).
The Structure of the Divine Society (Philadelphia: Westminster, 1951).
Christianity and Symbolism (London: Collins, 1955).
The Christian Faith (London: Hodder and Stoughton, 1964).
Myth and Symbol (London: SPCK, 1966).
The Christian Understanding of Atonement (London: Nisbet, 1967).
Traditional Symbols and Christian Faith (London: Epworth, 1973).
Charles Raven: Naturalist, Historian, Theologian (London: Hodder and Stoughton, 1975).
C. H. Dodd: Interpreter of the New Testament (London: Hodder and Stoughton, 1977).
Into All the World: A Biography of Max Warren (London: Hodder, 1980).
Religious Experience and Christian Faith (London: SCM, 1981).
The Power of Symbols in Religion and Culture (New York: Crossroad, 1986). (JW)

Dix, Gregory (1901–52) George Eglinton Alston Dix was born on 4 October 1901 and educated at Westminster School and Merton College, Oxford, where he graduated B.A. in Modern History in 1923. After a year at Wells Theological College, he was ordained to a fellowship at Keble College, Oxford, which he held for two years. In 1926 he went to the Anglican Benedictine community at Nashdom, where he tried his vocation, and eventually, after some years as a Priest Oblate, he took his solemn vows with the monastic name of Gregory in 1940. He was active in the Convocation of Canterbury from 1946 onwards, and held the post of Prior of Nashdom from 1948 until his death. He travelled widely in North America, where the fees accruing to his lecture tours helped to establish the sister-community at Three Rivers, Michigan. He was well known as a preacher and giver of retreats, and his quick-witted style permeated much of his work. He died on 12 May 1952.

His two major works are *The Apostolic Tradition of St Hippolytus* (1937) and *The Shape of the Liturgy* (1945). In the former, he demonstrated the breadth of his knowledge of ancient sources that pointed to a document which was attracting an increasing amount of attention among patristic scholars but which had as yet not appeared in a proper critical edition. Although dated now, and superseded by the more astringent study made by Dom Bernard Botte and others, Dix's work was published entirely in English, and it served to bring to a wider audience the way in which Christian communities in the third century might have been ordered in liturgy and life. In the latter, a lengthy study of the history of the eucharist which helped to earn him an Oxford D.D. in 1949, Dix drew together a vast range of scholarship from patristic, Medieval and Reformation studies and blended them into a book that, according to Edward Ratcliff, read like a novel but was in fact a serious contribution to scholarship. Dix was an Anglo-Catholic who celebrated a daily Mass according to the Roman rite. From that perspective, he could nonetheless see the coming impact of a fundamental reappropriation of the ancient past on the worship of the churches of the West, in particular his own part of it. He stood for a renewed Catholicism, based on a number of important foundations which come through in his works, but above all in *The Shape of the Liturgy*. Liturgy is about actions, interpreted by words, and his theory of the 'four-action-shape' has influenced nearly every revision of the eucharist since, even if his identification of Christ's 'taking' the bread and cup does not inevitably lead in the opinion of all to the 'offertory'. Moreover, it was he who brought home to many people the growing trend among scholars that the Jewish origins of the Church, in both ministry and worship, were to be taken seriously. For those nourished on the Book of Common Prayer, this insight had little direct bearing, except perhaps to question the unfortunately worded collect for Jews and heretics on Good Friday, already the subject of some debate. But his historical grasp of the evolution of the eucharist provided important clues for how liturgical revision should be reorientated. Dix was no fan of the (unsuccessful) proposed Prayer Book of 1928, for he could foresee a more radical climate ahead. For him, the eucharist in the West owed its main lines of development to the three classic environments in which it had been celebrated: the simple house-church (what he called 'stratum one'); the grand basilican mode (what he called 'stratum two'); and the medieval side-altar Mass (what he called 'stratum three'). The later medieval lay devotions, gazing at the distant eucharist in a meditative style, for Dix provided the background for the Reformation Lord's Supper, as it swept aside so much of the older traditions. In particular, Dix popularized the view that Cranmer, author of the English Prayer Book, was no crypto-Catholic, but a Zwinglian in his theology of the eucharist. In all these particulars, Dix was challenged, sometimes on detail, sometimes on questions of principle. With hindsight, one can see his influence behind much liturgical revision of recent years; and one can also note his lack of emphasis on style in language, as well as his lack of sympathy with much-loved Anglican devotions, such as the prayer of humble access, which would on his judgement be axed as a medieval-style devotion for a communicant hovering before the altar (it was in fact inspired by a prayer written by St Anselm). But two further trajectories in the Dix works have stood the test of time, even if they have been reinterpreted: the notion of eucharistic memorial, anamnesis, has been refined in the heady days of ecumenical agreement, but it is a foundation-stone for understanding origins as well as dialogue. Secondly, Dix had a strong social thrust to his vision of the eucharistic community, redeemed by God, the leaven in the lump of society, being the Body of Christ in the world, in which connection he was a partial fellow-traveller with Father Gabriel Hebert, SSM, whose *Liturgy and Society* (1937) made such an impact on Anglican social teaching. Dix's Catholicism made him uneasy with ecumenical moves that threatened to take the Church of England in any direction that he saw as more Protestant; he was an ardent opponent of the South India Reunion scheme, and contributed to Kenneth Kirk's collection of essays, *The Apostolic Ministry* (1946) with an at times humorous miniature study of the office of bishop down the ages. In today's world, it is not hard to picture him taking his stance on a number of controversial issues, armed with texts from the past, quick interpretations of accumulated evidence, and ready to lecture or preach at a moment's notice. His correspondence shows a man of God, who loved scholarship – and church controversy.

There are no collected editions of his works. A bibliography of his works appears in Kenneth Stevenson, 1977, *Gregory Dix 25 Years On*, Grove Liturgical Study 10 (Bramcote: Grove Books): 40f. His first published material consists of a long line of reviews in the Nashdom journal *Laudate*. From 1937, his main works appeared:

The Apostolic Tradition of St Hippolytus (vol. I only), Church Historical Society (London: SPCK, 1937); 2nd edn, Henry Chadwick (ed.) (London: SPCK, 1968).

The Question of Anglican Orders: Letters to a Layman (London: Dacre, 1944).

The Shape of the Liturgy (London: Dacre and A/C Black, 1945).

The Theology of Confirmation in Relation to Baptism, a lecture delivered at Oxford University, 22 January 1946 (London: Dacre, 1946).

'Ministry in the Early Church', an essay in K. E. Kirk (ed.), *The Apostolic Ministry* (London: Hodder and Stoughton, 1946) 183–303.

Jew and Greek: A Study in the Primitive Church (London: Dacre, 1953).

Holy Order, a paper read at a Priests' Convention, USA, 1950 (London: Church Literature Association, 1976), with introduction by Dr E. J. Yarnold, SJ.

In addition to Stevenson, *Gregory Dix 25 Years On*, there is also Simon Bailey's biography, *A Tactful God* (Leominster: Gracewing, 1995). (KS)

Donne, John (1572–1631), poet, Dean of St Paul's. God's praise, human frailty, and resurrection dominate his writings. Raised Roman Catholic, Donne left Oxford without a degree because of the Oath of Allegiance. Before ordination at 43, this worldling aggressively courted secular preferment. But death tinged his life. His father died in 1576; three siblings, his mother, his wife, and six of his twelve children predeceased him. 'A Valediction: Forbidding Mourning', 'The Funeral' and 'The Relique' demonstrate how resurrection faith pervades Donne's religious poetry.

Holy Sonnets and the Divine Poems explicate a whole theology. 'La Carona', a circlet of seven sonnets, bound together by the device of beginning each stanza with the last line of the preceding one, demonstrates the interrelationship of seven major doctrines from 'Annunciation' to 'Ascension'. The most vibrant of the Holy Sonnets, 'Death Be Not Proud', has a contemporary quality in its proclamation of the death of death.

Donne employs the stages of his 1623 illness and recovery as metaphors for sin, death and resurrection in 'A Hymn to God the Father' and *Devotions upon Emergent Occasions*. The hymn articulates the necessity of abject repentance. It unlocks the twenty-three devotions. Each has a tripartite structure: meditation, expostulation, prayer. Evidently, Donne imitates the prelude, meditation, colloquy of Loyola's *Spiritual Exercises* intended to discipline the three powers of the mind – memory, understanding, and will. 'Hymn' and *Devotions* deserve further exploration because they exemplify and inculcate Anglican spirituality.

Devotions and the tensile poems repay attentive reading almost immediately; theologically instructive, the sermons make scholarly

demands. Sermons and poetry complement each other with their identical theological themes. The 160 published sermons tend to be erudite
yet spiritually accessible, for Donne moved to tears his diverse audiences.
His last sermon, 'Death's Duel', is distinctive for profoundly inspiring
resurrection hope. It discloses how Donne shows the gateway of heaven
to those who traverse the Pilgrim's Way with Christ through his passion.

R. C. Bald, 1986. *John Donne, a Life* (Oxford: Clarendon).
John Carey, 1990. *John Donne* (London: Faber & Faber).
John Donne, *Sermons*, 10 vols., Simpson & Potter (eds.), 1953 (Cambridge: Cambridge
University Press. (WE)

DuBose, William Porcher (1836–1918), Episcopal clergyman and
theologian. Born in South Carolina, he graduated from the Military
College of South Carolina in 1855, and the University of Virginia in
1859. In 1861 he withdrew from seminary to serve in the Confederate
military during the Civil War. Ordained deacon in late 1863, he served
as an army chaplain for the remainder of the war. Ordained priest in
1866, he served as the rector of Trinity Church, Abbesville, S.C. from
1868, and chaplain of the University of the South, Sewanee, Tennessee
from 1871, where he served until his death. He was Dean of the
University's School of Theology from 1894 to 1908. Although influenced
early on by Evangelicalism, DuBose's mature theology is best described
as liberal Catholic. A creative philosophical theologian, his works stress
the doctrine of the incarnation and the evolutionary theories of the
time. In *The Soteriology of the New Testament* (1892) he argues for the
particular incarnation of God in Christ, and the generic incarnation of
humanity. That his philosophy employed the best Catholic emphases is
demonstrated by his great interest in the historic Christological defini-
tions as defending the full humanity of Christ (*The Ecumenical Councils*,
1896). Meanwhile his incarnational soteriology, rooted as it was in
Christ's representation of humanity, was delineated in such works as
The Gospel in the Gospels (1906), where he treats the soteriology of the
synoptic Gospels; *The Gospel According to Paul* (1907), dealing with Pauline
theology in the Epistle to the Romans, and *The Reason of Life* (1911), a
treatment of Johannine soteriology. Extremely influential in his own day
and widely recognized for his profound creativity and original thought,
he is often considered the greatest theologian that the American
Episcopal Church ever produced.

T. D. Bratton, *An Apostle of Reality* (London: Longmans, Green, and Co.).
Dictionary of American Biography, III.
Dictionary of American Religious Biography.
Dictionary of Christianity in America.

Eliot, Thomas Stearns (1888–1935), was an outstandingly important figure in the cultural life of the English-speaking world for a great part of the twentieth century. As poet, critic and editor, he helped to shape the sensibility of several generations; as a committed and articulate Christian of Catholic Anglican loyalties, he also exerted a significant influence on generations of Anglicans and others, not so much by his ideas as by the haunting and aphoristic quality of his poetry, much of which has come to express for many believers essential insights of their faith.

He was born in St Louis, Missouri into a cultivated and fairly prosperous Unitarian family with roots in New England. At Harvard, he studied philosophy and began to acquaint himself with oriental religion; the mystical tradition was already important to him; even in the years when he had abandoned formal religious affiliation. Further study in Paris and Oxford introduced him to two major philosophical influences, Henri Bergson and F. H. Bradley (he completed in 1910 a thesis on Bradley, originally intended as work towards a doctorate). His reputation as a poet grew steadily from 1914 onwards, but the publication of *The Waste Land* in 1922 established him as a major presence.

Profound personal turmoil, much of it connected with a disastrously unhappy marriage (to Vivien Haigh-Wood, in 1915), played some part in his return to religious practice in the 1920s. He was baptized and confirmed in the Church of England in 1927, and the prose and poetry of the years immediately following reflect his new commitments. The essay collection of 1928, *For Lancelot Andrewes*, signals his enthusiasm for the classical Anglican Divines, and the *Ash Wednesday* sequence of poems (1930) powerfully deploys echoes of Dante and the Latin liturgy, to evoke an elegiac and detached sensibility, a weary and still vulnerable repose and renunciation.

The poetry of the 1930s develops this vein; but Eliot was also increasingly active in ecclesiastical affairs: he was to become a churchwarden in his London parish (St Stephen's, Gloucester Road), and participated in several Anglican ventures in social critique, notably the 1936 Oxford Conference on Church, Community and State, and the informal group ('The Moot') which gathered around the remarkable figure of J. H. Oldham. The fullest exposition of his social ideals is *The Idea of a Christian Society* (1939), a short but densely argued tract of abiding interest. He experimented with the kind of para-liturgical drama quite popular in the 1930s – with uneven success: *The Rock* (1934) has fine passages but does not stand up in dramatic terms, while *Murder in the Cathedral* (1935), first produced in the Chapter House at Canterbury, has won a continuing reputation as a classic of its kind.

The war years saw the completion of what is agreed to be his master piece, the sequence of *Four Quartets* (1940–2), a subtle play of different voices and styles, exploring the themes of time and place, the significance of historical memory and the paradoxes of an incarnational faith. After the war, Eliot wrote hardly any more poetry; but he developed a new interest in drama, verse drama in a contemporary setting. The plays of this period have an unmistakable spiritual agenda; *The Cocktail Party* (1950), in particular, deals with conversion and sacrifice, alluding obliquely to the life and martyrdom of Charles de Foucauld. He received numerous international distinctions, including the Nobel Prize for Literature, continued his involvement in church affairs, attacking the reunion scheme in South India and, in the 1950s, advising on the prepa-ration of the Revised Psalter; and in 1957 he married Valerie Fletcher (Vivien had died in a mental hospital in 1947), with whom he enjoyed great happiness, celebrated in a brief dedicatory poem in the *Collected Poems* of 1963.

Eliot's famous summary of his loyalties (in 1928) as 'classicist, royalist and anglo-catholic' reflects the influence of the arch-conservative French writer, Charles Maurras; but Eliot, despite his inexcusable use of the rhetoric of anti-Semitism in the works of the 1920s and early 1930s, was not cast in the same mould as Maurras. Equally, he is not really to be aligned with the generation of post-war literary apologists for Christ-ianity such as C. S. Lewis and Dorothy Sayers (he had little time for Lewis – who reciprocated the sentiments – although they shared an admiration for Charles Williams, whom Eliot published in his time as an editor with Faber). What sets him apart from both French proto-Fascism and English Christian triumphalism is the abiding 'modernist' sense which he inherited from the French writers who so impressed him in his years in Paris – Baudelaire, Mallarmé and others. This is modernism in its literary meaning – the awareness of fragmentation, the apparent anarchy of the imagination, words escaping from the control of authorial intentions. Bradley's philosophy gave this a theoretical anchorage: truth-fulness, in this perspective, depends not on correspondence, economy and accuracy, but on the coherent interweaving of systems of representation, the ordering of an initially dissonant chorus. This casts light on Eliot's preferred technique, perfected in the *Quartets*, of allowing diverse voices full play (which is why the *Quartets* should not be read, as they often are, as a single statement of 'what Eliot thought'); and the gathering of the voices into coherence is done not by the imposition of an ideology or a vocabulary of orthodoxy, but by the subtle insinuation of the image of a God who accepts and 'owns' the fragility and vulnerability of the process of making meaning in words and history. Compared with the poetry of the 1930s, this is a 'renunciation of renunciation', a turn in to the inescapable reality of a present moment determined by the past, yet mysteriously open in its depths to the self-communication of God.

Eliot's cultural theories have found few followers, though some, like C. H. Sisson, have developed aspects of them with vigour and sophistication. The well-known early essay on 'Tradition and the individual talent' (1920) has, however, had some theological impact, especially on those concerned to build bridges between British and German hermeneutical reflection. Otherwise, there remains much to be done in reading Eliot theologically – the *Quartets* in particular, with their rich and distinctive interweaving of John of the Cross, the Bhagavad Gita, Julian of Norwich, Dante and (it has been argued) Kierkegaard. Few voices, even now, combine so fully an unconsoled contemporary vision with an obstinate and orthodox theological hopefulness.

The Complete Poems and Plays of T. S. Eliot (London: Faber, 1969).
For Lancelot Andrewes (London: Faber, 1928).
The Idea of a Christian Society (London: Faber, 1939).
Notes Towards the Definition of Culture (London: Faber,1948).
Peter Ackroyd, 1984. *T. S. Eliot* (London: Hamish Hamilton).
Helen Gardner, 1978. *The Composition of 'Four Quartets'* (London: Faber).
Lyndall Gordon, 1977. *Eliot's Early Years* (Oxford: Oxford University Press).
Lyndall Gordon, 1988. *Eliot's New Life* (Oxford: Oxford University Press).
Paul Murray, 1991. *T. S. Eliot and Mysticism: The Secret History of Four Quartets* (London: Macmillan). (RW)

Faber, George Stanley (1773–1854), Evangelical Divine and controversialist. Awarded his B.A. from University College, Oxford in 1793, he was elected a fellow and tutor of Lincoln College that same year. He received his M.A. and B.D. in 1796 and 1801 respectively. He delivered the Bampton Lecture for 1801, which was published as 'Horae Mosaicae'. After resigning his fellowship and his marriage in 1803, he served until 1805 as his father's curate in Calverly. He went on to minister in three parishes in Durham before being collated to a prebendal stall in Salisbury Cathedral in 1831. The next year he was given mastership of Sherburn Hospital, where he served until his death. Describing himself as an Evangelical High Churchman, he represented a 'just medium' between the Tractarian and the Low Church Evangelical positions. Faber was committed to the Evangelical doctrines of the necessity of conversion, justification by faith, and the sole authority of Scripture as the Rule of Faith, while at the same time interacting seriously with fathers of the first five centuries in his polemical works. His considerable involvement in the theological debates of the Oxford Movement represented what came to be known as the 'Evangelical High Church Party'.

Evangelical High Churchmen answered the Tractarian Party with the scriptures, the church fathers of the first five centuries, and the Reformers. His writings include a denunciation of Alexander Knox's teaching on Justification as essentially Roman Catholic in his *The Primitive Doctrine of Justification* (1837); a sharp attack on the doctrine of Reserve as found in Tract 80, and his *Primitive Doctrine of Regeneration* (1840), which were of more benefit at the time of their writing than for today. Nonetheless, his main importance comes from his hermeneutical principle, 'that Scripture is the sole Faith, but that, since no Rule can be practically used as a Rule until it be first interpreted and understood, we must . . . resort, not to the wantonness of our own arbitrary dogmatism, but to the ascertained Concurrence of the Primitive Church from the beginning'.

Dictionary of National Biography, XVIII (1885).
Peter Toon, 1979. *Evangelical Theology 1833–1856* (London: Marshall, Morgan & Scott), 33–42, 116, 132.

Fairweather, Eugene Rathbone (1920–), theologian and ecumenist, and a leading Canadian Anglican thinker. Educated in Montreal and at Trinity College, Toronto, he became divinity tutor at Trinity in 1944 and, apart from a brief spell of graduate work in New York, spent the rest of his career there until retirement in 1987. From 1964 he was Keble Professor of Divinity at the college.

Fairweather has published little by way of pure scholarship, although his edition of medieval theological materials in *A Scholastic Miscellany* is a justly celebrated standard text, as are other essays on patristic and medieval thinkers and themes. Most of his writings are more occasional in nature, emerging from his deep immersion in the life of the Church, and his involvement in both ecumenical and liturgical renewal. His influence on Canadian church life, both Anglican and non-Anglican, has been immense. Generations of Anglican priests were trained by him, and for many years he acted as the theological resource of the Anglican Church of Canada. He was one of the chief theological architects of the Canadian *Book of Alternative Services*, which, in many respects, reflects the moderate Catholic ethos of his theology. His advocacy of the ordination of women to the priesthood (after earlier opposition to the prospect) and of the communion of all the baptized, including children, was probably the single most important factor in commending such developments in Canada. As ecumenist, Fairweather is a figure of international stature: he was a major presence in the Canadian Council of Churches, and of the Faith and Order Commission of the World Council of Churches, and was an Anglican observer at the third and fourth sessions of Vatican II. In bilateral dialogues, he was a very significant member of

ARCIC I and played a large role in Anglican–Orthodox dialogue. He was a key consultant at the 1963 Anglican Congress in Toronto, and edited the report of its proceedings. He also published a great deal of religious journalism, which did much to shape the mind of the Anglican Church of Canada in the third quarter of the century and beyond.

(with R.F. Hettlinger) *Episcopacy and Reunion* (London: Mowbray, 1953).
(ed.) *A Scholastic Miscellany: Anselm to Ockham* (London: SCM Press, 1956).
Toronto Journal of Theology 3/1 (1987), Festschrift for Fairweather, including full bibliography. (JW)

Farrer, Austin Marsden (1904–68) was born the grandson of a learned, devout and lively Nonconformist family. At St Paul's School in London he developed his formidable literary and classical education, which together with the daily learning-by-heart of poetry was to bear fruit in his later life as priest-theologian. Preaching to his school in 1958 on the subject of St Paul's bitterness against the 'doctrine of limited liabilities' which foundered in human failure, he recalled his earlier life at school and then at Balliol as an exemplary student, with a taste for academic study, and a still more pronounced taste for academic success (Conti 1973: 120–4).

As an undergraduate he negotiated with his parents his transition to membership of the Church of England, and finding his vocation for ordination, he studied at Cuddesdon (in a group which included A. M. Ramsey). Words from a sermon on Keble describe himself too: 'a man must make up his mind what there is most worthy of love, and most binding on conduct, in the world of real existence. It is this decision, or this discovery, that is the supreme exercise of a truth-seeking intelligence' (Conti 1973: 157). After a curacy in Dewsbury between 1928 and 1931, during a period of severe economic 'slump', he was ordained to the priesthood by the Bishop of Wakefield in 1929. He learned German, and began a series of visits to German-speaking countries, acquainting himself (in person in some instances) with German theologians and biblical criticism. An invitation to work at St Edmund Hall, Oxford, as Chaplain and Tutor (1931–5) was followed by appointment as Chaplain and Fellow of Trinity College, Oxford (1935–60). Return to Oxford made possible his acquaintance with Katherine Newton, whom he married in 1937. One daughter was born in 1939. From Trinity he went as Warden to Keble College, Oxford (1960–8) and visited the USA.

Two essays 'The Christian doctrine of man' (1938) and 'The theology of morals' (1939) may be read as prolegomena to his sermons, as exceptional for their moral wisdom as for their wit and sheer verbal elegance and vitality. To the years at Trinity belong some major publications. As unpredictable as *Finite and Infinite* (1943) was a quite different kind of book, the 1948 Bampton lectures, *The Glass of Vision*. Between the two he took the degrees of B.D. and D.D. on one day.

Finite and Infinite is an exercise in 'rational theology', and whatever the shifts of emphasis in his later work, the bones of his theology are already clear. He thinks about cosmological relating (God) to 'being-as-activity' (substance), and attends to the analogies which make possible the climbing of the scale within ourselves which yields knowledge of God. Ever alert to what was going on in other disciplines, his 1958 Gifford Lectures, *The Freedom of the Will*, explored his conviction that central to what it is to be a human person is to be free to become what we will. 'Rational theology' was related to the revealed knowledge of God with scrupulous care in *Faith and Speculation: An Essay in Philosophical Theology* of 1967, with a treatment of grace in relation to free will, revelation and history (and criticism of Alan Richardson). His intention was to maintain a climate in which belief could flourish.

The Glass of Vision is the work of a theologian thinking systematically and with great originality about revelation, specifically the thought of Christ as 'expressed in certain dominant images', e.g. those of the Kingdom of God and the Son of Man, and 'displayed in the action of the supper, the infinitely complex and fertile images of sacrifice and communion, of expiation and covenant' (42). These images, and their interplay, were 'given', that is to say, inspired by the Holy Spirit, and yet like analogy, drawn from human life. The coincidence of image and event together constitutes revelation, which continues in the existence of the apostles, and in the life of the Church, authoritative whilst ever corrigible. The themes of his work on the authors of two synoptic Gospels are already clear, though the most astonishing (for an Anglican theologian, given its lack of prominence in the lectionary) was his work on the Apocalypse, of which a foretaste is given in the Bamptons.

In *A Rebirth of Images* (1949), Farrer held that just as St Mark had produced a new form of writing appropriate to God's revelation in Christ, so St John wrote in a 'poetic' form appropriate to the prophecies he uttered, though in the subsequent writing of his Gospel, and then of his Epistles, inspiration took a different mode. Above all, Farrer was concerned for the communication of an Easter and Paschal faith, and it was revelation through images, and not the results of current biblical 'scholarship' (for which he had scant, if any respect) which needed to be appreciated.

Farrer was also what would now be called a 'systematic' theologian too, given his capacity to think through the implications of his beliefs from one topic to another. Thus works such as *Love Almighty and Ills*

Unlimited (1961), *A Science of God?* (1966) and above all, *Saving Belief* (1967) between them treat many of the major themes of Christian faith.

Farrer was a 'Catholic' and robustly confident and critical member of the Church of England. His classicism made it possible for him to use and translate the Christian texts of the past with ease, and to transmit them to others. So familiar with the Book of Common Prayer that his own prayers and collects themselves exhibit its style, he also valued the spiritual power of the Authorized Version of the Bible. Further, he came to teach how to use the rosary, unexpectedly explained as the conclusion to *Lord I Believe: Suggestions for Turning the Creed into Prayer* (1955: but see the second edition of 1958). His theological and pastoral creativity detached the use of the rosary from 'an exclusive connection with the scenes of Mary's life', however, since identification with our redeemer is more vital. His admiration for St Paul as a theologian was unqualified, as is clear from his sermons. His address to his old school was a brilliant and succinct statement of 'justification by faith'. On the other hand, 'of course the most conservative of us do and must rethink the theology of the saints if we are to use it or live by it. We are bound to rid St Paul's pages of elements which we can only regard as First-Century period junk' (*A Science of God?*: 119).

Farrer was a Trinitarian theologian, unsurprisingly for one who lived liturgically, whilst giving full weight to the particularity of the incarnation (as in 'Galilean carpenter, turned freelance rabbi' (*Saving Belief*: 69)). He learned everything he could from natural and social scientists, alert to every possible conceptual option if it serves 'saving faith and the objectives of its belief' (*Saving Belief*: Preface). And since, for Farrer, 'the work of the Church is to incorporate men into the life of Incarnate God, and the Church is itself the means and the form of such an incorporation', he was blessed to be a member of a church whose Catholicism had been preserved in form and substance by merciful providence, whilst remaining free from papal usurpation (Conti 1973: 48–52). His intellectual and priestly catholicity was nourished by the tradition to which he contributed so remarkably.

Full bibliographies of Farrer's works may be found in two books marked ★ below.
Finite and Infinite (Westminster: Dacre, 1943).
The Glass of Vision (Westminster: Dacre, 1948).
A Rebirth of Images: The Making of St. John's Apocalypse (Westminster: Dacre, 1949).
A Study in St. Mark (Westminster: Dacre, 1951).
St. Matthew and St. Mark (Westminster: Dacre, 1954) .
The Freedom of the Will (London: A. & C. Black, 1958).
Lord I Believe (London: Faith, 1958).
Love Almighty and Ills Unlimited (New York: Doubleday, 1961).

The Revelation of St. John the Divine: Commentary on the English Text (Oxford: Clarendon, 1964).
Saving Belief (London: Hodder & Stoughton, 1964).
A Science of God? (London: Bles, 1966).
Faith and Speculation (London: A. & C. Black, 1967).

There are several collections of Farrer's papers edited by Charles Conti, including *The End of Man* (London: SPCK, 1973) and Leslie Houlden. Richard Harries has also edited *The One Genius: Readings through the Year with Austin Farrer* (London: SPCK, 1987).

Key Secondary literature
Philip Curtis, 1985. *A Hawk among Sparrows: A Biography of Austin Farrer* (London: SPCK).

Conference papers
Jeffrey C. Eaton and Ann Loades (eds.), 1983. *For God and Clarity: New Essays in Honor of Austin Farrer* (Allison Park, Penn.: Pickwick).★
Brian Hebblethwaite and Edward Henderson (eds.), 1990. *Divine Action: Studies Inspired by the Philosophical Theology of Austin Farrer* (Edinburgh: T. & T. Clark), especially David Brown, 'God and Symbolic Action', 103–22.
Ann Loades and Michael McLain (eds.), 1992. *Hermeneutics, the Bible and Literary Criticism* (London: Macmillan).
See also the special issue on Austin Farrer of *Modern Theology* 1.3 (1985): 165–242.

Two important essays
To read with Brown (as above), Basil Mitchell, 1990. 'The Places of Symbols in Christianity' in his *How to Play Theological Ping-Pong, and other Essays on Faith and Reason* (London: Hodder and Stoughton): 184–97.
Vincent Brümmer, 1992. 'Farrer, Wiles and the Causal Joint', *Modern Theology* 8.1: 1–14.

Two single-authored works
Charles C. Hefling, 1979. *Jacob's Ladder: Theology and Spirituality in the Thought of Austin Farrer* (Cambridge, Mass.: Cowley).
Charles Conti, 1995. *Metaphysical Personalism: An Analysis of Austin Farrer's Metaphysics of Personalism* (Oxford: Clarendon).★ (AL)

Field, Richard (1561–1616) theologian and Dean of Gloucester. Educated at Magdalen College, Oxford, he earned an M.A. from Magdalen Hall in 1584. In this same year he was appointed to an otherwise unimportant position lecturing within Magdelen Hall, but the quality of these lectures attracted a wide audience from throughout the university. In his career he held a series of significant posts including Divinity Reader at Winchester Cathedral, Rector of Burghclere, chaplain ordinary to Queen Elizabeth I, Prebendary of Windsor, and in 1609 was appointed Dean of Gloucester. *Of the Church Five Books* (1609; reprinted by the Ecclesiastical History Society, 4 vols, 1847–52), was his significant theological contribution, which he wrote to contrast errors that he saw in the Roman church with the Church of England. In this book the Roman church's demand of submission to papal authority is compared by Field to the demands of the Donatists, of the early church, who made

123

excessive requirements concerning purity which led to exclusivity and schism. In this work he also outlines five qualities of a true church: Antiquity, Succession, Unity, Universality, and the name 'Catholic'. This book ranks along with that of Hooker's *Treatise on the Laws of Ecclesiastical Polity* as one of the most significant works of Anglican polemical divinity. He was one of the most penetrating theologians of his time, and although his learning was remarkable, Field's success can also be attributed to his disposition and fine character, which earned him many supporters.

Oxford Dictionary of the Christian Church, 512.
R. Hooper in *Dictionary of National Biography*, XVIII (1889), 410–12.

Figgis, John Neville (1866–1919) was a leading theologian, preacher and political theorist active in the early years of the twentieth century. Originally from a Nonconformist family, he studied history at Cambridge, where he subsequently taught. After a few years as a country parson, he joined the Community of the Resurrection and rapidly acquired a wide reputation as a speaker. Most of his subsequently published work consists of courses of sermons and lectures delivered in Britain and the USA. In 1918, he was on a transatlantic voyage when his ship was torpedoed; he never recovered either physical or mental health.

In addition to his influential monographs on Renaissance political thought, completed before his entry into the Mirfield community, and a brief but penetrating study of Augustine's *City of God*, his books deal with issues for the contemporary Church of England. He writes as a Christian Socialist and an Anglo-Catholic, critical alike of the English religious establishment and of the centralism of the Roman Catholic Church. His ideal is a non-confessional state, in which churches have the right to determine their own business, as do other 'voluntary' communities. Drawing on his knowledge of continental political theory and history, Figgis argues that the state must not be thought of as a monolithic sovereign entity, but as a 'community of communities', an administrative system assisting independent voluntary associations, such as churches, trade unions and educational institutions, to negotiate their goals. Authority is not delegated from the state downwards but is intrinsic to the voluntary association. A high valuation of what we might now call grass-roots political action and of the local church go hand in hand in his thought. Unlike most earlier Anglican Christian Socialists, Figgis (though no more alert than they were to strictly economic issues) is sceptical of appeals to a natural (let alone national) basis for the distinctive identity of the Church.

The Divine Right of Kings (Cambridge: Cambridge University Press, 1896).
Churches in the Modern State (London: Longmans,1913).
The Fellowship of the Mystery (London: Longmans, 1914).
Mark D. Chapman, 1995.'Concepts of the voluntary church in England and Germany, 1890–1920: A study of J. N. Figgis and Ernst Troeltsch', *Zeitschrift für Neuere Theologiegeschichte* 2: 37–59).
David Nicholls, 1975. *The Pluralist State* (London/Basingstoke: Macmillan).
Maurice G. Tucker, 1950. *John Neville Figgis: A Study* (London: SPCK). (RW)

Frith, John (1503–33), Protestant martyr who died for denying the doctrines of purgatory and transubstantiation.Educated at King's College, Cambridge, he was appointed a junior canon at Cardinal College, which was to become Christ Church College, Oxford. Though influenced by the German Reformation, Cardinal Wolsey brought him as a promising young scholar from Cambridge to Oxford in Wolsey's attempt to establish his new college. After being convicted for traffic in forbidden Protestant literature, he was imprisoned for a period in 1528. A friend of William Tyndale, he assisted him in translating the New Testament into English with the shared hope of eventually transforming the Church. Sir Thomas More wrote a tract against Frith's theology of the sacraments. Frith's views were basically fourfold: that transubstantiation was not an article of faith to be held under punishment of death; that if Christ was truly human, he could not be in two or more places at once; that Christ's words of institution were analogy and not literal with reference to his body and blood; that the sacrament should be received after the institution of Christ not in the prescribed order of the day. These views were eventually incorporated into the Book of Common Prayer. His major works include *Fruitful Gatherings of Scripture* (nd), which was Frith's translation into English of the basic expressions of the Lutheran teaching of justification by faith; *A Pistle to the Christen Reder* (nd), which also teaches justification by faith along Lutheran lines; *Antithesis wherein are compared together Christ's Acts and our Holy Father the Pope's* (1529) similar to Luther's work on the subject but with a detailed analysis by Frith. His championing of the doctrines of the Reformers led to various imprisonments for heresy and eventual death by burning at Smithfield on 4 July 1533.

Oxford Dictionary of the Christian Church, 539.
A. C. Bickley, 1889. 'Frith, John', in *Dictionary of National Biography*, XX (Oxford: Oxford University Press), 278–80.
F. L. Clarke, 1978. *John Frith, Kentish Martyr 1503–1533* (Kent: F. L. Clarke).

Gore, Charles (1853–1932) was the most important Anglican theologian and church leader between the beginning of the twentieth century and the end of the First World War. The editor of *Theology*, E. G. Selwyn, declared on Gore's death that he was 'the greatest theologian of our time'. Adrian Hastings, in his *History of English Christianity 1920–1985*, credits Gore more than anyone else with the 'vast transformation of consciousness' that had taken place in the Church of England as the Catholic movement had moved into the mainstream. In his lifetime, there was no more powerful force than Gore in English Christianity. He was the most famous – and at one point the most notorious – churchman of his day.

Biographical sketch

Gore was born to privilege. He belonged to the Irish aristocracy, but grew up in a large Victorian house at Wimbledon. His religious upbringing was conventional Low Church, but at the age of eight or nine he was given a Protestant tract which described the conversion of a Roman Catholic priest to the Protestant faith. But the book's effect was the reverse of what was intended. 'The book described confession and absolution, fasting, the Real Presence, the devotion of the Three Hours, the use of incense, etc, and I felt instinctively and at once that this sort of sacramental religion was the religion for me.'

Gore went to Harrow, where he came under the influence of B. F. Westcott, the New Testament scholar and later Bishop of Durham, who taught him the vocation of scholarship and a rule of life. A series of academic triumphs took him to Balliol and then to a fellowship at Trinity, Oxford. After ordination, Gore was made vice-principal of Cuddesdon at the age of 26 and then became the first principal of Pusey House. There Gore was at the centre of a movement of radical renewal in the Church which resulted in the Community of the Resurrection with Gore as superior or 'Senior', the Christian Social Union, with Westcott as President, and the study group the Holy Party – a cross between a research seminar and a vicarage tea party which produced the sensational symposium *Lux Mundi* in 1889. Gore was a disaster as a parish priest and was rescued from collapse by being made a canon of Westminster Abbey, from where he published some of his most original books. In 1901 Lord Salisbury made him Bishop of Worcester, and he was consecrated by the aged Archbishop Frederick Temple amid a storm of protest – some opponents regarding him as a destructive radical who undermined the Bible, others as a treacherous monkish Romanizer.

Gore's heart was in the great commercial centre in his diocese, the city of Birmingham. Gore set about dividing the diocese of Worcester and helped to endow the new see of Birmingham, becoming its first bishop. He gave his energies to the pastoral care of the clergy, the building of churches and parsonages, the impartial exercise of patronage, and the development of constitutional, representative structures for the diocese, in which vision of conciliarity he was ahead of his time. He was firm about liturgical experiment. Gore had no delusions of episcopal grandeur and lived simply.

Translated to be Bishop of Oxford in 1911, Gore seemed to be involved in ceaseless controversy. Against 'advanced' Anglo-Catholics, he insisted on strict use of the Book of Common Prayer and would only countenance Reservation for communicating the sick. Against ecumenically minded Anglicans, he opposed expressions of intercommunion with Protestants. Against more progressive biblical scholars – Anglo-Catholic though they sometimes were – who questioned the virginal conception and the physical resurrection, Gore insisted that the creed be interpreted literally, on these points. His open letter of 1914, *The Basis of Anglican Fellowship*, is the definitive statement of his position.

Gore stuck to his post during the First World War, but by 1919 he had had enough. He despaired of getting Archbishop Davidson and the bishops to take a stand on principle. Gore resigned his see, lived in London and became honorary assistant curate at Grosvenor Chapel, Mayfair. During this period, Gore devoted himself to writing. There followed a period of remarkable productivity. *Belief in God*, the first volume of his trilogy *The Reconstruction of Belief*, appeared in 1921. The second and third volumes, together with a fourth dealing with objections and reinforcing his conclusions, entitled *Can We then Believe?* soon followed. In the late 1920s Gore was an editor and contributor to *A New Commentary on Holy Scripture* and gave the Gifford Lectures, *The Philosophy of the Good Life*, an impressive testament. After extensive missionary travels in India, which he had first visited nearly fifty years before – at one point attracted by the idea of becoming Bishop of Bombay – Gore's health deteriorated rapidly and he died early in 1932.

Theological synthesis and conflict

As a theologian, Gore was radical in his methodology but conservative in his presuppositions. He was committed all his life to facing up to the most daunting challenges to the faith: evolution, biblical criticism, imperialistic philosophies such as Hegel's. Gore grappled with these ideas and eventually, through much mental anguish, overcame them and assimilated them. But his starting-point was the Christian Church, its life of sacramental worship, its faith and teaching given in Scripture and tradition and expounded with authority by its commissioned officers, the clergy and bishops in succession from the apostles.

Gore's aim was the integration of knowledge from whatever source, a synthesis of belief, resulting in a worldview that – though grounded in faith – did justice to all the evidence and satisfied the reason. Gore called this synthesis drawn from Scripture, tradition and reason 'liberal Catholicism'. Gore was not defensive about the word 'liberal'. It stood for freedom in the search for truth and distinguished his interpretation of Catholicism from authoritarian and obscurantist forms of it. It was also a Catholicism with a strong social conscience.

The great paradox of Gore's life and the source of so many of the conflicts that engaged him was the tension between the Reformation principle of the supremacy of Scripture over tradition as the sole arbiter of binding belief and practice, on the one hand, and Gore's intransigent insistence on aspects of tradition on the other. He could not justify his unchurching of non-episcopal communions on the basis of Scripture, and it is doubtful whether there is sufficient biblical evidence to support Gore's insistence on the literal interpretation of the virginal conception. On these and other points, it seemed that the radical theologian of *Lux Mundi*, who had accepted evolution and biblical criticism and on those grounds had challenged the orthodox and traditional interpretation of the incarnation, had given way to an intolerant reactionary who denied to others the liberty he had claimed for himself. Gore's own convictions remained unchanged – he was perfectly consistent – but the argument moved on, leaving Gore the lonely prophet of an impressive but actually static orthodoxy.

Gore's synthesis drew on a rich and diverse range of sources. Second only to the Bible were the early Fathers of the Church, both Western and Eastern. The patristic theology of the Western tradition – particularly Tertullian, Cyprian and Augustine – taught him the Catholic principle that the Church is a visible society with an ordered life, sustained through a sacramental ministry that is validated by authority. But Gore did not accept the need for a centralized primacy and believed that the papacy had proved itself an inveterate enemy of spiritual and theological liberty. He was virulent in his criticisms of the papacy and said that he wanted Catholicism without Rome and what it stood for – in other words, his version of Anglicanism.

From Eastern patristic theology Gore drew a more dynamic and mystical understanding of the life of the Church as a participation in God, the crucial role of the Holy Spirit and the emphasis on divine immanence that enabled him to recognize the truth of God in the theory of evolution and the principles of biblical criticism.

Gore was not vainly searching for an unbroken tradition. He was dismissive of much medieval scholastic theology which he believed was speculative and unreal. What Gore demanded was deep roots in patristic theology. His appeal was to Scripture and the primitive Church, interpreted by reason in the light of all our knowledge. 'I want to find myself, in the Church of England, now in the twentieth century, of one mind across the ages with the ancient Christian Church.'

Though, like the Tractarians, Gore's knowledge of Reformation theology was sketchy, he nevertheless held to certain principles of the Reformation: the paramount authority of Scripture, the fiduciary nature of faith, justification by grace through faith, the universal priesthood of the baptized, the non-sacerdotal, representative character of the ordained ministry, the right and duty of private judgement, and the importance of scrutinizing tradition in the light of historical criticism and moral principles. However, Gore believed that in breaching the rule that authority in ordained ministry is given only by devolution from above, and by renouncing the historic succession, the Protestant churches had flouted a fundamental law of Catholicity. 'I believe that in repudiating this principle the Reformed churches were – with whatever excuse – repudiating a law of spiritual authority in the church and also an essential principle of the Church's continuous life.' Though Gore readily acknowledged the grace of God at work in the non-episcopal Protestant churches, he could not recognize them as true churches of Christ with genuine ministries and sacraments.

While conservative in biblical interpretation, defending for example the Pauline authorship of the Pastoral Epistles and virginal conception of Jesus, Gore learned from biblical criticism the importance of taking seriously the human figure of the Gospels, who could be mistaken about the authorship of the biblical texts he quoted. This entailed a doubt as to Jesus' omniscience and led Gore to his doctrine of a kenosis or self-emptying of divine attributes in the incarnation.

The physical sciences taught Gore the truth of evolution, and the human sciences schooled him in the historical method which was characteristic of Gore's way of arguing a case. The personalist Idealism of the Platonic and Hegelian tradition in philosophy contributed the centrality of personality and the overarching authority of moral considerations to his worldview.

Gore on Anglicanism
Gore understood Anglicanism as a biblical and rational Catholicism. 'The character of the Anglican Church', he wrote, 'has been from the first that of combining steadfast adherence to the structure and chief

formulas of the Church catholic with the "return to Scripture" which was the central religious motive of the Reformation.' Anglicanism, according to Gore, therefore bears witness to a scriptural Catholicism – 'a catholicism in which Scripture is enthroned in the highest place of controlling authority in the Church'. But the revival of classical learning at the Renaissance had contributed a third component to the Anglican synthesis, the appeal to sound learning, to the findings of dispassionate scholarship. Gore affirmed:

> It is the glory of the Anglican Church that at the Reformation she repudiated neither the ancient structure of catholicism, nor the new and freer movement. Upon the ancient structure – the creeds, the canon, the hierarchy, the sacraments – she retained her hold while she opened her arms to the new learning, the new appeal to Scripture, the freedom of historical criticism and the duty of private judgement.

Scripture, insisted Gore, constitutes 'the sole final testing ground of dogmatic requirement'.

But Gore was far from triumphalist about Anglicanism. The history of the Church of England, he confessed, 'fills me with a profound humiliation. I find its continuous Erastianism, its complacent nationalism, its frequent deafness to the most urgent and obvious moral calls, its long-continued identification of itself with the interests and tastes of the "upper classes" . . . depressing and humiliating.' Gore's faith was not in the empirical Church but in the power of the Holy Spirit to bring the Church to perfection.

Gore's significance today

Gore could be fanatical, intransigent, unreasonable and was incapable of compromise. He had a consuming need of certainty. He wrestled with the arguments and the evidence continually. A characteristic utterance was, 'I am profoundly convinced, with a certainty that is unshakeable . . .'. Gore presents us with the case of an irreducibly paradoxical figure, a true enigma, who baffled his contemporaries, friends and enemies alike: a fastidious aristocrat who would insist on lodging in a working man's home on his episcopal visitations; a man filled with self-doubt and a depressive sense of his own unworthiness who was resolute and unflinching in contests over principle; the most eminent of all the bishops who resigned in order to write books; the radical young theologian who denied a similar freedom to others and in later life seemed to be an arch-reactionary; an Anglo-Catholic who antagonized other

Anglo-Catholics by insisting on scrupulous use of the Book of Common Prayer; an Anglican leader held in respect and affection by Nonconformists yet who was unbending about apostolic succession; a religious who lived in the world; a scholar whose life was filled with constant activity and who did his reading late at night.

Gore's impact as a theologian stretches down the century and touches us today. William Temple admitted he had learned more from Gore than from any other living teacher. Gore exerted a masterful influence on the young Michael Ramsey, who was awed by him and internalized Gore's prophetic voice and visage into his theological conscience, so that in years to come, as Archbishop of Canterbury, Ramsey would find himself asking, What would Gore say about this or that? In one of the last things he wrote, Ramsey recalled that in the years between the wars Gore's influence over him waned. He began to seem a rather outdated figure (he was a high Victorian, after all), and William Temple seemed to have more to offer. 'Today,' Ramsey went on, 'when I read and recall these two great men, it is Temple who now seems rather dated in thought and idiom while Gore speaks with the mysteriousness of a timeless authority.'

Select bibliography of works by Gore
Roman Catholic Claims (1884; 11th edn, London: Longmans, 1900).
The Church and the Ministry (1886; 2nd edn, London: Murray, 1889).
The Incarnation of the Son of God (Bampton Lectures 1891; 2nd edn, London, 1892).
Dissertations on Subjects Connected with the Incarnation (1895; 2nd edn, London: Murray, 1896).
The Body of Christ: An Enquiry into the Institution and Doctrine of Holy Communion (1901; 3rd edn, London: Murray, 1902).
The New Theology and the Old Religion (London: Murray, 1907).
Orders and Unity (London: Murray, 1909).
The Reconstruction of Belief (new edition in one volume of *Belief in God* (1921), *Belief in Christ* (1922), and *The Holy Spirit and the Church* (1924) (London: Murray, 1926).
Christ and Society (London: Allen and Unwin, 1928).
The Philosophy of the Good Life (Gifford Lectures 1929–30; London: Murray, 1930).

Works about Gore's life and thought
P. Avis, 1988. *Gore: Construction and Conflict* (Worthing: Churchman).
J. Carpenter, 1960. *Gore: A Study in Liberal Catholic Thought* (London: Faith Press).
G. L. Prestige, 1935. *The Life of Charles Gore* (London: Heinemann).
A. M. Ramsey, 1960. *From Gore to Temple* (London: Longmans). (PA)

Grant, Fredrick (1891–1974). After attending Lawrence College and Nashotah House, he earned his B.D. in 1913 from General Theological Seminary. He received his S.T.M. in 1916 and was awarded a D.D. in 1922 from Western Theological Seminary. In 1912 he was ordained deacon, and the following year he was ordained to the priesthood. His literary contribution was particularly evident in his role as Editor in Chief of the *Anglican Theological Review*. His writings appeared in the *Biblical World*, the *American Journal of Theology*, the *Journal of Biblical Literature*, the *American Church Monthly*, the *Church Quarterly Review*, and the *Anglican Theological Review*. At the age of thirty-six, Grant was instrumental in the reorganization of Western Theological Seminary, moving it to Evanston. From 1927 to 1938 he presided over the seminary and was largely responsible for its merger in 1933 with Seabury Divinity School. In 1938 he was called to Union Theological Seminary, where he assumed responsibilities as chair of Biblical Theology. Recognized for his contribution in New Testament studies, he was chosen as a member of the revision committee which produced the Revised Standard Version of the New Testament. His proper placement as a New Testament theologian is difficult to characterize. Grant accepted the basic methods of form criticism, relying heavily upon his knowledge of the Jewish background of Christianity. Much of his writing was therefore preoccupied with the synoptic Gospels and life of Jesus, interpreted largely through rabbinic and intertestamental literature. He belonged to a group known as 'Erasmians', who believed in the continuity of the Church and the duty to bring new learning into it. In *An Introduction to New Testament Thought* Grant suggests that Jesus was 'neither Messiah nor Son of Man (He was too sane to think of himself as the latter)' and he tends to view the teachings of Christ as eschatological but not apocalyptic.

Stowe's Clerical Directory of the American Church 1929–30.
Sherman E. Johnson, 1951. *The Joy of Study* (New York: Macmillan Co.).
Sherman E. Johnson, 1975. *Anglican Theological Review* 57: 3–13.

Guilbert, Charles Mortimer (1908–) Educated at the University of Chicago, Ph.D. (1934), and Seabury-Western Theological Seminary, S.T.B. (1936), he was made S.T.D. *honoris causa*, in 1959. Ordained to the priesthood in 1937, he served in pastoral positions in Oregon (1937–49) and California (1957–61). Among non-pastoral duties, Guilbert served as diocesan staff person, secretary of the Executive Council, and of the General Convention. Guilbert has been Custodian of the Standard Book of Common Prayer and Member of the Standing Liturgical Commission since 1963, serving as chair of the editorial committee. He retired in 1975, though he has remained an Honorary Canon of Grace Cathedral, San Francisco. He authored a small dictionary of liturgical terms which is comprehensive in scope, *A Dictionary of Liturgics* (New York Church Hymnal Corporation).

Hall, Arthur Crawshay Alliston (1857–1932), Anglo-Catholic bishop. Born in Berkshire, he attended Oxford University from which he took his B.A. in 1869, M.A. in 1872, and honorary D.D. in 1893. Ordained priest in 1871, he was consecrated bishop in 1894. Considered a preacher of rare ability and eloquence, and also a well-read theologian; he served as a licensed preacher in Oxford before moving to the United States in 1874. An early member of the Society of St John the Evangelist, he was eventually promoted as the head of its American province. He remained an avid Anglo-Catholic while maintaining respect from all church parties. When chosen for Bishop of Vermont he was released from his obligations to the Society. He was a prolific writer, whose work included *Notes on the use of the Prayer Book* (1896) and *The Use of Holy Scripture in the Worship of the Church* (1903). Theologically a High Churchman, Hall's writings reflect a Catholic tone with attention to detail in holy worship. Aware of the diverse practices which had entered into the Episcopal Church after the Oxford Movement, Hall penned some practical advice to the clergy in his *Notes on the use of the Prayer Book*. The purpose of the book was to 'guide a clergyman, according to the rubrics, to an intelligent and reverent use of the Prayer Book Services'. Bishop Hall's historical work, tracing the use of Holy Scripture in the Church; is not only masterful in accuracy but also instructive in laying a foundation for liturgical orthodoxy. 'The reading of the Scriptures (with which naturally follows some exposition of their meaning, or exhortation based upon them) is an integral part of the Eucharistic service. The communication of Truth must accompany the ministration of Grace.' Dedicated to historic orthodoxy and liturgical worship, Hall's influence as a beloved bishop and respected theologian is unquestionable.

Stowe's Clerical Directory of the American Church, 1929–30.
George DeMille, 1941. *The Catholic Movement in the American Episcopal Church* (Philadelphia: The Church Historical Society).
William Stevens Perry, 1895. *The Episcopate in America* (New York: Christian Literature Co.).

Hall, Francis (1857–1932). After receiving his B.A. in 1882 from Racine College, he went on to earn an M.A. in 1885. In 1898 he was awarded Doctor of Divinity (D.D.) from Kenyon College and then again from General Theological Seminary in 1910. After a year in the diaconate he was ordained to the priesthood in 1886. From 1886 until 1905 he served as an instructor of dogmatic theology at Western Theological Seminary, at which time he was promoted to Professor of Dogmatics, a position he held for eight years. He ministered in the same capacity at General Theological Seminary from 1913 to 1928. Hall's theological influence is particularly important as the author of a ten-volume set of dogmatic theology, known to many as the 'Anglican Summa'. The work was begun in 1907 and continued until 1922. Hall's *Dogmatic Theology* stands alone as the most comprehensive Anglo-Catholic presentation of Anglicanism in the twentieth century. The volumes consist of an Introduction, and volumes on: Authority; The Being and Attributes of God; The Trinity; Creation and Man; The Incarnation; The Passion and Exaltation of Christ; The Church; The Sacraments, and a volume on Eschatology. There is little originality in Hall's work as it was intended to collect the thinking of Catholic theologians before him. His work is thoroughly patristic, though not negligent of the scholastics. Where Hall interjects some originality, it is in his treatment of creation and the fall of man. Influenced by Darwinism and the evolutionary view of mankind, Hall builds a bridge which attempts to explain how the progress of mankind's evolution was effected by sin and the fall. Francis J. Hall's *Dogmatic Theology* remains the most thorough Anglo-Catholic work of its kind in the twentieth century.

Stowe's Clerical Directory of the American Church, 1929–30.
Dogmatic Theology (New York: Longmans, Green and Company).

Hammond, Henry (1605–60), Fellow of Magdalen College, Oxford, 1625, Rector of Penshurst, 1633, Archdeacon of Chichester, 1643, and chaplain to Charles I, 1647, was regarded even in his own time, as by John Owen, and by subsequent historians since, as a major single factor in the survival and invigoration of Anglicanism during the Interregnum. Gilbert Burnet (*History of His own Time, 1724*, vol. I) described Hammond's death just before the Restoration, when his appointment to the diocese of Worcester was proposed, as 'an unspeakable loss to the Church'. Deprived of his parish and imprisoned in 1647, he spent two years at the house of a friend, Sir Philip Warwick, and moved in 1650 to Westwood, Worcestershire, the home of Sir John Pakington, where he spent the remainder of his time. Over the following decade his enforced retirement bore fruit in many books – biblical studies, work on aspects of moral theology, controversial books and apologies for Anglicanism, for episcopacy and for infant baptism. More than this, he set others to work, and the Anglican theological output during the decade was a striking tribute to Hammond's influence and to those who supported his scheme, laymen like Sir Robert Shirley and clerics such as Bishop Duppa. His biographer, John Fell, who published his *Life* (1661) the year after Hammond's death, records that he had 'a perfect hate of idleness'. Hammond was a linguist, a classicist and 'no stranger in modern writers

. . . and learned in school divinity, and a master in Church antiquity, perfect and ready in the sense of the fathers, councils . . . and liturgies'. Attractive and humble, he was for ten years a model parish priest at Penshurst, visiting, relieving the poor and the sick, catechizing and writing, his day built around the daily services. He had 'an ardent love of souls', says Fell, and not surprisingly moral/ascetic theology was for him a practical necessity, as witness his *Of Conscience* (1644), *Of Scandal* (1644), *Of Will-Worship* (1644), *Of Sinnes of Weakness and Wilfulness* (1645), *Of a late or a Death-bed Repentance* (1645), *The Power of the Keys* (1647), *Spiritual Sacrifice* (1660), *The Daily Practice of Piety* (1660). Regarded then and later as 'the embodiment of Anglicanism', he was, as Fell records, profoundly anxious about 'the securing a succession to the Church' as death removed some of the surviving bishops, a concern actively pursued by the exiles Hyde, Bramhall and others. Hammond's writings influenced many, including George Bull and Simon Patrick, to seek episcopal ordination in 'a proscribed and persecuted Church'. His theological commitment to Anglicanism was as total as his life-commitment. The result was a positive theology in the round, setting out the position of the Church of England in *A Paraenesis* (1656), *Of Schism* (1653) and affirming episcopacy in his *Dissertationes Quatuor* (1651) in which he used the Ignatian epistles proved genuine by Ussher and Voss. Among his many other works, such as *Of Fundamentals* (1654) and *Of the Reasonableness of Christian Religion* (1650), his *A Practical Catechism* (1644) laid the intellectual basis of the faith for practising Anglicans and was widely used not least by Charles I. Hammond stands out as the great and influential promoter of Anglican apologetic 'in this sad conjuncture of affairs' (*A Paraenesis*).

Works, Library of Anglo-Catholic Theology edn (1847), is far from complete; the best modern study of Hammond is J. W. Packer, 1969, *The Transformation of Anglicanism 1643–1660*; See also H. R. McAdoo, 1949, *The Structure of Caroline Moral Theology*; and R. S. Bosher, 1951, *The Making of the Restoration Settlement*; though I. M. Green, 1978, *The Re-Establishment of the Church of England 1660–1663* rejects aspects of Bosher's thesis. John Spurr, 1991, *The Restoration Church of England, 1646–1689* also elaborates on Hammond's role as leader of a group called 'To take up the Anglican torch'. (HM)

Hammond, Thomas Chatterton (1877–1961), Irish theologian and churchman; Principal of Moore College, Sydney, 1935–54. Thomas Hammond was born in Cork on 20 February 1877, the son of a retired naval captain who had been a Church Missionary Society missionary to Sierra Leone in the 1850s. From his earliest days he was plunged into the heat of the Catholic–Protestant debates in Ireland, living with a Catholic aunt after his father's death in 1883. In 1890 he became a railway clerk for the Cork, Bandon & South Coast Railway, and joined the YMCA. Two years later, he was converted and was quickly plunged into a life of street evangelism. Aware of his need to train, he left Cork in 1895 to take a course in Anglican theology, practical ministry and the 'Roman Controversy'. The course was provided by the Irish Church Missions (ICM) in Dublin. This led to three years of itinerant evangelism, from 1897 to 1899. Next, he began study in preparation for the ordained ministry at Trinity College, Dublin, where he won the Gold Medal in Philosophy. He was ordained in the Church of Ireland on 20 December 1903.

Hammond served St Kevin's, Dublin, from 1903 until 1919, first as Curate and then as Rector. It was during this period, coinciding with the Anglo-Irish War and the sectarian violence which accompanied it, that he established a reputation for himself as an Evangelical Protestant leader. His intellect, prodigious memory and impressive debating skills marked him out as the obvious choice when the ICM were searching for a new Superintendent in 1918. Hammond took up the post early the next year.

The work associated with the ICM was varied. Hammond headed a team of evangelists, ran meetings which challenged the doctrines of Catholicism, was responsible for schools and children's homes, and represented beleaguered Protestants in their legal battles with the Catholic authorities. He was a regular speaker at lunchtime meetings at Trinity College and was a keen supporter of the Bible Churchmen's Missionary Society and the Keswick Convention. Whether on a conference platform or in print, he played a prominent role in addressing the pressing issues of the moment in the Church of Ireland and Anglicanism at large. He did not fear controversy or censure. Even those who did not always want to be identified with him were often prepared 'to shelter behind his guns'. In 1921 his argument for checks and controls on episcopal authority was published as *Authority in the Church*. His trenchant opposition to the proposals for liturgical revision, which threatened to reintroduce into Anglican church practice some of the more objectionable elements of medieval Catholicism, gained him international attention. In 1926 he toured Canada and Australia, giving a series of lectures on the subject, financed by the Vickery Trust.

The impression left by Hammond during this tour was a contributing factor in the decision to invite him to become Principal of Moore College, Sydney, in late 1935. The college had been run down in recent years; it was in debt and had been weakened by the incursions of Liberal Evangelicalism. Hammond's appointment was part of Archbishop H. W. K. Mowll's larger strategy to secure and clarify the Evangelical character of the Diocese of Sydney. While on the ship to Australia, in March 1936, Hammond corrected the proofs of his most enduring work, a handbook of basic Christian doctrine entitled *In Understanding be Men*. It had been originally commissioned as part of the follow-up to an Inter-Varsity Fellowship mission to the University of London. Upon his arrival in Sydney, at the age of 59, he set about raising the morale as well as the academic standards of the college. He lectured most of the subjects in the curriculum, extended the course, instituted a daily sermon, and began the practice of an annual college convention. His practice in teaching doctrine was to work through E. J. Bicknell's *On the Thirty-nine Articles* paragraph by paragraph, commenting and correcting along the way. Years later a similar approach would be adopted with his own *In Understanding be Men*.

As well as rebuilding Moore College, Hammond was involved in the wider affairs of the Diocese of Sydney. He became a member of its Standing Committee in 1939, acted for the Archbishop in the Red Book controversy of 1942–7, advised him at Lambeth in 1948, and was himself made an archdeacon in 1949. He made significant contributions to the debates about a Constitution for the Anglican Church of Australia, as well as advising the Anglicans in South Africa as they drafted their own Constitution. Throughout this period he continued writing. As well as regular contributions for *The Australian Church Record*, in 1938 he produced *Perfect Freedom*, an introduction to Christian ethics, and five years later, *Reasoning Faith*, an introduction to apologetics. His last book, *The New Creation*, was a biblical examination of the doctrine of regeneration and appeared in 1953.

T. C. Hammond finally retired at the end of 1953, at almost 77 years of age and after an extraordinarily influential ministry on both sides of the world. He continued to pastor a congregation in the centre of Sydney until his death on 16 November 1961. It is a measure of the agility of his mind right up to the end of his life that when his son went into his study after his death, he found a Latin edition of Bellarmine open on his desk.

Hammond's theological contribution did not lie in new and novel insights into any of the doctrines of the faith. He did not see himself as an innovator, but as one who passed on the authentic teaching of Scripture as it has been understood throughout the history of the Church. Nevertheless, his firm stand for biblical truth contributed to the intellectual regeneration of Evangelicalism in the second half of the twentieth century. On foundations built largely by him, a robust Evangelical witness was secured in Sydney which remains influential throughout the world.

Authority in the Church (London: IVF, 1921).
In Understanding be Men (London: IVF, 1936).
Perfect Freedom (London: IVF, 1938).
Reasoning Faith (London: IVF, 1943).
The New Creation (London: IVF, 1953).
Warren Nelson, (1994). *T. C. Hammond: His Life and Legacy in Ireland and Australia.* (MT)

Harwood, Edwin (1822–1902), Rector of Trinity Church, New Haven, Connecticut. It is unfortunate that very little biographical information survives regarding Harwood concerning his education and background, despite his influence in the American church later in life. His contribution to the development of Anglican theology is primarily evident in the role he took as a signer of the '1853 Memorial', drawn up by W. A. Muhlenberg. The purpose of the Memorial which Harwood signed was seen as a call urging the bishops to provide 'as much freedom in opinion, discipline and worship as is compatible with the essential Faith and order of the Gospel' for the sake of effecting greater church unity among Protestant Christendom in America. Harwood supported the idea that the Episcopal Church in the nineteenth century required a significant re-evaluation of its policy in regard to public worship, holy orders, and the historic episcopacy. In *The Historic Episcopate and Apostolic Succession*, Harwood's historical analysis of apostolic succession suggested that 'the Episcopate is historic, [and] is the normal type of the highest office in the church of Christ, but it is an *institutio ecclesiastica* and not an *institutio divina*. The ministry, as such, is a divine institution, but the form of its constitution is subject to the decisions and actions of the Church. The church has the right to order the form of its government, subject only to Christ, its adorable head.' The purpose of his work, originally read before the Church Congress, Louisville, October 1887, was to provide an apologetic supporting the movement towards the restoration of lost unity among Protestants.

Edwin Harwood, 1887. *The Historic Episcopate and Apostolic Succession* (New York: Whittaker).
William Stevens Perry, 1885. *History of the American Episcopal church 1587–1883* (Boston: James R. Osgood).

Headlam, Arthur Cayley (1862–1947), administrator, theologian, and Bishop of Gloucester. Educated at New College, Oxford, he went on to obtain a fellowship at All Souls. Subsequently he served the parish of Welwyn until he was elected principal of King's College, London, the same year he was awarded the prestigious Doctor of Divinity degree in 1903. He was elected Regius Professor of Divinity at Oxford in 1918 after 15 years of significant but controversial service at King's College. He was consecrated as Bishop of Gloucester in 1923 and used his position to further ecumenical discussions, an issue which concerned him for most of his adult life. His major theological work outlined his views on the issue of church union, the 1920 Bampton Lectures, entitled *The Doctrine of the Church and Christian Reunion*, which were subsequently published. He served the editorship of *The Christian Quarterly Review* (1901–21), where his extensive biblical and theological knowledge found expression. His other works consist of a commentary on the *Epistle to the Romans*, with William Sanday (1895); *St Paul and Christianity* (1913); *The Life and Teaching of Jesus the Christ* (1923); *Christian Theology* (1934); and *The Fourth Gospel as History* (1948, posthumous, with biographical essay by Agnes Headlam-Morley). Considered an enlightened conservative, he also supported the proposed revision of the Prayer Book which was eventually defeated by Parliament. A central churchman, he refused to be associated with any party within the church; nonetheless he was one of the most influential bishops of his day.

A. T. P. Williams in *Dictionary of National Biography, 1941–50*, 369–71.
Oxford Dictionary of the Christian Church, 623.
R. C. D. Jasper, 1960. *Life and Letters of Arthur Cayley Headlam* (London: Faith Press).
E. C. Prichard, 1989. *Bishop Arthur Cayley Headlam* (Worthing: Churchman).

Hebert, Arthur Gabriel (1866–1963), liturgical and biblical theological writer. Member of the Society of the Sacred Mission, a religious community for men in the Church of England. Taught in their theological colleges at Kelham (England) and Adelaide (Australia). In *Liturgy and Society* (1935), he declared that liberalism was theologically bankrupt and, against propositional dogmatism, argued that Christian doctrine was enshrined in the worship forms of the Church, and that the corporate activity of worship was the touchstone of Christian life and prayer. His collection of essays, *The Parish Communion* (1936), arguing for the centrality of the eucharist in the Sunday worship on the basis of the educational model of the Church as the Body of Christ, was the most singular influence on the worshipping patterns of the Church of England in the latter half of the twentieth century. A committed ecumenist, Hebert translated Swedish Lutheran theology and introduced English readers to the work of Yngve Brilioth (*Eucharistic Faith and Practice*) and Gustav Aulén (*Christus Victor*). He forged contacts with Roman Catholics on the continent, particularly the leaders of the Liturgical Movement, and towards the end of his life became an ecumenical figure. A key category in his ecclesiology was the elusive term 'catholicity'. No church could claim to be fully catholic. The term 'catholic' was a predicate of God, and denoted the inclusivity and universal scope of God's redemptive purposes. All churches, he claimed, fell short of the fullness of catholicity. Most of his published writings were in the field of biblical theology. His work, particularly *The Throne of David* (1941), and *The Authority of the Old Testament* (1947), anticipates a kind of canonical criticism, seeking to hold together the Hebrew and Greek scriptures by offering a liturgical hermeneutic. The canon itself, he asserted, was established by the needs and usage of the worshipping community, and he took the use of Scripture in the context of worship as the principle key for a Christian reading of the Bible.

Donald Gray, 1986. *Earth and Altar* (Norwich: Alcuin Club).
Christopher Irvine, 1993. *Worship, Church and Society* (Norwich: Canterbury Press).

Henson, Herbert Hensley (1863–1947), Broad Church Divine and Bishop of Hereford and then Durham. In 1884 he received a first in modern history at Oxford and earned a fellowship at All Souls. This fellowship proved to be a time of significant transition for him as it was during this period that he shifted away from his Nonconformist background to Anglicanism. In 1884 he was ordained a deacon and worked in Bethnal Green. He spent 7 years at the living of Barking, where he served after being ordained priest in 1888. An early sympathizer with the Anglo-Catholic party, he was given the chaplaincy of Ilford Hospital, but only with the understanding that he would check the 'Roman tendencies' there. At his next post as the rector of St Margaret's, his reputation grew and he was nominated to a canonry at Westminster. His liberal thinking grew still more until he became an ardent critic of Anglo-Catholicism and even defied his old friend and bishop, Charles Gore, by preaching in a Nonconformist church in 1909. After going on to serve as a dean in Durham, he was appointed to the see of Hereford in 1917 despite significant opposition. Anglo-Catholics regarded his liberal views concerning the virgin birth and miracles as unorthodox. In fact, *Creed and Pulpit* (1919) was largely responsible for two separate books written by Bishop Weston against his modernist views. In 1920 he was elevated to the see of Durham, where he served for 19 years before he retired. An early critic of the episcopate, despite his serving in this office later, he was a proponent of closer relations with the various churches that were not established by law (Methodists, Presbyterians, Baptists, etc.). He is at his best in *Ad Clerum* (1937) and *Bishoprick Papers* (1946) but the 1935–6 Gifford Lectures on 'Christian Morality' are also noteworthy. As a preacher and latitudinarian thinker he was greatly admired even by those who disagreed with him.

A. T. P. Williams in *Dictionary of National Biography, 1941–50*, 378f.
Owen Chadwick, *Hensley Henson* (Norwich: Canterbury Press, 1994).
E. F. Bradley (ed.), 1950. *Letters* (London: SPCK).

Hooker, Richard (1554–1600) was born at Heavitree near Exeter in April 1554 and died 2 November 1600 at Bishopsbourne near Canterbury in Kent. Educated first at Exeter Latin School, Hooker went to Corpus Christi College, Oxford, in 1569, under the patronage of John Jewel, Bishop of Salisbury. In 1579 he was made Deputy Professor of Hebrew and a full fellow of his college, where he lectured on logic. In 1581 he preached at Paul's Cross, the preaching station outside St Paul's Cathedral, causing some controversy by declaring that it was God's primary will that all be saved. In 1584 Hooker was presented to the living of Drayton-Beauchamp in Buckinghamshire, but resigned a year later when appointed by the Crown to be Master of the Temple, at the Inns of Court. There he entered into a controversy with the Puritan disciplinarian Walter Travers, the Reader of the Temple, who enjoyed a considerable following among the lawyer-parishioners. Hooker preached in the morning on Sundays and Travers in the afternoon, the Reader using the pulpit to attack the Master for, among other things, his teaching on assurance (assurance 'is not so certain as that we perceive by sense') and his lenient attitude toward Roman Catholics (some were saved). The controversy was brought before the Privy Council, where judgement was made in favour of Hooker and against Travers, who was silenced. Then highly regarded by the Archbishop of Canterbury, John Whitgift, Hooker received preferments, to Boscombe in Wiltshire, to the prebendary of Netheravon, and to the subdeanship of Salisbury Cathedral. But his chief efforts were employed from 1591 on in writing a defence of the Church of England against the disciplinarian Puritans, a work to be called *Of the Laws of Ecclesiastical Polity*. In this work he was supported by the Churchman family, whose daughter, Joan, he married in 1588, and by former students, George Cranmer and Edwin Sandys. In 1595 Hooker was presented to the living of Bishopsbourne, near Canterbury, where he continued his work on the Laws until his death in 1600.

It is now believed that by the winter of 1592/3 all eight books of Hooker's *Of the Laws of Ecclesiastical Polity* were written and ready for publication in some form. In 1593 the Preface and Books I–IV were printed by John Windet with a subsidy from Edwin Sandys. The publication of the rest of the books was delayed in part by the dissatisfaction of Cranmer and Sandys, who believed that Hooker was not sufficiently polemical, his writing deficient in detail and vigour. Book V, published in 1597, originally may have been the length of one of the first four books, but when printed was 270 pages (compared to 209 pages from the Preface to Books I–IV). Books VI–VIII were published posthumously, Books VI and VIII in 1648 and Book VII in 1662. In the latter year the entire work was published for the first time as compiled by John Gauden, Bishop of Exeter. The authenticity of the final three books has been debated, but it is generally believed at present that the books in question were written by Hooker and belong in the *Laws*. In addition to the *Laws* there survive notes made by Hooker in preparation for a response to the Puritan attack on the Preface to Books I–IV (*A Christian Letter*, 1599); writings involved in the controversy between Hooker and Travers at the Temple and before the Privy Council; several sermons; and the theologically important *A Learned Discourse of Justification*, first published in 1612.

Of the Laws of Ecclesiastical Polity was written as a defence of the Church of England against its critics, specifically those Puritan members of the Church of England who demanded a further reformation: a reinforcement and extension of the authority of Scripture; worship patterned after that of Calvin's Geneva; and, in place of the episcopal government of the church, the Genevan polity of pastors, elders and deacons. There was also a concern that the civil government not interfere with the church in matters of religion, challenging royal supremacy and the Elizabethan Settlement. Hooker's *Laws* dealt with all of these matters. The Preface discusses the nature of the controversy, Books I–IV concern law in general and scriptural authority in the context of the national church in particular, with the assertion that the Church of England was lawful, according to both God's law and civil law. Book V concerns the worship of the church and in defending the legality of the Book of Common Prayer provides a theological commentary on that book. Book VI concerns church discipline and against the background of Genevan discipline provides a discussion of the nature of repentance in traditional terms but with modifications dictated by the Book of Common Prayer. Book VII is on episcopacy and the episcopal polity of the church in its ideal form. Book VIII provides a defence of royal supremacy. With the new light shed on Book VIII by manuscript notes recently discovered at Trinity College, Dublin, and through a careful comparison of the existing manuscripts of Book VIII, it is now believed that Hooker, with his strong convictions concerning law, was no avid proponent of the divine right of kings, a doctrine then developing. Hooker's *Laws* contributed to the controversy begun with the Admonitions to Parliament in the 1570s and continued by the literary struggles between the Puritan Thomas Cartwright and the conformist John Whitgift during the 1580s. But the books of the *Laws* also contributed to the development of legal theory, theological scholarship and the literary works from Donne and Herbert to S.T. Coleridge in the nineteenth century and beyond. The *Laws* were required reading for theological students at the universities into the nineteenth century.

Hooker's insistence on grounding his defence of the practices of the Church of England in fundamentals, beginning with the universe of laws, and in relation to his extensive study of the scriptures, the church fathers, Greek and Latin, the schoolmen, especially Thomas Aquinas, and the most profound insights of the Renaissance and Reformation Divides, including John Calvin, ensured that the *Laws* would influence the development of English theology and survive the controversy for which it was written. Hooker began with a description of the universe of laws, encompassing all that is from God to inanimate objects. In tune with prior descriptions of the Great Chain of Being, Hooker refuted the idea that God and creation, nature and grace, were radically separated and insisted upon the interdependence of all. Citing Scripture, and in accord with Thomas Aquinas and others, Hooker emphasized this: 'God hath created nothing simply for itselfe: but each thing in all thinges and of everie thing ech part in other hath such interest that in the whole world nothing is found whereunto anie thing created can saie, I need thee not' (Sermon on Pride, *Works*, Folger Library edn, 5:333.16–19).

Deeply involved in Hooker's understanding of the universe of laws was his teleological point of view. This is expressed in his definition of law as 'that which doth assigne unto each thing the kinde, that which doth moderate the force and power, that which doth appoint the forme and measure of working' (*Laws*, I.2.1). His attention was focused on the purpose for which any thing existed and above all on the great purpose of human existence, which is communion, union with God, so that 'we live, as it were, the life of God' (*Laws*, I.11.2). From birth, humans are drawn toward this end, through the senses, the intellect and above all the spirit. But their progress toward deification is frustrated by sin, rooted in the source of all evil, pride. Hooker did not subscribe to the doctrine of total depravity, rather he argued that there is in every person an 'aptness' toward the true and the good. However, as sinful beings, we lack the ability to ascertain and hold the truth and do the good. The light of reason whereby we perceive the true and the good is 'slothful'. God provides 'the medicine of grace' in Jesus Christ, by whom we are justified and set on the way of sanctification, drawn out of pride into communion with God and with one another in Christ.

The means whereby this salvation occurs are provided by word and sacrament in the context of the Church. The key here is that through word and sacrament in the Church we are conjoined to Christ in his death and resurrection: we have the participation of Christ, enter into communion with God and realize the joys of communion with all creation. Scripture, as the revelation of God and Christ, is instrumental to this end and is not to be regarded as a new Leviticus. Indeed, Scripture 'presupposes' diverse sources of wisdom (*Laws*, II.1.4) and is itself illuminated by wisdom, Egyptian, Chaldean, Greek, and Jewish (*Laws*, III.8.9). The sacraments are means instrumental to our participation in Christ. The purpose of the eucharist is '*reall participation* of Christe and of life in his bodie and bloude' (*Laws*, V.67.2). The purpose is not the transformation of things but of persons, liberation from sin and death to live 'as it were, the life of God'. The Church, according to this understanding, is not a company of the perfect but a community of persons, including heretical and evil people, on the way toward perfect communion with God, enabled by grace to repent their sins and lead new lives in Christ. The purpose of the ministry of the Church is the 'ministerie of holy thinges', the ministry of word and sacrament. All else is subservient to this. The purpose of civil government is to provide for the commonwealth, in particular by promoting true religion and protecting the Church that it may rightly administer word and sacraments. The teleological perspective, the concern for purpose, the breadth of understanding, the emphasis upon the interdependence of all creation, are among those things basic to Hooker's theology which are still of importance.

Major editions of Hooker's Works:
The Works of Mr. Richard Hooker . . . in Eight Books of Ecclesiastical Polity (London: J. Best, for Andrew Crook, 1662). Compiled by John Gauden.
The Works of . . . Mr. Richard Hooker: With an Account of his Life and Death by Isaac Walton, John Keble (ed.), 7th edn, rev. R. W. Church and F. Paget, 3 vols. (Oxford: Clarendon Press, 1888). Contains sermons, etc., as well as *Laws*.
The Folger Library Edition of the Works of Richard Hooker, W. Speed Hill (ed.), 6 vols. Vols. I–V (Cambridge, Mass.: Harvard University Press, 1977–90); vol. VI (Binghamton, New York: Medieval and Renaissance Texts and Studies, 1993). A final volume containing indexes is yet to appear.

Life of Hooker:
Izaak Walton, *The Life of Mr. Rich. Hooker, The Author of those Learned Books of the Laws of Ecclesiastical Polity* (London: Richard Marriott, 1665). Often reprinted. Major corrections are found in C. J. Sisson, *The Judicious Marriage of Mr. Hooker and the Birth of 'The Laws of Ecclesiastical Polity'* (Cambridge: Cambridge University Press, 1938), and in David Novarr, *The Making of Walton's 'Lives'* (Ithaca, New York: Cornell University Press, 1958). See also George Edelen's Chronology in vol. VI of the Folger edn, pp. xvii–xxv.

Commentary:
Robert K. Faulkner, 1981. *Richard Hooker and the Politics of Christian England* (Berkeley: University of California Press).

W. Speed Hill (ed.), 1972. *Studies in Richard Hooker: Essays Preliminary to an Edition of his Works* (Cleveland and London: The Press of Case Western Reserve University).

W. J. Torrance Kirby, 1990. *Richard Hooker's Doctrine of Royal Supremacy*. (Leiden: E. J. Brill).

Peter Lake, 1988. *Anglicans and Puritans? Presbyterianism and English Conformist Thought from Whitgift to Hooker* (London: Unwin Hyman).

Olivier Loyer, 1979. *L'Anglicanisme de Richard Hooker*, 2 vols. (Lille: Université de Lille III; Paris: Librarie Honoré Champion).

Peter Munz, 1970. *The Place of Hooker in the History of Thought* (London: Routledge and Kegan Paul).

Francis Paget, [1899] 1907. *An Introduction to the Fifth Book of Hooker's Treatise of the Laws of Ecclesiastical Polity*, 2nd edn (Oxford: Clarendon Press). (JB)

Hort, Fenton John Anthony (1828–92), scholar and theologian. Educated at Trinity College, Cambridge, there he became acquainted with his lifelong friends Wescott and Lightfoot. In the 1850s his personal acquaintance with F. D. Maurice proved a great influence in his thought, particularly through Maurice's support of his doubts on eternal punishment, and he remained sympathetic to Maurice, yet not a Christian Socialist. Serving as incumbent of St Ippolyts from 1857 to 1872, all the rest of his adult life was spent at Cambridge in various capacities including a Fellowship at Trinity, and the Hulsean and Lady Margaret Professorships. During the years 1852–81 much of Hort's effort was focused on the Greek text of the New Testament which he had worked on with Wescott. The introduction to this text is considered exceptional for its precision and reserve concerning his involvement in this monumental work. Some of his other substantial work can be found in *Two Dissertations* (1876), *Judaistic Christianity* (1897) and *The Christian Church* (1897). It is quite unfortunate that his deep appreciation and insight into the natural sciences and theology did not find expression in his publications. The 1871 Hulsean Lectures, *The Way, The Truth, and The Life*, display the depth of his philosophical theology, as well as Coleridge's lifelong influence, in his contention that truth is not appropriated by logical processes alone but rather by the whole person. In these lectures he examines the teaching of Christ in John 14.5–6. Christ is the 'Way' both to God the Father and the way or model which men must follow. Christ is the 'Truth', its very embodiment, and Christianity insists on Truth receiving pre-eminence both in its pursuit as knowledge and in the person and work of Christ. The implications of this allow for the Church to embrace all truth in whatever disciplines to enrich theological truth, but truth is apprehended morally as well as intellectually. 'I am the Life' describes the quality of life which is emphasized in John's Gospel and which Jesus made possible through the incarnation.

Oxford Dictionary of the Christian Church, 667–8.

Graham Patrick, 1987. *F. J. A. Hort, Eminent Victorian* (Sheffield: Sheffield Academic Press).

Huntington, William Reed (1838–1909), priest of the Episcopal Church in the USA, ecumenical theologian, liturgical reformer. A graduate of Harvard University, he was assistant at Emmanuel Church, Boston, Mass., was married in 1863 and was rector of All Saints Church in Worcester, Mass. (1862–83), then rector of Grace Church on Broadway, New York City (1883–1909), the most influential member of the House of Deputies of the Episcopal Church's General Convention in the late nineteenth century. His *The Church-Idea* (1870) is the most creative and significant work of ecclesiology yet to emerge from the Episcopal Church in the USA. His feast day in the calendar of the American Book of Common Prayer is 27 July. In this same book, the Chicago–Lambeth Quadrilateral which he originated is now printed on pages 876–78.

The four points of Huntington's Quadrilateral have been one of the distinctive characteristics of Anglican ecclesiology since it was adopted by the Lambeth Conference of 1888, and they remain the Anglican basis for discussion of unity with other churches. Huntington was also the inspiration and principal author of the 1892 revision of the Episcopal Church's Book of Common Prayer, which owes more to him than to any other single person. This revision he pursued because he was convinced it would aid the cause of church unity, not only by attention to patristic sources but also by the principles of flexibility, adaptability and revisability. His progressive ideas on the role of women in the Church were far ahead of their time, and it was he who established the order of deaconesses in the Episcopal Church. He also helped to found the Cathedral of St John the Divine in New York City, contributing its iconographic plans and serving as trustee for twenty-two years. Its chapel of St Ansgar (consecrated 1918) is a memorial to him. No one label defines Huntington's school or churchmanship adequately, but he is sometimes called 'liberal' or 'broad', although the latter is an epithet that he denied.

The Chicago–Lambeth Quadrilateral is generally understood to have had its immediate origins not in England but in the USA, in a resolution from the American House of Bishops meeting in General Convention at Chicago in 1886, stimulated by the ideas and writings of Huntington, who was the leading presbyter of the House of Deputies at that time. While rector of All Saints in Worcester, Mass., Huntington was the co-founder, together with his neighbour Fr John Power of St Paul's Roman Catholic parish, of a local ecumenical clergy fellowship, and it has been suggested that he first articulated his Quadrilateral idea to these colleagues at their gatherings in the late 1860s and in a sermon that he preached there in 1870 entitled 'The Church of the Reconciliation'. Then he developed and committed the idea to writing in his seminal book *The Church-Idea: An Essay towards Unity*, published later in the same year.

The front cover of the original (1870) edition of *The Church-Idea* depicted an imaginative drawing of the seamless robe of Christ, with the words 'Now the coat was without seam woven from the top throughout' (John 19.23). In the key passage of this volume Huntington likens 'the absolutely essential features of the Anglican position' to the four fortress cities of Lombardy (Mantua, Verona, Peschiera, and Legnano) that had provided Austria a means to keep northern Italy under its control from 1815 to 1859; but the four points of the Quadrilateral that he develops are quite different:

> What are the essential, the absolutely essential features of the Anglican position? When it is proposed to make Anglicanism the basis of a Church of the Reconciliation, it is above all things necessary to determine what Anglicanism pure and simple is. The word brings up before the eyes of some a flutter of surplices, a vision of village spires and cathedral towers, a somewhat stiff and stately company of deans, prebendaries, and choristers, and that is about all. But we greatly mistake if we imagine that the Anglican principle has no substantial existence apart from these accessories. Indeed, it is only when we have stripped Anglicanism of the picturesque costume which English life has thrown around it, that we can fairly study its anatomy, or understand its possibilities of power and adaptation.
>
> The Anglican *principle* and the Anglican *system* are two very different things. The writer does not favour attempting to foist the whole Anglican system upon America; while yet he believes that the Anglican principle is America's best hope. . . .
>
> But what if it can be shown that the Anglican system has failed in just so far as it has been untrue to the Anglican principle? And what if it can be shown that here in America we have an opportunity to give that principle the only fair trial it has ever had?
>
> The true Anglican position, like the City of God in the Apocalypse, may be said to lie foursquare. Honestly to accept that position is to accept –
>
> 1st. The Holy Scriptures as the Word of God.
> 2nd. The Primitive Creeds as the Rule of Faith.

3rd. The two Sacraments ordained by Christ himself.

4th. The Episcopate as the key-stone of Governmental Unity.

These four points, like the four famous fortresses of Lombardy, make 'the Quadrilateral' of pure Anglicanism. Within them the Church of the Reconciliation may stand secure. Because the English State-Church has muffled these first principles in a cloud of non-essentials, and has said to the people of the land, 'Take all this or nothing', she mourns today the loss of half her children. Only by avoiding the like fatal error can the American branch of the Anglican Church hope to save herself from becoming in effect, whatever she may be in name, a sect. Only by a wise discrimination between what can and what cannot be conceded for the sake of unity, is unity attainable. . . .

If our whole ambition as Anglicans in America be to continue a small, but eminently respectable body of Christians, and to offer a refuge to people of refinement and sensibility, who are shocked by the irreverences they are apt to encounter elsewhere; in a word, if we care to be only a countercheck and not a force in society; then let us say as much in plain terms, and frankly renounce any and all claim to Catholicity. We have only, in such a case, to wrap the robe of our dignity about us, and walk quietly along in a seclusion no one will take much trouble to disturb. Thus may we be a Church in name, and a sect in deed.

But if we aim at something nobler than this, if we would have our Communion become national in very truth, – in other words, if we would bring the Church of Christ into the closest possible sympathy with the throbbing, sorrowing, sinning, repenting, aspiring heart of this great people, – then let us press our reasonable claims to be the reconciler of a divided household, not in a spirit of arrogance (which ill befits those whose best possessions have come to them by inheritance), but with affectionate earnestness and an intelligent zeal.

Writing in the spirit of late Romantic nationalism as well as in the wake of the American confidence that was celebrating a newly found national unity in the years since the Civil War's end in 1865, Huntington was one of several Anglicans in mid-nineteenth-century America (including William Augustus Muhlenberg, Thomas H. Vail and Edward A. Washburn) who turned their attentions to the question of the unity of the churches in the United States. The original content of his four-point Quadrilateral does seem to have been rather national and optimistically American, somewhat minimalist and reductionist, rather anti-confessional and anti-British. What he said of liturgical revision he also thought of church unity: 'We certainly do not want to Americanize the Prayer Book in any vulgar sense, but at the same time we cannot forget that it is in America we live, and to Americans that we minister.' Yet he had an answer to the charge of narrowness and nationalism, for in the same book he also wrote: 'While, therefore, we seem to be narrowing the broad question of Catholicity when we thus fence it within national limits and subject it to local conditions, we are in reality only putting to the test principles which have an interest and an application as wide as the Christian world.' This prediction of worldwide applicability would eventually be fulfilled when the four points of his Quadrilateral were adopted by the Lambeth Conference of 1888.

Echoing but altering the six visible signs of the Church that had been developed by Frederick Denison Maurice in *The Kingdom of Christ* (1838), Huntington came to believe that he could 'determine what Anglicanism pure and simple is', could identify the essential principles that would serve as the doctrinal basis for a national church. All three of his books that comment upon the Quadrilateral (*The Church-Idea*, 1870; *The Peace of the Church*, 1891; and *A National Church*, 1898) were designed to serve the purposes of reconciliation among Christians in the United States. In the last of these three books, Huntington expanded the fourth point of his Quadrilateral, 'the episcopate as the key-stone of governmental unity', along national but non-denominational lines, proposing an organic union of American churches on the basis of territorial units by state and county. This union, never endorsed by higher authority, was to comprise a national bicameral assembly of a smaller house consisting of one or two county 'overseers' or 'chief pastors' from each state and a larger house consisting of pastors and lay people proportionate to state populations.

American national church unification, Huntington also believed, was to be accomplished on the basis of the Quadrilateral's four points rather than upon the time-honoured quasi-confessional Anglican doctrinal basis of the Thirty-Nine Articles. Let the Articles, he wrote in *The Church-Idea*, 'not continue to be considered . . . one of the essentials of the Anglican position'. And even uniformity of worship, so central to the Anglican Prayer-Book tradition, was for Huntington not an essential to be included in the Quadrilateral. He reasoned:

> Strong as is the argument for liturgical worship upon grounds of expediency and fitness, there are good reasons for not reckoning a strict uniformity in this regard among the first principles of Church unity. It is true that liturgical worship was universal at the

earliest date in the history of the Christian Society of which we have any authentic post-Scriptural record. But it is equally true that the liturgies of that age existed in wonderful variety. Upon this point all scholars are agreed. Indeed, so numerous were the early formularies of worship that they can be distributed into groups and families, genera and species, very much as naturalists classify animals and plants.

At the Episcopal Church's General Convention of 1907, Huntington's final agenda was revealed in his twofold proposal to add the Quadrilateral by way of a preamble to the national, written Constitution of the Episcopal Church but also to remove the Thirty-Nine Articles from their place within the Book of Common Prayer. In the end both proposals were defeated, and Huntington died within two years at the age of seventy-one.

Nonetheless, Huntington's Quadrilateral had been adopted overwhelmingly by the American House of Bishops at Chicago, Illinois, on 20 October 1886, and the American House of Deputies in the same year established a commission to communicate it to the other 'organized Christian bodies of our country' for study, action and 'brotherly conference'. The Chicago form of the four points introduced the word 'Historic' to the fourth point about the Episcopate, an adjective that had not been present in the words of Huntington's original Quadrilateral but a term that he later accepted and defended. Huntington had said of the episcopate that it 'has a strong historical presumption in its favor, – a presumption which nine-tenths of contemporary Christendom respect, and which must be wholly overthrown before any other form of polity can put forward a reasonable claim to general acceptance'. Here, remarkably, he anticipated what the Lima Statement on Baptism, Eucharist and Ministry of the World Council of Churches' Faith and Order Commission would say much later (1982), when it agreed that the threefold ministry is, historically, 'the generally accepted pattern'.

The four points of Huntington's Quadrilateral went to the Lambeth Conference of 1888, where they were eventually endorsed as Resolution number 11. However, now Huntington's original words, as well as the terminology of the American bishops from 1886, were transposed to an international, and especially British, context, and once again changes were made. Point 1 of the Chicago form of the Quadrilateral was embellished with material from article 6 of the Thirty-Nine, point 2 from article 8, and point 3 from article 25. The Lambeth Conference, interestingly, did not change the wording of point 4, thus leaving intact the term 'historic episcopate', even though it would have been possible, on the same principle, to draw upon article 36 and alter the fourth point to read 'an episcopal ministry consecrated according to historic church order'. The four points were also at the 1888 Lambeth Conference very clearly described as a basis for an approach to reunion, that is, as a starting-place or *terminus a quo* from which other matters might be discussed, and not as a *terminus ad quem* or sufficient basis for reunion in themselves.

At the American General Convention of 1895, finally, the 1888 Lambeth form of Huntington's Quadrilateral was formally adopted and received by the American Church to replace the 1886 Chicago form as authoritative, and in the 1888 form it has been endorsed by subsequent Lambeth Conferences. For over a century, therefore, from the late nineteenth on into the last years of the twentieth, the 1888 Lambeth text of Huntington's Quadrilateral has remained the cornerstone and standard by which the Episcopal Church and most of the Anglican Communion approach questions of unity with other churches. Huntington in his theology had advocated a broad inclusiveness, responsible scholarship, balanced moderation, concentration upon essentials, and generosity of interpretation which influenced the thought and action of many within his own church and beyond. Not only practical but also somewhat mystical in temperament, he declined many elections as bishop at the same time that he crafted an Anglican doctrine of church unity which has lasted well into the closing years of the most ecumenical of centuries. He was recognized by honorary doctorates from Princeton, Harvard, Hobart, Union, Columbia, Yale, and the University of the South.

Key works

The Church-Idea: An Essay towards Unity (New York: E. P. Dutton and Company, 1870; 5th edn, Boston: Houghton Mifflin Company, 1928).

'National Churchmanship', *Virginia Theological Seminary Magazine* (July 1888).

The Peace of the Church (New York: Charles Scribner's Sons, 1891).

Popular Misconceptions of the Episcopal Church (New York: Thomas Whittaker, 1891).

A Short History of the Book of Common Prayer, Together with Certain Papers Illustrative of Liturgical Revision, 1878–1892 (New York: Thomas Whittaker, 1893).

A National Church (New York: Charles Scribner's Sons, 1898).

Twenty Years of a New York Rectorship (New York: The DeVinne Press, 1903).

'Tract No. XCI: The Articles of Religion from an American Point of View', *The Hibbert Journal* 5 (1906–7); 808–20.

An extensive bibliographical essay including hundreds of his published sermons, addresses, poems, etc. is printed on pp. 213–23 of J. Robert Wright (ed.), *Quadrilateral at One Hundred* (see below). The most extensive collection of his printed works is located in the archives of Grace Church on Broadway in New York City, and the most extensive collection of his original manuscripts is kept in the national archives of the Episcopal Church at Austin, Texas.

Important secondary studies

Anglican Consultative Council, 1984. *The Chicago–Lambeth Quadrilateral*, ACC

Dogmatic and Pastoral Study Series (London: ACC).

Stephen H. Applegate, 1981. 'The Rise and Fall of the Thirty-Nine Articles: An Inquiry into the Identity of the Protestant Episcopal Church in the United States', *Historical Magazine of the Protestant Episcopal Church* 50: 409–21.

Clyde H. Cox, Jr, 1985. 'William Reed Huntington: Uniting the Church', *The Living Church* 191 (3) (21 July): 8–9.

Gunther Gassmann, 1988. '100 Jahre Lambeth-Quadrilateral: Die anglikanische Einheits-charta und ihre okumenische Wirkung', *Oekumenische Rundschau* 37 (3) (July): 301–11.

H. G. G. Herklots, 1968. 'The Origins of the Lambeth Quadrilateral', *Church Quarterly Review* 168 (January–March): 61–8.

Max Keller-Huschemenger, 1976. *Die Lehre der Kirche im Urteil der Lambeth Konferenzen* (Gutersloh: Mohn).

Charles J. Minifie, 1966. 'William Reed Huntington and Church Unity', *Historical Magazine of the Protestant Episcopal Church* 35: 155–66.

Lesley A. Northup, 1993. 'William Reed Huntington: First Presbyter of the Late Nineteenth Century', *Anglican and Episcopal History* 62 (2) (June): 193–213.

Lesley A. Northup, 1993. *The 1892 Book of Common Prayer*, Toronto Studies in Theology, vol. LXV (Lewiston: Edwin Mellen Press).

Paul T. Phillips, 1986. 'The Concept of a National Church in Late Nineteenth-Century England and America', *Journal of Religious History* 14 (June): 26–37.

John Wallace Suter, 1925. *Life and Letters of William Reed Huntington: A Champion of Unity* (New York: Century).

John F. Woolverton, 1970. 'Huntington's Quadrilateral: – A Critical Study', *Church History* 39: 198–211.

John F. Woolverton, 1986. 'W. R. Huntington: Liturgical Renewal and Church Unity in the 1880's', *Anglican Theological Review* 48 (2) (April): 175–99.

J. Robert Wright (ed.), 1988. *Quadrilateral at One Hundred* (Cincinnati: Forward Movement; London: Mowbray). Also published as *Anglican Theological Review*, Supplementary series no. 10 (March 1988). (JRW)

Jewel, John (1522–71), Protestant theologian and Bishop of Salisbury. Beginning at Merton College, he transferred to Corpus Christi College, Oxford, and was elected a fellow of Corpus Christi in 1542. In 1547, Peter Martyr came to the university and influenced him significantly towards Protestantism. Eventually Jewel was forced to flee Oxford and escaped to Frankfurt because of his doctrine. After the death of Queen Mary, he returned to England and was chosen by Elizabeth to be trained as a potential bishop. He was consecrated as Bishop of Salisbury in 1560. He eventually published his *Apologia pro Ecclesia Anglicana* in 1562, which was a defence of the Anglican Church and provides the basis of all following controversy with the Church of Rome. In this Jewel maintains that the Catholicity of the Church of England is proved by its doctrinal succession from the apostles. Evidence for this claim of Catholicity is gathered through comparing the Church of England's doctrine to that of the Church of the first six centuries. Subsequently, he contrasts the positions of Anglicanism with the 'perversions' of Roman Catholic doctrine. True unity is found only in Christ and essentials of doctrine, and not in conformity with the see of Rome and her 'heretical' doctrines. Jewel also believed in *a* holy church but not in *the* holy church, in that the Church could not make one article of faith but can only embrace the authority of the scriptures. The *Apologia* is of serious importance for understanding the logical basis by which Anglicanism was instituted and conceived.

Oxford Dictionary of the Christian Church, 738–9.
J. Ayre (ed.), 1845–50. *The Works of John Jewel* (Cambridge: Cambridge University Press).
J. E. Booty, 1963. *John Jewel as Apologist of the Church of England* (London: SPCK).
W. M. Southgate, 1962. *John Jewel and the Problem of Doctrinal Authority* (Cambridge, Mass.: Harvard University Press).

Johnson, Samuel (1696–1772), American clergyman and educator, was the son of Samuel and Mary (Sage) Johnson of Guilford, Connecticut. Members of Johnson's extended family were active in the Congregationalist Church; a great uncle was a clergyman. Johnson entered Yale College in 1710, and after graduation in 1714, served briefly as a teacher in Guilford. In 1716 he returned to Yale as a tutor. Jonathan Edwards would be one of his students during this period.

In 1720 Johnson accepted a call to serve as pastor of a Congregational Church in nearby West Haven. By that time, however, Johnson had begun to have doubts about three elements of his Congregational heritage: the free form of liturgy, the doctrine of predestination, and non-episcopal form of ordination. He and Yale faculty and graduates with similar concerns formed a book club to investigate the matters further. The group included Timothy Cutler, who became Yale's rector in 1719, and Daniel Browne, who became a Yale tutor in 1719. Members of the group read such Anglican writers as William King (1650–1729), Daniel Whitby (1638–1726), Benjamin Hoadley (1676–1716) and John Potter (*c.* 1674–1747). They read works by Presbyterians and Congregationalists as well, such as Edmund Calamy (1600–66). Johnson and several other members of the group became gradually convinced of the legitimacy of a fixed liturgy and episcopal ordination, and increasingly uncomfortable with the doctrine of predestination.

At the time that the book discussions began, there were no Anglican clergy in Connecticut. In 1722, however, a Society for the Propagation of the Gospel (SPG) missionary, George Pigot, paid a visit to Stratford, Connecticut, where a group of Anglican families were desirous of forming a congregation. Johnson invited Pigot to meet with the members of the book club in New Haven. Pigot accepted the invitation and encouraged the book club members to seek ordination in the Church of England.

News of the meetings soon spread. In September the Trustees of Yale College requested interviews with members of the book group. Seven members of the group admitted their reservations about the Congregational Church. Four – Johnson, Cutler, Browne and James Wetmore – resigned their positions and travelled to England for reordination. Browne died of smallpox while in England, but Johnson, Cutler and Wetmore returned to North America to serve in Anglican parishes. Their reordination marked an important turning-point for the Anglican Church in New England, which to that point had relied primarily upon missionary clergy sent from the British Isles.

On his return to Connecticut in 1723, Johnson served as an SPG missionary in Stratford, forming a congregation with the Anglican families that George Pigot had first visited. The congregation, which opened its first building in 1724, was the first continuing Anglican congregation in Connecticut, and initially the only one. Despite the relative modesty of the parish, Johnson quickly became one of the leading Anglican clergymen in New England. He corresponded regularly with Anglican clergy in other colonies. One important correspondent was the philosopher George Berkeley, whom he befriended during the latter's stay in New Port, Rhode Island (1729–31). He also lobbied the SPG and the Bishop of London for the introduction of a bishop in America.

Johnson remained in Stratford until the mid-1750s. Anglicans in the cities of Philadelphia and New York were at that point playing important roles in two new colleges: the College of Philadelphia (later the University of Pennsylvania, first charter in 1740, revised charter in 1755) and King's College (later Columbia University, first charter in 1753). Because of his earlier teaching experience at Yale, his lifelong habit of study and writing, and his reputation as a leader of the Anglican Church in New England, Johnson was sought after by both schools. He corresponded with the backers of the College of Philadelphia, and arranged to have a text book on philosophy published by Ben Franklin in Philadelphia in 1752. It was the earliest text on philosophy printed in British colonial America. Johnson, however, ultimately declined an offer from Philadelphia and, in 1754, became the first president of King's College in New York.

The years in New York were hard on Johnson. While there, smallpox claimed the lives of two wives (Charity Nicoll, who had been a widow when he married her in 1725, and Sarah Hull Beach, also a widow when he married her in 1761), a son, and a stepdaughter. Johnson elected to return to his parish in Stratford, following the death of his second wife in 1763. He stayed there for the remainder of his life.

Although Johnson wrote a great deal, only a relatively small amount of his writing appeared in print during his lifetime. The most important published works concerned philosophy: *Introduction to Philosophy* (1731) and *Elementa Philosophica: Containing Chiefly, Noetica, or Things Relating to the Mind or Understanding; and Ethica, or Things Relating to the Moral Behaviour*, the philosophy text book published by Franklin in 1752. The second half of *Elementa Philosophica* had initially been published separately with the title *Ethices Elementa, or the First Principles of Moral Philosophy* (1746).

A number of Johnson's works, including an autobiography, were not published until the twentieth century.

The earliest of Johnson's philosophical works may have been a manuscript in a question-and-answer format, which he titled 'A Synopsis of Natural Philosophy or Physics'. It was written around the time of his graduation from Yale in 1714. He explained in the prologue that his work was based upon certain 'catholic rules' that were 'brought together by the light of the sacred scriptures, of human reason, of sense observation, of induction and experience' (question 4). This premise of compatibility of biblical and scientific data made it possible for him to move easily from discussion of angels (question 70), to a discussion of the void that preceded creation (questions 71 to 74), to a discussion of the qualities of matter (questions 75 to 79).

While Johnson had less to say about angels in his later works, he never lost his moderate enlightened confidence in the compatibility of scientific and theological truth. In his essay on 'A division of the Sciences' (1716), he subdivided wisdom into two broad categories. Semiotical or rational philosophy concerned Logic and Grammar; Theology was, however, paired with 'Physic' as the topic of 'Real' philosophy. Physics and Theology dealt with two sides of the same proposition – the first with the creation and the second with the creator. The Bible provided the data for the exploration of theology. Biblical languages were important as research tools. At King's, Johnson would require the study of Hebrew and arrange for the publication of a Hebrew grammar.

Johnson trusted in the basically benevolent character of the world and had little place for vengeance or tragedy in his thought. Theology, he explained in his *Encyclopedia of Philosophy* (1714), concerned 'the goodness in things'. It may have been this conviction that led him to reject the Reformed doctrine of predestination. In the *Encyclopedia*, written before his conversion to the Church of England, he identified three characteristics of the image of God (in which humans were made) as wisdom, holiness and justice. In his later works, he would expand this list considerably, including liberty of the will as an essential part of God's image. This was the position that he took in *Elementa Philosophica* (1.2.5). Human beings shared God's liberty of the will 'for without liberty I should be destitute of one of the chief excellencies of my natural nature, and should not be capable of either duty or sin, properly speaking' (1.2.23).

Johnson was attracted by the Idealism of George Berkeley. He dedicated his *Elementa* to Berkeley and incorporated some elements of the philosopher's thought. Human knowledge of the world outside, Johnson explained, came through a series of perceptions that were assigned to the objects by the creator. The perceptions 'have the nature of a wonderful language, whereby the great author of Nature appears to be continually present with me, discovering his mind and will to me (and that is a stable and invariable manner, which I find I can always depend upon) and, as it were, speaking to me, and directing me how to act, and conduct myself in all affairs of life' (*Elementa*, 1.2.13).

Johnson's strongest effect on the colonial Anglican Church would not be his philosophy; his advocacy of Berkeley did not make serious inroads into the stronger appreciation of colonial Anglicans for John Locke. Herbert Wallace Schneider, co-author of Johnson's collected works, suggested that *Elementa Philosophica* was little read, except by the students at King's during the years Johnson was president. Johnson's personal experience of leaving the ordained ministry of the established Congregational ministry for the Anglican Church did, however, leave a lasting mark. It gave a character that would mark Anglicanism in New York and New England for several centuries: an absolute conviction about the importance of episcopal ordination, a militant rejection of the Westminster Confession's position of predestination, a marked dislike for extemporaneous prayer, and a willingness to evangelize active Congregationalists aggressively. This High-Church emphasis would contrast with a more latitudinarian or evangelical character to the churches in the southern colonies (where the Anglican Church was established) and in Pennsylvania (where there was no establishment).

Herbert and Carol Schneider edited the four-volume *Samuel Johnson, President of King's College, His Career and Writings* (New York: Columbia University Press, 1929). It includes Johnson's autobiography, his letters, his major philosophical works, and documents relating to King's College. Joseph Ellis's *New England Mind in Transition* (New Haven: Yale University Press, 1973) traces the evolution of his thought. (RP)

Jowett, Benjamin (1817–93), liberal theologian, philosopher, and Master of Balliol College, Oxford. Educated at Balliol, he spent the rest of his adult life there, eventually becoming Master of the college in

1870. His most important academic work is considered to be his translations of Plato and of Aristotle's *Politics*. In 1855, his theological ideas
were first expressed in *Commentaries of the Epistles of St Paul* (Thessalonians,
Galatians and Romans, 2 vols). Jowett's approach to this work was a radical departure from the past. 'Can it truly be said, that much has been
done in this place for Scriptural interpretations, which seems to be the
most hopeful mine in theology, and strangely enough the least explored?
It would hardly have been an unreasonable hope that the meaning of
Scripture, like that of any other book, might by this time have become
fixed, and raised above the fancies of sects or individuals.' In this he was
following a 'scientific' and inductive approach which started with the
conviction that there were human and divine elements of Scripture and
that they were to be distinguished and discerned. Doctrine should be
the fruit of this 'critical' approach, not something held *a priori*. This
approach reveals his indebtedness to Arnold, Schleiermacher, and F. C.
Baur. By consciously taking the authority of interpretation away from
theologians and tradition, and placing it in the hands of academics and
their rational and critical study of the text itself, Jowett was understood
by many as diminishing the authority of the scriptures altogether. He
also abandoned the *textus receptus* in favour of a more scholarly edition
of the text and departed from any objective theory of the atonement
in favour of a subjective and moral view, clear only to himself. Jowett's
article on 'The Interpretation of Scripture' in *Essays and Reviews* (1860)
advanced his earlier ideas and was so controversial, and therefore his
orthodoxy so suspect, that he was forced to stop writing theology
altogether.

E. Abbott in *Dictionary of National Biography*, suppl., III: 49–56.
Peter Hinchliff, 1987. *Benjamin Jowett and the Christian Religion* (Oxford: Clarendon
Press).

Kirk, Kenneth Escott (1886–1954), Bishop of Oxford, author and
moral theologian. Educated at St John's College, Oxford, he was
ordained priest in 1913. After serving at the University of London for
four years, he was elected to a tutorship at Keble College, Oxford, in
1913. Elected a fellow and chaplain of Trinity College, Oxford, in 1922,
and Regius professor of moral and pastoral theology in 1933, he was
awarded D.D. in 1926. In 1937, Kirk was appointed Bishop of Oxford
and excelled in this pastoral role. In *Some Principles of Moral Theology*
(1920), he established his name as an authority in moral theology, and
his indebtedness to Thomas Aquinas was openly acknowledged. 'The
standing problem of all ethics', he wrote in *Conscience and its Problems*

(1927), 'is the reconciliation of . . . the principles of law and liberty.' For Kirk, the attempt to effect such a reconciliation was the Catholic inheritance of Anglicanism, exemplified in such writers as Hooker, Taylor and the Caroline Divines. He was quick to apply this principle in his day to the Church's tension between ecclesiastical authority and tolerance of freedom of thought. Thus the prior study of casuistry became the focus of his methodology. Among his other works are *Ignorance, Faith, and Conformity* (1925), *The Vision of God* (the highly acclaimed 1928 Bampton Lectures), and a commentary on Romans (Clarendon Bible, 1937). He also edited *Personal Ethics* (1934), *The Study of Theology* (1939), and *The Apostolic Ministry* (1946). This last work compiled the scholarship of prominent Anglo-Catholic thinkers of the day (such as Dix, Hebert and Farrer) in defence of the Church's historic and apostolic continuity in the context of the proposed union of non-episcopal bodies and the Anglican Church of South India, a controversy which consumed much of Kirk's energy in his later years.

Oxford Dictionary of the Christian Church.
E. W. Kemp, 1959. *The Life and Letters of Kenneth Escott Kirk: Bishop of Oxford, 1937–1954* (London: Hodder and Stoughton).
The Times. 'The Bishop of Oxford: Scholar and Pastor', an obituary (9 June 1954).

Knox, David Broughton (1916–94), Australian theologian and churchman, Principal of Moore College, Sydney 1959–85. Broughton Knox, the eldest son of an Anglican clergyman trained and ordained in the Diocese of Sydney, was born in Adelaide, South Australia on 26 December 1916. The family returned to New South Wales in 1922, and Broughton was educated at Knox Grammar School and the University of Sydney (B.A.). After a year as a full-time catechist in his father's parish of Gladesville, he travelled to England in 1938, where he studied at St John's Highbury (A.L.C.D.) and the University of London (B.D.). In 1941 he was ordained by the Bishop of Ely, serving as a curate in Cambridge while he began study towards the theological tripos under C. H. Dodd and W. Knox. During that period he joined the Inter-Varsity Fellowship's Biblical Research Committee, which sought to counter the charge of 'anti-intellectualism, if not outright obscurantism' which had been regularly levelled against Evangelicals. At Kingham Hill in July 1941, during a small conference organized by this committee to plan a strategy for the future, Broughton suggested the establishment of a residential research library (which would later materialize in the form of Tyndale House, Cambridge). However, his academic involvements were interrupted in 1943 by his chaplaincy in the Royal Naval Reserve, which saw him present during the D-Day landings.

On his discharge in 1947, Broughton was appointed a tutor and lec-turer at Moore College, Sydney, then under the principalship of T. C. Hammond. The next four years were eventful as he played a pivotal role in a controversial legal struggle with the neighbouring Bishop of Bathurst in 1947, received his M. Th. from the University of London in 1949 and was married to Ailsa Lane in 1950. From 1951 to 1953 he was engaged in doctoral study at the University of Oxford, simultaneously holding down the posts of Assistant Curate at St Aldates and Tutor in New Testament at Wycliffe Hall. Receiving his D.Phil. in 1953 for a thesis on the doctrine of justification in the early English Reformers, Broughton returned to Australia in 1954, resumed teaching theology at Moore College, and was appointed Vice Principal in the same year under a new principal, M. L. Loane. When the latter took up the position of an assistant bishop in the diocese, Broughton was appointed the tenth principal of Moore College from February 1959. This was the post he was to hold with distinction over the next twenty-six years, and from which he was profoundly to influence the shape of Evangelicalism in the Diocese of Sydney and beyond. He expanded the College's teaching programme and its campus, raising its academic standards without compromising the gospel in the process. However, throughout his period as Principal he remained heavily involved in church affairs. He was a member of the Standing Committee of the Diocese of Sydney for thirty years (1954–84), played a critical role in the development of a constitution for the Anglican Church of Australia (1961) and edited *The Australian Church Record*, an independent Christian newspaper which presented an uncompromisingly Evangelical commentary on church and national affairs. Upon his retirement in 1985, he continued teaching theology at Moore College before becoming founding Principal of George Whitefield College, a theological college for the Church of England in South Africa, in 1988. He retired from this post in December 1992 and died just over a year later on 16 January 1994.

Broughton Knox's most profound influence was through over three decades of teaching at Moore College. Gifted with a powerful and orig-inal mind, he was never satisfied with glib answers or an unthoughtful acceptance of Evangelical orthodoxy. Through rigorous questioning, he delighted in pushing his students back to the Bible to think through issues afresh and for themselves. He broke with the established pattern of teaching Christian doctrine in terms of comments on the views of others. This was not because he was unaware of profound theological contributions down through the ages. Rather, he was demonstrating the centrality of the Bible in the theological task, a centrality which is demanded by the nature of the Bible as the living and active Word of

God to us. To put it another way, the Bible is God's personally directed speech, addressed to us. In it God defines his own character, explains his own actions and delineates his desired response from us. All Christian reflection must begin and end at this point. When we deal with the Bible we are not just dealing with print on a page: God is his Word. Broughton's goal was a coherent and thoroughly biblical theology, which is nothing less than the true knowledge of God himself.

From this secure theological foundation, Broughton could radically explore the nature of revelation, faith, the Church, and even the canon of Scripture itself. In many of these areas his writing calls us back to neglected aspects of theological truth: the univocal nature of God-talk, the propositional nature of revelation, faith as the distinguishing mark of the whole Christian life, the Church as a gathering around Christ, and the important distinction between the fact and content of the biblical canon. Above all, however, his understanding of the Christian world-view, in terms of the sovereignty of God and the centrality of the cross, arises directly from the pages of the Bible and remains a challenge to the modern tendency to define theology in terms of ourselves, whether through human religious experience or human metaphysical speculation.

A number of Broughton Knox's articles and books remain important contributions, including: 'Propositional Revelation the Only Revelation' *Reformed Theological Review* 19 (1) (1960); *The Doctrine of Faith in the Reign of Henry VIII* (1961); 'The Church and the Denominations' *Reformed Theological Review* 23 (2) (1964); *The Thirty-Nine Articles* (1967); 'Demythologising the Church' *Reformed Theological Review* 32 (23) (1973); 'Problems of the Canon' *Reformed Theological Review* 36 (1) (1977); *The Everlasting God* (1982); *The Lord's Supper from Wycliffe to Cranmer* (1983). In 1986 a collection of essays was published in his honour: Peter T. O'Brien and David G. Peterson (eds.), *God Who is Rich in Mercy* (MT)

Lampe, Geoffrey William Hugo (1912–80), liberal Evangelical theologian. Having won a scholarship to Exeter College, Oxford, he went on to earn honours degrees in *literae humaniores* and theology in 1935 and 1936. From 1938 to 1941 he served as assistant master and assistant chaplain at King's School, Canterbury. For the next four years he served the Forces in the war, and his service in this capacity was recognized when he received an award for bravery under fire. Theological teaching and research occupied the rest of his life. He was chaplain and fellow of St John's College, Oxford (1945–53); Edward Cadbury professor of theology at Birmingham University (1953–9), Ely professor of divinity at Cambridge (1959–70); was a fellow of Gonville and Gaius College (Cambridge) from 1960; and Regius Professor at Cambridge from 1970 until his retirement in 1979. He gained both a B.D. and D.D. from Oxford in 1953, an Honorary D.D. from Edinburgh in 1959, and a

D. Theol. from the University of Lund, Sweden, in 1965. His theological contribution is largely remembered through his three primary books, *A Patristic Greek Lexicon* (5 vols. which he edited, 1961–8); *The Seal of the Spirit* (1951), a study of Christian initiation in the early church, and the 1975–6 Bampton Lectures, *God as Spirit* (1977), in which his knowledge of patristic thought greatly enhanced this work on the Christian doctrine of God. Concerned to communicate faith in a way relevant to the modern world he was not always appreciated by others who felt in doing so he compromised historic truth. A proponent of women's ordination he also was determined to achieve greater ecumenical cooperation, which he saw as the aim of a new reformation that he tried to lead.

Maurice Wiles, in *Dictionary of National Biography*, 1971–80, 481–2.
Adrian Hastings, 1986. *A History of English Christianity 1920–1980* (London: SCM Press).
C. D. F. Moule (ed.), 1982. *G. W. H. Lampe, Christian Scholar, Churchman – a Memoir by Friends* (London: Mowbrays).

Laud, William (1573–1645), was born on 7 October 1573 in Reading and was educated at Reading Grammar School and St John's College, Oxford, an institution recently founded for merchants' sons by Sir Thomas White, a native of Reading himself. After graduation, Laud was made a Fellow, was ordained in 1601, and in 1611 succeeded John Buckeridge as President of the College on his elevation to the See of Rochester. Laud was a bright and ambitious man, a stern disciplinarian, as his students knew well. Ecclesiastical preferment came his way in the form of the Deanery of Gloucester in 1616, and in 1621 he was consecrated Bishop of St David's, from which he went on to Bath and Wells in 1626, London in 1628, and finally Canterbury in 1633. He had attracted the attention of King James I, who liked his strong theological views that upheld the position of the King and the Church. While Bishop of London, he virtually ran the Church of England, owing to the sequestration of Archbishop George Abbot after an unfortunate shooting incident while out hunting. As very much King Charles I's man, Laud was closely associated with the new monarch's ecclesiastical and political programme, in particular in connection with the Court of High Commission. In December 1640, he was taken to the Tower of London, and after a lengthy imprisonment there was tried for high treason by the Long Parliament. On 10 January 1645 he was executed.

Of his publications, four deserve particular mention. The first concerns his role as joint-editor, with John Buckeridge, of the *Ninety-six Sermons of Lancelot Andrewes* (1629). Both Laud and Buckeridge stood under the theological shadow of Andrewes, and many of the badges of what was later termed 'Laudianism' owed their origin in reality to the more original and less provocative personality of Lancelot Andrewes. On the latter's death in 1626, King Charles instructed Buckeridge and Laud to make a collection of the best sermons Andrewes had preached. The resulting volume was reprinted several times, and the sermons are still studied as the embodiment of classical Anglicanism. Second, in 1639, Laud published *A Relation of the Conference between William Laud and Mr Fisher the Jesuit by the command of King James*. Public disputations were a common occurrence at the time, and James, no mean theologian himself, relished a good religious debate. In a sense it was in part a re-run of Andrewes's controversy in publisher form with Cardinal Bellarmine, for it centred on whether the Church of England was a true church. Laud's line concerned its agreement with the Church of antiquity. Third, Laud wrote a personal diary (published posthumously in 1649) and during his imprisonment and trial wrote at length of his circumstances, including the lengths to which his accusers went in order to ensure that his guilt was proven. The diary is detailed in content and cool in style, though it nonetheless protests the man's innocence, and his loyalty to the Church of England. Fourth, he had his own *Summarie of Devotions*, which were also published posthumously, this time at the Restoration, in 1667. Unlike Andrewes, these prayers are simpler, more akin to Prayer-Book language in their style, and they even include the prayer Laud composed commending himself to God before his death.

Laud's influence on the church of his time was greater than his enduring legacy to Anglicanism. Theologically, he belonged to the Andrewes–Overall school, devoted to the Prayer Book, suspicious of the liturgical practices of extreme Puritans, and deeply loyal to the monarchy. At his trial he was accused of using incense and wafer-bread in his private chapel, and defended himself by denying both charges and pointing out that Andrewes and John Cosin had indulged in both. Whatever the rights and wrongs of these particulars, Laud was nevertheless an enthusiast for altar-tables placed at the east end of chancels and being railed off, a move that sets the eucharist in visual terms both in continuity and discontinuity with the tradition of the pre-Reformation Church. Energetic and industrious as he was, he also toiled hard to ensure that church property was maintained to a high standard and that the clergy were properly paid: beautiful services needed to be performed in fitting surroundings and by a priesthood who were cared for. Moreover, many of the liturgical and theological presuppositions Laud took for granted were hurled at him, when he was on trial, for being signs of popery, when in fact they were carefully worked-out ways of projecting an image of the Church of England that was both Catholic and Reformed. That was the nub in his controversy with Fisher the Jesuit: the Church of England, he maintained, was nearer the primitive Church than any other, and that was enough for him. In this regard, for example, he followed Andrewes in rejecting transubstantiation in favour of a middle road that affirmed a real presence of Christ in the elements but which at the same time placed a due emphasis on faithful reception. Here is continuity and development that does not throw off strong legacies from the past but can still be critical of them. As one of his own eucharistic devotions puts it: 'His mercy [i.e. Christ's] hath given it, and my faith hath received it into my soul.' It is in the devotions that we see another flavour of Anglicanism, namely the blending of liturgy and piety with a dash of developing doctrine. Laud stands in a long tradition, stretching back to the Middle Ages, of supplementing public liturgy with private piety. But the particular Anglican style draws together time and sacrament, daily prayer and the eucharist, in a language adjacent to that of the Prayer Book. As a theologian and a devotional prayer-writer, Laud is not in the same league as Andrewes. And although the final verdict of history is to link him with a monarchy that was becoming increasingly distant from the climate of public opinion, he is nonetheless part of a significant strand of Anglican thought and practice, albeit at a time of unfortunate polarization.

He is often (misleadingly) linked with the 1637 Book of Common Prayer for the Scottish Church, the hostile reception of which helped pave the way for the rebellion in Scotland against Charles I. In fact, it was the work of Scottish bishops, who were intent on producing a Prayer Book yet more in tune with seventeenth-century High Churchmanship than the English Prayer Book of 1604.

The works of Laud were collected and edited by W. Scott and J. Bliss and published as *The Works of Archbishop William Laud*, 7 vols., Library of Anglo-Catholic Theology (Oxford: Parker, 1847–60). For a modern biography, see Charles Carlton, *Archbishop William Laud* (London and New York: Routledge and Kegan Paul, 1987). (KS)

Law, William (1686–1761), mystical theologian of the High Church School and nonjuror. Educated at Emmanuel College, Cambridge, he received his B.A. and M.A. before being elected a Fellow of the college in 1711. After declining to take the oath of allegiance to George I, because he felt bound to the Stuart line of kings, he became a nonjuror and eventually published his *Three Letters to the Bishop of Bangor*, which express the essentials of his High Church position. This position included the doctrine of the Divine Right of Kings, allegiance to the oath made to James II (and therefore the Stuarts), and passive obedience. His most famous and enduring work, *A Serious Call to a Devout and Holy Life*, was published in 1728. John Wesley and his brother Charles were his disciples for six years between 1732 and 1738 prior to John's famous conversion. After his conversion, John rebuked Law for not teaching the correct doctrine of faith in Christ, upon which Law replied that he had recommended Thomas à Kempis for him to read and had taught consistently the same doctrine of faith. Law's mystical tendencies were fuelled by his study of Jakob Boehme (the German Lutheran), and later in Law's response to Hoadly's *Plain Account* of the Lord's Supper these tendencies are full-blown. Late in life he kept busy with correspondence, practical theological writing, and work for charities including a school for girls which he established. The thrust of his thought was on glorifying God in every aspect of life by moral living and ascetical practices which included meditation and guidance by the 'inner light'. His vast writings were collected in nine volumes in 1762.

See Canon Overton, 1881, *Wm Law, Nonjuror and Mystic*.
Oxford Dictionary of the Christian Church, 805.
L. Stephen in *Dictionary of National Biography*, XXXII, 236–40.
A. K. Walker, 1973. *William Law: His Life and Thought*.

Leighton, Robert (1611–84), Archbishop of Glasgow. Educated at the University of Edinburgh, he went on to receive his M.A. in 1631. Subsequently he spent several years in France and learned French, Latin, Greek and Hebrew while reading large amounts of theological literature. He was ordained by the presbytery of Dalkeith in 1641 and served the parish of Newbattle for twelve years. In 1653 he began his duties as elected Principal of Edinburgh University, which he served for nine distinguished years while also serving as professor of divinity. Upon the restoration of the episcopacy in Scotland (1661), he accepted this change as not inconsistent with the National Covenant or his latitudinarian principles. He was offered the office of bishop and after being reordained in episcopal orders was consecrated Bishop of Dunblane in 1661. In 1665 he went to London to resign this office to King Charles II, over the brutality of forced conformity to the episcopal system in Scotland. The King refused his resignation and promised to reform his policy. In 1669 a more conciliatory policy, which respected the political and religious realities of Scotland, was finally put into place, and Presbyterian ministers were allowed to resume their duties in certain conditions. He resigned his episcopal office in 1674 and returned to Edinburgh after being unable to make peace with the Presbyterians even after gaining huge concessions for them. The Presbyterians refused his offer, which included: placing episcopal powers in presbyteries and synods, with bishops merely as moderators; no requirement of an oath of canonical obedience; and ministers of Presbyterian convictions being allowed openly to declare it. His writings, though not published in his lifetime, reflect his love of Thomas à Kempis and the virtues of humility, meekness and charity. Besides commentaries and sermons his *Rules and Instructions for a Holy Life*, with its mysticism and other-worldliness, has been well received by a broad audience. His legacy is a noble commitment to church unity.

Oxford Dictionary of the Christian Church, 810.
G. W. Sprott, *Dictionary of National Biography*, XXXIII, 4–7.
E. A. Knox, 1931. *Robert Leighton, Archbishop of Glasgow* (London: James Clarke).

Liddon, Henry Parry (1829–90) was one of the leading representatives of the second phase of the Oxford Movement, noted for his competent defence of traditional Christian doctrines, especially in relation to Christology. Liddon was a convinced High Churchman, who was deeply influenced by the Oxford Movement, and held an especially high regard for E. B. Pusey. After a curacy in the Oxfordshire village of Wantage (1852–4), Liddon became vice-principal of Cuddesdon Theological College (1854–9). His rise to fame dates from the 1870s, when a combination of positions allowed him to achieve prominence in both church and academic circles. In 1870, he was appointed to a canonry at St Paul's Cathedral, and shortly afterwards to the Dean Ireland professorship of biblical exegesis at Oxford University. At this stage, Oxford was becoming increasingly sympathetic to a more liberal approach to Christian theology, which Liddon regarded with deep concern. His 1864 Bampton Lectures, entitled *The Divinity of our Lord and Saviour Jesus Christ*, are widely regarded as a classic statement of High Church orthodoxy, setting out a coherent justification of the Chalcedonian definition of the identity of Jesus Christ in the face of a growing tide of scepticism. Liddon was particularly alarmed by the views set out in the *Lux Mundi* (1889), which appeared the year before his death, and seemed to him to bode ill for the future. Liddon's major work was a four-volume biography of E. B. Pusey, which was published posthumously (1893–7).

The Divinity of Our Lord and Saviour Jesus Christ (London: Longman, 1867).
J. O. Johnston, 1904. *Life and Letters of Henry Parry Liddon* (London: Longmans).
Jude V. Nixon, 1994. *Gerald Manley Hopkins and His Contemporaries: Liddon, Newman, Darwin and Pater* (New York and London: Garland Press) (AM)

Llewelyn Davies, John (1826–1916), 'Muscular Christian Socialist' and successor of F. D. Maurice. Llewelyn attended Trinity College, Cambridge, and was friends with Westcott, Hort, and David Vaughan, with whom he translated Plato's *Republic* (1852). Davies *incarnated* Maurice's theology of the earthly redemption of mankind via the *imitatio* of a Johannine (and Platonized) Christ, who as Living God stood as Head of his universal Catholic Church and Nation. He emphasized redemptive sacrifice via the (anti-penal) atonement of Christ as well as the fellowship of the Holy Spirit. Ameliorist on social issues but no democrat, he supported the Queen, for whom he served as chaplain. He became Maurice's disciple while working on 'Christian Socialist' endeavours with Kingsley, Ludlow and Thomas Hughes. Their cooperative movement culminated with the founding of the Working Men's College (1854). Davies's marriage to Mary Crompton brought him Positivist and scientific sparring partners like her brother Henry, brother-in-law E. S. Beesley, and T. H. Huxley, whom he cordially challenged. In 1882, he joined Frederic Harrison's Anti-Aggression League, but left it over the doctrine of 'peace at any price'. During struggles over Forster's Education Act, Davies formed the National Church Reform Union (1870). Then, after presiding at Maurice's deathbed and funeral in 1872, he filled Maurice's shoes as Principal of Queen's College (1873–4; 1878–86). His *Social Questions* (1885) discuss 'Maurice's Christian Socialism'. With his sister Emily Davies, he laboured to secure for women university degrees and the right to vote. He also replaced Huxley on the first London School Board; and subsequently presided at his funeral (1895). For Smith's *Dictionary of the Bible*, he wrote on 'Paul'. Robert Browning admired his *Sermons on the Manifestation of the Son of God* (1864). With Westcott, he contributed to Smith's *Dictionary of Christian Biography* the entry on 'Ambrosius', who, like Davies, was 'fearless and large hearted' and had a 'truly episcopal spirit of humanity'. His 1891 Hulsean lectures, *Order and Growth*, and published selections from Maurice entitled *Lessons of Hope* (1891), were accomplished while in retirement after losing favour with the Queen. During Balfour's term, Davies drafted the 'Cowper-Temple clause' favouring non-denominational religious teaching. Davies's legacy lives through adult education, cooperatives, and the Anglo-Catholic movement.

Macquarrie, John (1919–), was born in Renfrew, Scotland, attended Paisley Grammar School and was reared in what he later called 'rather dreary evangelical Protestantism'. Alongside this he claims always to have had a sense of the divine presence, associated with the ancient Celtic Christian tradition, of a more mystical character. In 1936 he began his theological pilgrimage at Glasgow University by way of preparation for ordination in the Church of Scotland. Already, however, he was drawn to the more liturgical and symbolic emphases of the Scottish Episcopal Church, and rejected the Barthian criticism of religion which was fashionable.

Ordained in the Kirk, he served as an army chaplain and then in a parish in the north-east of Scotland. He was lured back into theology to undertake doctoral research, a study of Heidegger's influence on the theology of Bultmann. The resulting thesis was published as his first book, *An Existentialist Theology* (1955). After lecturing in the University of Glasgow (1953–62), he was appointed Professor of Systematic Theology at Union Theological Seminary, New York (1962–70). In 1965 he was ordained an Anglican priest by the Bishop of New York, having felt the lure of communion 'broader, richer . . . more catholic'. He was a consultant at the Lambeth Conferences of 1968 and 1978. In 1969 he was awarded the degree of Doctor of Divinity, and 1970 saw his appointment as Canon of Christ Church and Lady Margaret Professor of Divinity at Oxford University, the post he held until his retirement in 1986, having been made a Fellow of the British Academy in 1984.

As a teacher he was known for his gift with words, a lecturer who could charm his audience. A devoted churchman, he willingly gave talks to small parish groups as well as participating in international ecumenical dialogues.

Macquarrie's theology was influenced early on by Idealist philosophical tradition, in particular F. H. Bradley's *Appearance and Reality*, teaching a version of Hegelian thought leading to the absolute which was beyond our thought and beyond personhood. This philosophical tradition criticized both materialist empiricism as self-eroding, and traditional Christianity whose dogmas and historic claims were at best picture-language for the truths of Idealism, C. A. Campbell, Professor at Glasgow, who wrote *On Selfhood and God* (London: Allen and Unwin, 1957) also influenced Macquarrie theologically.

Having developed an interest in Bultmann's theology, Macquarrie became a world authority on Martin Heidegger's thought, translating his *Being and Time* in collaboration with the American Edward Robinson. Bultmann drew almost exclusively on 'the early Heidegger', the more Kierkegaardian and subjectivist side of his philosophy. Macquarrie's Idealist heritage found a counterpoint in this pure version of existentialist thought, concrete experience of the present balancing earlier panentheistic tendencies. The 'later Heidegger' seeks to articulate 'Being', which is not 'at hand' but transcends all our categories and yet is mystically experienced through language and nature, succinctly described in his small book *Martin Heidegger* (London: Lutterworth Press, 1968). Macquarrie's constructive theology takes up both 'earlier and later' aspects of Heidegger to forge an 'existential-ontological' theology. Theology is cast into this dynamic, modern framework in something of an apologetic systematic theology, expressed primarily in his *Principles of Christian Theology* (London: SCM, 1966, revised edition 1977). In his astonishingly erudite *Twentieth Century Religious Thought* (1963; rev. 1971, 1981), Macquarrie shows his growing appreciation of Roman Catholic theologians, notably Rahner and von Balthasar, who share his orientation for the post-Kantian 'transcendental' philosophical tradition as a background for reinterpretation of Christian dogmatic themes.

Macquarrie never found the Evangelical theologies of the word congenial, rejecting the 'I–Thou' model of God's relationship with humanity. His theology is Anglican, 'catholic and critical', in the nine-teenth-century tradition of *Lux Mundi* and *Essays and Reviews*, and more recently William Temple's *Nature Man and God*. His 1983–4 Gifford Lectures *In Search of Deity* advocate the mystical, immanentist view of God, pressing for an 'essentialist' rather than 'voluntarist' understanding of God and the world. He changed his mind about the term 'panentheism', preferring 'dialectical theism' to characterize his doctrine.

Macquarrie engages with modern philosophy in forging a theology which is deeply appreciative of patristic doctrine, and in this he points ahead as well as continuing a tradition. Never a Biblical theologian, but with a keen pastoral sense, he has steered a subtle path through con-temporary thought for trinitarian Christianity. His focus on human sense of the divine in non-religious contexts will continue to assist Anglican theologians in their efforts to reach a synthesis with modernity, although some will wonder whether his theology has also sufficiently dealt with the discontinuities of sin and redemption.

Macquarrie, for a long time, was unquestionably Anglicanism's most distinguished systematic theologian in the second half of the twentieth century.

His works include:
An Existentialist Theology (London: SCM, 1955).
The Scope of Demythologizing (London: SCM, 1960).
Twentieth Century Religious Thought (London: SCM, 1963, 1988).
God and Secularity (London: Lutterworth Press, 1967).
God Talk (London: SCM, 1967).
The Concept of Peace (London: SCM, 1973).
Principles of Christian Theology (London: SCM, 1966; revised and enlarged edn 1977).
Christian Hope (London: Mowbrays, 1978).
In Search of Humanity (London: SCM, 1982).

In Search of Deity (London: SCM, 1984).
A New Dictionary of Christian Ethics (London: SCM, 1986), (co-editor with James F. Childress).
Theology, Church and Ministry (London: SCM, 1986).
Jesus Christ in Modern Thought (London: SCM, 1990).

Appraisals of his work include:
Alistair Kee and Eugene Long, 1986. *Being and Truth: Essays in Honour of John Macquarrie* (London: SCM).
Eugene Thomas Long, 1985. *Existence, Being and God: An Introduction to the Philosophical Theology of John Macquarrie* (New York: Paragon House).
David Jenkins, 1987. *The Scope and Limits of John Macquarrie's Existential Theology* (Stockholm, Academia Uppsaliensis: Almquist and Wiksell International). (TB)

Manning, William Thomas (1866–1949), bishop. Born in England, he moved to the United States with his family in 1882. Educated at the University of the South, Sewanee, Tennessee (1888–91), he was influenced both personally and theologically by William DuBose. He was ordained to the priesthood in 1891, only two years before he was appointed as Professor of Systematic Divinity, University of the South. He left Sewanee after only a year to take up parish work, eventually becoming rector of Trinity Parish, New York City, in 1908. Turning down two prior episcopal elections, Manning was elected Tenth Bishop of New York and consecrated in 1921, a fitting choice for a Diocese still reverberating from the war-cry of beloved former Bishop J. H. Hobart: 'Evangelical Truth and Apostolic Order'. The two great interests of Manning's career were the building of the Cathedral Church of St John the Divine in New York City, and the work of Christian reunion. The latter he approached warily as a traditional Catholic theologian who, though fully committed to the cause of reunion, was compelled to oppose any proposal which diluted apostolic order, faith and practice. In 1915 Manning wrote, 'The Episcopal Church has been much influenced by her contact with Protestantism . . . But her own faith and order as judged by the standards of the undivided Church are fundamentally and definitively Catholic.' Thus he objected to any 'pan-Protestant' proposal which excluded the great ancient communions of Rome and Orthodoxy, firmly believing that Anglicanism held a unique position in Christendom as the communion best able to bring about a great synthesis between Protestant and Catholic Christianity. He led the opposition against both proposed concordats with the Presbyterians and the Congregationalists. An ardent defender of traditional Christian belief and morality, Manning was often the pre-eminent voice against the growing liberalism of his denomination, in which he contributed an element of sobriety, but in the end failed to persuade.

'The Protestant Episcopal Church and Christian Unity', *Constructive Quarterly* (December 1915).

W. F. Hughes, 1963. *Prudently with Power: William Thomas Manning, Tenth Bishop of New York* (New York: Holy Cross Publications).

Mascall, Eric Lionel (1905–93) was born in London. He was a brilliant student at Cambridge University, where he read mathematics and had the distinction of being a wrangler. After teaching mathematics for three years, he decided that his interests lay in theology, and he was ordained to the priesthood in 1932. He did not regret the years he had spent on mathematics and believed that the discipline of that subject was a considerable help in his theological work.

It was obvious that someone with intellectual qualifications as impressive as Mascall's was superbly fitted for a teaching career in the Church, and for thirty-five years he held appointments, first in Lincoln Theological College (1937–45), then in Christ Church, Oxford (1945–62) and finally at King's College, London (1962–72). He continued writing after his retirement, and died in 1993.

A convinced Anglo-Catholic, he was perhaps the most influential in a group of like-minded theologians of the Church of England, all approximately his contemporaries, including Austin Farrer, Gregory Dix, Michael Ramsey and Gabriel Hebert. He worked in the Thomist tradition and was well acquainted with the thinking of Catholic theologians on the continent, especially France.

His first important work, establishing his reputation as a major British theologian, was entitled *He Who Is*, and appeared while he was still at Lincoln. The title is, of course, the expression used by St Thomas as 'the most appropriate name' for God, and the subtitle of the book is 'A Study in Traditional Theism'. The book was written at a time when the old natural theology was being severely criticized both by philosophers and by theologians of the Barthian school. Mascall did not simply restate the old arguments, but infused a new dynamism into them, foreshadowing the 'transcendental' Thomism, which was so influential at Vatican II. So we find Mascall saying that 'in St Thomas' whole metaphysic it is existence, not essence, that is primary'. Several times he cites Joseph Maréchal, whose pioneering work in reinterpreting Thomism had laid the foundation on which later and better-known exponents of transcendental Thomism would be building twenty years further on.

The arguments of *He Who Is* were developed and expanded in *Existence and Analogy* (1949), where the expression 'He who is' is interpreted 'as signifying not a static perfection but the absolutely unlimited Act and Energy'. Mascall's philosophical theology reached its highest development in his Gifford Lectures, entitled *The Openness of Being*

(1971). The first two chapters of this book are explicitly devoted to an exposition of transcendental Thomism and of its emergence in the previous generation. The main argument of the book is a sophisticated restatement of the traditional Thomistic claim that when we attentively consider finite being, we grasp that ontologically it is dependent on God. At this point we also see how in Mascall rational theology is linked with spiritual experience. 'Awareness of God', he claims, 'is closely linked with the capacity for contemplative wondering.'

In other writings Mascall strengthened his case for theism by attending to some related questions. *The Importance of Being Human* (1959) takes up the age-old question 'What is man?' and stresses that in the Christian conception, the human being is not a fixed nature but an open nature, an idea which he develops in a way similar to what we find in Rahner and some of the existentialists. At a time when logical positivism was still a powerful influence in the English universities, Mascall offered a defence of theological language in *Words and Images* (1957), which recognizes the limitation of human concepts in their applicability to God, while stressing the function of imagery and indirect language. Mention should be made also of his Bampton Lectures, *Christian Faith and Natural Science*, hailed at the time of its publication as a breakthrough in this area, and still worth reading today.

But it was not only problems of philosophical theology that Mascall tackled. His contributions ranged over the whole area of theology. Problems of ecclesiology, sacramental theology and ecumenical theology are treated in such books as *Corpus Christi* and *The Recovery of Unity*.

In his last period, troubled by the increasing liberalism of the Church of England and the corresponding decline of Anglo-Catholicism, Mascall became increasingly polemical in his writings. *The Secularisation of Christianity* (1965) was a vigorous attack on the views of John Robinson and other secular theologians. The writing was brilliant and exposed some of the superficialities of the views criticized. But perhaps it failed to address some of the real concerns which Robinson and his allies had espoused. Similar judgements could be passed on most of the other books which Mascall produced in the final years of his life. They lack the constructive qualities of his earlier work. An exception is the short book, *The Triune God*, in which he reflected on the deepest mysteries of Christian faith. Some critics believed that this book made an important contribution toward reconciling Eastern and Western doctrines of the Trinity.

Mascall's final book was *Saraband*, published shortly before his death. The title of the book is taken from the name of a stately dance popular in the sixteenth and seventeenth centuries, also used for the slow but rhythmical music which accompanied such a dance. Presumably Mascall thought that his own theology had characteristics similar to the dance or its music. In the book, he gives a fascinating picture of the Church of England and some of its leading personalities, drawn from his long career in the service of that church. Not only *Saraband* but his writings as a whole give the impression of a man who drew his inspiration from the perennial wisdom of the past and yet was aware of a dynamic rhythm that carried us on into the future. He remains as a witness to whatever is enduring in the conception of a Catholic Anglicanism. (JM)

Meade, William (1789–1862), bishop. Born into a prominent Evangelical family from Virginia, his mother's concern over the influence of deism at the College of William and Mary led him to attend Princeton, graduating in 1808. Ordained in 1811 when the Episcopal Church in Virginia was perhaps at its lowest point in history, he became a passionate Evangelical churchman. He appeared and acted more like a Methodist circuit-rider than the typical Latitudinarian churchman of the previous generation. Meade was influenced as a child by English Evangelicals Wilberforce and Simeon. He credited the former's *Practical View* with the transformation of Latitudinarian Virginia into an Evangelical diocese. But this was no doubt a self-effacing view. In 1829 Meade became assistant bishop under the Evangelical Richard Channing Moore, succeeding Moore as bishop of Virginia in 1841. The effects of Meade's Evangelical fervour while bishop have been described in no less terms than the resurrection of the church in Virginia from the dead. His character was firmly imprinted upon both the diocese and the Protestant Episcopal Seminary in Alexandria (founded 1823). Ardently Protestant in theology, and consequently an outspoken opponent of the Oxford Movement, he was nevertheless a convinced Anglican who valued both episcopal succession and the historic liturgy. He supported the *Muhlenberg Memorial* at the General Convention of 1853, a proposal for Protestant unity based on the extension of episcopal ordination to non-episcopal clergy. Among his numerous writings he is best remembered for *Old Churches, Ministers, and Families of Virginia* (1857) a tribute to the diocese and Commonwealth which he loved and served to the end. Opposed to secession in principle, he nevertheless followed his beloved Virginia when the state seceded from the Union, and he served as presiding bishop of the Protestant Episcopal Church in the Confederate States until his death in 1862.

Dictionary of American Biography, VI.
Dictionary of Christianity in America.
A. C. Guelzo, 1994. *For the Union of Evangelical Christendom. The Irony of the Reformed*

Episcopalians (University Park: Penn State University Press).
R. Nelson, 1873. *Reminiscences of the Rt. Rev. William Meade.*

Mozley, James Bowling (1813–78), professor of divinity and Tractarian theologian. Educated at Oriel College, Oxford, he was influenced greatly by Pusey, whom he lived with while seeking a Fellowship which he eventually received in 1840 at Magdalen College. In 1871 he was appointed to the prestigious position of Regius Professor of Divinity at Oxford, in the same year in which he received his D.D. A Tractarian of the inner circle, he was the joint editor of the *Christian Remembrancer*, which was the High Church party paper after the demise of the *British Critic.* He began to feel less positively about Tractarianism only after the succession of Newman in 1845 and the Gorham case, which brought about the secession of Manning and of Robert and Henry Wilberforce. Serving from 1856 until his death in the parish of Old Shoreham in Sussex, he wrote three works prompted by his modification of High Church principles during the Gorham crisis: *On the Augustinian Doctrine of Predestination* (1855); *On the Primitive Doctrine of Baptismal Regeneration* (1856); and *A Review of the Baptismal Controversy* (1862). In these, Mozley concludes that regeneration of all baptized infants is not an article of faith and that therefore the Church of England should not insist on this belief in all its members as it has never been received as an article of faith or proved in Scripture. In response to the direct statements of the Prayer Book, for example 'this child is now regenerate', he suggests that this type of statement is 'literal in form and hypothetical in meaning'. His other significant works were the 1865 Bampton Lectures *On Miracles*; *University and other Sermons* (1876); and *Essays Historical and Theological* (2 vols, 1884) which was a compilation of his journalistic writings. Dean Church, the Anglo-Catholic nineteenth-century historian, estimated him next to Newman the most forcible and impressive writer of the Oxford Movement.

Oxford Dictionary of The Christian Church, 948.
W. A. Greenhill in *Dictionary of National Biography*, XXXIX, 249–51.

Neale, John Mason (1818–66). While attending Trinity College, Cambridge, he founded the Cambridge Camden Society for the study of ecclesiastical art. He was ordained priest in 1842. In 1846 Neale was offered the wardenship of Sackville College, East Grinstead, where he remained for twenty years. At East Grinstead he founded the Society of St Margaret, a sisterhood that was devoted to the education of girls and care of the sick. Neale's influence upon Anglicanism is most evident in four fields: church architecture, liturgies, hymnody and ceremonialism.

Neale was also a gifted preacher whose bibliography includes numerous volumes of penetrating sermons. In all, his published material comprises well over one hundred volumes. Though hymns were only a small part of Neale's literary contribution, it is as a hymn writer that he is generally best known. Frustrated with a lack of hymns for the Church of England, Neale translated Latin medieval hymns and sequences for the church. Because of the beauty and accuracy of his translations, these hymns have found a permanent place in the hymnody of Anglicanism. Neale's most important influence is in his contribution as an apologist for Catholic symbolism and ritualism in Christian worship. His translation of Durandus's *Symbolism of Churches* included an introduction which marked the earliest attempt in the nineteenth century to explain the value and need for proper church architecture, symbols and ornaments. Neale also provided the post-Oxford Movement Ritualists with a thorough historical lineage of ornaments used in the Church of England. The *Hierurgia Anglicana* (1848) allowed early Ritualists to appeal to continuity with earlier Anglican bishops and priests for the use of the chasuble, altar frontals, candles, and credence tables. As Pusey and Newman were the theological force of the Oxford Movement, Neale was the driving influence behind the revival of Catholic symbolism in the Church of England. He was among the first to wear a chasuble in the nineteenth century, and suffered greatly at the hands of rioters who sought to end such visible Catholic principles.

Hierurgia Anglicana (London: Rivington, 1848).
A. G. Lough, 1962. *The influence of John Mason Neale* (London: SPCK).

Neill, Stephen Charles (1900–84), as he never tired of telling his friends, was born on the last day of the nineteenth century, 31 December 1900, as the third of six children. Although his family traced its origins back to the north of Ireland, Neill's childhood was largely spent in the south of England. He attended Dean Close School in the English Cotswolds town of Cheltenham, where he experienced a form of conversion experience. By the age of 15, he was able to read parts of the Old Testament in Hebrew. Neill's gift for languages would prove to be one of his most valuable assets in the form of ministry which lay ahead of him. He was awarded a classical scholarship to Trinity College, Cambridge, in 1918 and was subsequently elected to a prize Fellowship in October 1924. During his period at Cambridge, Neill found himself equally attracted to both the Cambridge Inter-Collegiate Christian Union and the Student Christian Movement. Although troubled by the former's intransigence and the latter's liberalism, Neill managed to bridge what seemed to many to be a growing gulf between two increasingly divergent styles of student Christianity.

Neill's election to a Fellowship at Trinity seemed to many to mark the beginning of what was confidently predicted to be a stunning academic career, in which classical scholarship would be taken to new heights of excellence. Neill's 100,000-word study of the relation of Plotinus and the Cappadocian fathers gained him a prize Fellowship in October 1924 – the first ever at Trinity in a theological area of scholarship. Yet even before he submitted the thesis, Neill had purchased a passage to India, where he believed his future lay. By the end of 1924, he had arrived in the southernmost region of India, known to the English as 'Tinnevelly' (but more correctly as Tirunelveli). His career as a missionary would last more than twenty years, during which he mastered the Tamil language. He was ordained deacon in 1926, and spent a period working as a missionary before being appointed warden of the local theological college. He became Bishop of Tirunelveli in 1939, and remained in that position until 1945. Following a serious breakdown (which may have been linked with his homosexuality), Neill returned to England. Despite his remarkable gifts, he never achieved high academic or ecclesiastical office. It is known that his name was considered for the Regius chair of divinity at Cambridge University in 1950. His 1962 Firth Lectures, published as *The Interpretation of the New Testament, 1861–1961*, is widely regarded as a landmark in New Testament studies. Although he held academic appointments at the Universities of Hamburg (1962–7) and Nairobi (1969–73), he never gained the academic recognition he deserved. He ended his days as scholar-in-residence at Wycliffe Hall, Oxford.

Neill's contribution to Anglican thought and practice during the twentieth century has been substantial. His *Anglicanism* (1958) has been widely thought of as a classic contemporary statement of the Anglican ethos. Although dealing especially with the historical origins and distinctive nature of the Church of England, the work allows ready extension of its approach to the Anglican Communion as a whole. Neill was instrumental in ecumenical affairs, most notably the creation of the Church of South India. Although he was active in the work of the World Council of Churches during its early period, he gradually became disillusioned with its drift into theological liberalism, and its increasing emphasis on social action rather than theological reflection.

Neill's specific contribution to the continuing development of the Anglican ethos can be thought to focus particularly on the area of mission. Perhaps the most important and enduring aspect of Neill's legacy to Anglicanism is his persistent emphasis upon the importance of mission. His *History of Christian Missions* (1964) and *Colonialism and Christian Missions* (1966), though primarily works of history, show a strong commitment to the importance of mission in the life of the Church. Neill's assessment of the importance of this theme, linked with his experience of the Church in India, led him to explore the complexities of the relationship between Christianity and other faiths. His 1960 Moorehouse Lectures, originally delivered in Australia, examined this question. Eventually published as *Christian Faith and Other Faiths* (1961), the work remained influential, in various revisions, for more than two decades. Neill's approach ran counter to the forms of relativism which were gaining currency at that time, in that he vigorously maintained the distinctiveness of the Christian faith, and its ultimacy in the face of other faiths. For Neill, conversion is 'necessarily present in any religion which claims to be the truth'.

Yet alongside this stress on mission in the life of the Church, we find Neill continuing to advocate the importance of personal conversion. His own experience as a schoolboy convert in the 1910s remained formative, even in his later period. In 1922, Neill spoke of the importance of personal conversion as a prerequisite to credible and convincing preaching. In 1934, he explored the intricacies of the relationship between baptism and conversion. It was an important theme, not least on account of its ecumenical implications. In 1950, he noted how conversion brought together both intellect and emotions. Even as late as 1978, Neill argued for the continuing importance of both the term 'conversion' and its implications for Christian life. Noting that some Christians in effect treated the term 'as a dirty word', Neill argued for its continuing importance in authentic Christian thought and life.

For Neill, Christianity was a missionary religion on account of its realization that it possessed the truth, and was therefore under obligation to proclaim it. As Anglicanism moves into a situation in which evangelism is the norm rather than the exception, Neill's concerns and approaches are likely to continue to be of relevance for many years to come.

Anglicanism (London: Mowbrays, 1958; rev. edn 1977).
Christian Faith and Other Faiths (London: Oxford University Press, 1961).
Colonialism and Christian Missions (London: Lutterworth, 1966).
A History of Christian Missions (Harmondsworth: Penguin Books, 1964).
The Interpretation of the New Testament, 1861–1961 (London: Oxford University Press, 1964).
Jesus through Many Eyes (London: Lutterworth, 1976).
The Supremacy of Jesus (London: Hodder & Stoughton, 1984).
Towards Church Union (London: SCM Press, 1952).
God's Apprentice (London: Hodder & Stoughton, 1991).

A. K. Cragg and W. O. Chadwick, 1985. 'Stephen Charles Neill', in *Proceedings of the British Academy* 71, 603–14.
Christopher Lamb, 1987. 'The Legacy of Stephen Neill', *International Bulletin of Missionary Research* 11 (2) (April): 62–6.
Timothy Yates, 1988. 'Stephen Neill: Some Aspects of a Theological Legacy', *Anvil* 5: 151–61. (AM)

Newman, John Henry (1801–90), although eventually received into the Roman Catholic Church, was – and remains – of major importance to the development of Anglican theology and church life. He was born into a banking family in London. He attended school at Ealing, where he underwent some form of conversion experience, partly through the influence of an Evangelical member of the teaching staff, Walter Mayers. After Ealing, he was awarded a scholarship at Trinity College, Oxford, and was subsequently elected to a Fellowship at Oriel College in 1822. It was during this period that he established friendships with a number of significant Anglican writers, including John Keble, Hurrell Froude and Robert Isaac Wilberforce.

Newman was ordained deacon in 1826, and priest a year later. In 1828, he became vicar of St Mary the Virgin, generally known as the 'university church'. He would remain in this position until 1843, when he finally resigned this position as a consequence of his increasing disillusionment with the Church of England. He was received into the Roman Catholic Church in 1845. Newman's relationship with his new church authorities was not entirely happy, not least on account of his misgivings concerning the First Vatican Council's definition of papal infallibility. Despite continuing suspicion from the ultramontanist wing of the church, Newman was created a cardinal in 1879.

Newman's historical importance to the development of Anglicanism is immense. There are, for example, excellent reasons for suggesting he was instrumental in popularizing the use of the hitherto unfamiliar term 'Anglican' to refer to the distinctive ethos of the Church of England. His deep involvement (along with Keble and E. B. Pusey) in the rise of Tractarianism (subsequently more widely known as the 'Oxford Movement') ensured that it would be impossible to write any future history of Anglicanism without reference to his name. He was responsible for the series of Tracts for the Times (1833–41), which fostered the vision of a recovery of a Catholic vision of the Church, and made available theological and spiritual resources designed with this end in mind. Although Newman's withdrawal from Anglican circles, initially precipitated by strong reaction within both the Church of England and the University of Oxford over the contents of Tract 90, diminished his influence over a rising generation of Anglican thinkers, there is no doubt that his long-term influence exceeds that of any other Anglican writer of the period.

Newman's continuing importance for Anglican theology rests on a number of considerations, of which this essay will focus on three: the importance of tradition; the concept of a *via media*; the development of doctrine. We shall consider these individually in what follows.

The importance of tradition

At an early stage, Newman became aware of the importance of the role of tradition in the life of the Church. His *Lectures on the Prophetical Office of the Church* (1837) (subsequently republished as *The Via Media of the Anglican Church* (1877)) stressed the importance of both Scripture and the patristic witness to the contemporary life and thought of the Church. Believing that Roman Catholicism was wedded to a concept of authority which minimized the authority of the fathers, and Protestantism to a concept of the authority of Scripture which had the same effect, Newman affirmed the importance of the first five centuries of Christian tradition to the self-understanding of the Church. In some ways, this can be seen as an extension of the views of some of the Caroline Divines (for whom Newman had great regard), such as Launcelot Andrewes. However, Newman brought new theological acumen to this issue. His use of the 'Vincentian Canon' allowed him to explore the notion of the critical reception of tradition in terms of that which 'has been believed always, everywhere and by everyone'. Increasingly concerned about the tendency towards individualism which he discerned in Protestantism, Newman came to see tradition as a means of safeguarding the corporate nature of the Christian faith, and establishing appropriate authorities (such as bishops, creeds, councils and liturgies, to name a number of different authority-bearing traditions) by which the life and thought of the Church might be governed. The work also began to develop the idea of Anglicanism as a *via media* between Roman Catholicism and Protestantism, to which we may now turn.

The concept of a via media

At quite an early stage, Newman began to formulate the idea of the Church of England as a 'middle way' between the extremes of Protestantism and Roman Catholicism. The concept can be seen in a number of writings from the late 1830s, such as his *Lectures on the Prophetical Office of the Church* (1837), which argued that the Church of England was able to avoid the shortcomings of both Roman Catholic and Protestant approaches to authority. His *Lectures on Justification* (1838) argued that the Reformation of the sixteenth century threw up two diametrically opposed manners of understanding the doctrine of justification by faith. Arguing that both the Protestant and Roman Catholic approaches to the nature of justifying righteousness were defective, in different ways, Newman advocated a mediating position which he believed to safeguard what was good in the two approaches, while allowing their weaknesses to be eliminated. This *via media* approach, which he found exemplified in some of the Anglican Divines of the Caroline period, was able to lay claim to the strengths of the two extreme positions, while setting to one side their less palatable teachings.

The importance of Newman's approach was that it laid the foundations for a renewed affirmation of the theological and ecclesiological distinctiveness of the Church of England, and thus allowed it to see itself as a church which could not be categorized simply as yet another Protestant denomination. For Newman, the Church of England possessed a self-understanding which was capable of justification at both the theological and historical levels. Newman's reaffirmation of the *via media* encouraged further reflection on the nature of the Church, and found particular application in the 'three branch' theory of the Church, which gained a considerable following in later Oxford Movement circles. While this theory is open to some criticism, it nevertheless pointed to the need – which continues to be important today – for a rigorously *theological* understanding of the nature of Anglicanism, as opposed to a purely sociological (mis)interpretation of that church as the 'British empire at prayer'.

The development of doctrine

Newman's earliest work – *The Arians of the Fourth Century* (1832) – was essentially a historical study of the Arian controversy, which raised the issue of the way in which Christianity is obligated to formulate doctrines in order to safeguard its distinctive identity. In dealing with the controversy, Newman found himself wrestling with the issue of how Christianity could maintain its identity while at the same time developing. The issue received his most sustained attention in the 1845 work *Essay on Development of Doctrine*. Newman assumed that the fact of the 'development of doctrine' was evident from the history of the Church. What required to be established was the means by which authentic developments were to be distinguished from those which distorted or corrupted the original. Newman, in effect, affirmed that it was necessary to change in order to remain the same. However, he argued that seven principles (initially referred to as 'tests', and later as 'notes') could be identified as means by which true could be differentiated from false developments.

1. The preservation of a type or idea
2. Continuity of principles
3. Power of assimilation
4. Early anticipation of development
5. Logical sequence of development
6. Additions which preserved matters of importance
7. Chronic continuation

Although Newman provided historical illustrations of each of these points, it is clear that a strongly prescriptive understanding of what doctrine is and should be lay behind his historical descriptions of certain developments. The Arian controversy, surveyed in an earlier work, was a case in point.

The issue remains of importance to Anglicanism, which has witnessed considerable tension between theological preservationists (who insist on speaking the same language – often complete with its specific vocabulary – as their forebears in the fourth or sixteenth centuries) and theological modernizers (who insist on the radical elimination of traditional theology as an irrelevance from the past). Newman offers a means by which the essence of a traditional faith may be carried over from one generation to another, without surrendering its distinctiveness on the one hand, or lapsing into the language and logic of a bygone era on the other. The task of correlating past and present remains of critical importance to Anglicanism, especially in the developing world; Newman remains an important voice in this conversation.

Apologia pro Vita Sua (Oxford: Clarendon Press, 1967).
Lectures on Justification (London: Rivingtons, 1874).
The Via Media of the Anglican Church (Oxford: Clarendon Press, 1990).
I. T. Ker (ed.), *The Genius of John Henry Newman: Selections from his Works* (Oxford: Clarendon Press, 1989).

Sheridan Gilley, 1990. *Newman and his Age* (London: Darton, Longman and Todd).
Ian T. Ker, 1990. *The Achievement of John Henry Newman* (London: Collins).
Ian T. Ker, 1993. *Healing the Wound of Humanity: The Spirituality of John Henry Newman* (London: Darton, Longman and Todd). (AM)

Packer, James Innell (1926–) is widely regarded as one of the most distinguished Evangelical theologians within Anglicanism. Born in 1926 in the English cathedral city of Gloucester, he initially studied classics at Oxford University. As a result of his conversion in October 1944, Packer was moved to study theology, and subsequently to undertake doctoral research in the theology of Richard Baxter. After serving his title in the diocese of Birmingham, he served as tutor at Tyndale Hall, Bristol, before assuming the position of Warden of Latimer House, a newly established Evangelical Anglican research centre in Oxford. He was instrumental in convening and providing theological direction to the National Evangelical Anglican Congress (Keele, 1967), which gave a new sense of direction to Evangelical presence within the Church of England. After further periods in theological education at Bristol, he moved to Canada to become professor of systematic theology at Regent College, Vancouver.

At an early stage, Packer showed himself to be a vigorous and capable defender of orthodox Evangelical theology, seeing the theological trends of the 1950s and 1960s as destructive of much that was essential to Christian integrity. His earliest book *'Fundamentalism' and the Word of God* (1958) was a strident defence of the views of the authority of Scripture against the criticisms directed against them by Gabriel Hebert in *Fundamentalism and the Church of God* (1957). Packer's most significant contribution, however, is widely regarded as lying in the area of Christian spirituality. His 1973 work *Knowing God* has achieved classic status. This book demonstrated the manner in which theology, rightly understood and applied, is of fundamental importance to Christian living. One of its most distinctive features is its ability to bring together the intellectual and affective (to use a term much favoured by the Puritans) aspects of faith.

Packer's literary output shows a consistent concern to relate theology to the life of the Church. Firmly persuaded of the 'primacy of theology', Packer (often using the Puritans as mentors) stressed the way in which theology was an integral part of a coherent approach to the Christian life, bringing together matters as diverse as spirituality, liturgy, church polity and social ethics. Packer's insistence that theology cannot be divorced from the life and witness of the Church remains an important counterbalance to the prevailing tendency to isolate theology as a purely academic discipline.

'Fundamentalism' and the Word of God (London: Inter-Varsity Fellowship, 1958).
Knowing God (London: Hoddert & Stoughton, 1973).

Christopher Catherwood, 1985. 'J. I. Packer', in *Five Evangelical Leaders* (London: Hodder & Stoughton; and Wheaton, Ill.: Harold Shaw), 169–204.
A. McGrath, *To Know and Serve God* (London: Hodder, 1997).
Roger Nicole, 1993. 'J. I. Packer', in W. A. Elwell (ed.), *Handbook of Evangelical Theologians* (Grand Rapids: Baker), 379–87. (AM)

Palmer, William (1803–85), High Church theologian and ecclesiastical historian. Educated at Trinity College, Dublin, he went to Magdalen Hall, Oxford, where he earned his M.A. in 1828. In 1831 he moved to Worcester College where he published *Origines Liturgicae*, a flawed but important work on the English liturgy which provoked great interest in this field of study. This significant liturgical work brought him into close association with the High Church party at Oxford, including such figures as Keble, Froude, Rose and Newman, just prior to the start of Oxford Movement. His interest and study of the Roman Church's apologists brought polemical skills to Oxford which were unique in his day. In 1833 he published *Remarks on Dr. Arnold's Principles of Church Reform*, an attack on the idea that the Church is the religious aspect of the state. Palmer was a founding member of the Association of Friends of the Church, which went on to serve as Newman's vehicle for circulating the theology of the Oxford Movement, the 'Tracts for the Times'. One of these was written by Palmer himself. In 1838 he published a two-volume work that set forth the 'Branch Theory' of the Anglican Church in *Treatise of the Church of Christ*. This theory maintains that although there is schism within the true Church of Christ there are legitimate 'branches' of this Church as long as the doctrine of the undivided Church and apostolic succession of bishops is maintained. In the early 1840s, he wrote polemic treatises against Cardinal Wiseman. His *Narrative of Events connected with the Publication of Tracts for the Times* and *Doctrine of Development, and Conscience considered in relation to the Evidences of Christianity and of the Catholic System*, were important works. In the latter he answered both Ward's *Ideal of a Christian Church* and Newman's *Development of Christian Doctrine*. Newman remarked that he was the only thoroughly learned man among the initiators of the Oxford Movement.

Oxford Dictionary of the Christian Church, 1026.
G. Goodwin in *Dictionary of National Biography*, XLIII, 168–70.
Peter Nockles, 1994. *The Oxford Movement in Context* (Cambridge: Cambridge University Press).

Parsons, Edward Lambe (1868–1960), bishop, theologian and liturgiologist. After attending Yale, where he received his B.A. in 1889, he went on to study at Union Theological Seminary in 1892 and Episcopal Theological Seminary in 1894, and to receive two D.D.s, from Pacific Theological School (1914), and Yale (1924). Ordained deacon in 1894, he was ordained priest the following year, and twenty-five years later was consecrated bishop in 1919. He was well respected for his versatility as a preacher, liturgiologist, historian and professor of theology at the Church Divinity School of the Pacific. His greatest contribution is evident in his work on the 1928 Book of Common Prayer. In *The American Prayer Book, its Origins and Principles*, Parsons and Bayard Hale Jones set forth the hopes, designs and reasons for the 1928 Book of Common Prayer. The work is a fine historical presentation of the history of the Book of Common Prayer, along with an attempt to deal with the controversial matters which accompany a Prayer Book revision. Parsons gives an informative glance into the theology and philosophy which guided the liturgical revision committee. Commenting on the Invocation during the Canon of Consecration, Parsons writes, 'As to the Invocation, there is really a certain hollowness in the controversies between proponents of subjective and objective ideas of the Consecration. Obviously it is not possible to "receive" anything which is not in some sense objectively real; and on the other hand, it is of no importance what the Elements may be alleged to have been made in themselves, unless they are subjectively realized within the soul of the communicant.' Bishop Parsons' scholarly liturgical commentary, along with numerous articles written for the *Historical Magazine*, reflect theological conservatism with an eye towards the needs of future generations of Episcopalians. His important written work reflects his wide interests: *Bishop Tuttle, a Portrait*; *William Ingraham Kip*; *The Church Rush in the God Rush*; and *The Hale Lectures*.

The American Prayer Book, its Origins and Principles (New York: Scribner & Sons, 1950). *Historical Magazine of the Protestant Episcopal Church* 29 (September 1960).

Pearson, John (1613–86), born at Great Snoring, Norfolk, where his father was rector, was educated at Eton and Cambridge, where he became Fellow of King's in 1634. He was ordained in 1639, became a prebend of Salisbury the following year and was presented to the parish of Thorington, Suffolk, as the troubles began, during which he spoke out on religion and politics. In 1645 he was chaplain to George Goring's forces in the West. During the Commonwealth he resided chiefly in London, acting from 1654 as unpaid weekly preacher at St Clement's, Eastcheap. At the Restoration he received various preferments and became Master of Jesus College, Cambridge, Margaret professor, and in 1662, Master of Trinity College, where he remained until his consecration as the bishop of Chester in 1673, a diocese he served with care and devotion.

Throughout the ups and downs of his career, Pearson was constantly active, defending the Church against the claims of both Roman Catholicism and Puritanism, but chiefly by his very numerous writings, for he was one of the group of Anglicans led by Sheldon and Hammond committed to the defence of the Anglican tradition during the Interregnum. A man of personal integrity and devotion, he was pre-eminently a scholar. He frequently appears in the diary of John Evelyn, who held him to be 'the most learned Divine of our nation' (*Diary*, 1673), an opinion shared by contemporaries and later by such as J. B. Lightfoot. Pearson was an active assistant at the Savoy Conference of

1661, at which Baxter praised his patient courtesy and learning. In the same year, as Lady Margaret professor, he delivered his *Determinationes Theologicae*, setting forth the apostolic succession. Two years earlier he had published two books, the first being *The Golden Remains of the Ever Memorable Mr. John Hales*, a member of the Great Tew Circle of liberal and rational theologians whom he knew from Eton days onwards and greatly admired: 'a man never to be truly expres'd but by himself' (Preface). The second book was his renowned *An Exposition of the Creed*, translated into other languages and constantly reprinted appearing in many editions down to 1899 (Sinker's revision of Chevallier's edition of 1849). It became a classic of Anglican theology, and characteristically the notes to the *Exposition* demonstrate an extraordinary range of patristic scholarship. It was in this area that Pearson also achieved fame with his *Vindiciae Epistolarun S. Ignatii* (1672), a defence of Ussher on the genuineness and dating of the Ignatian epistles and in which he paid tribute to Hammond's work on the subject. Pearson's vindication, a piece of outstanding scholarship, was evoked by a real-life situation in which the French Reformed theologian, Jean Daillé, had attacked Ussher's recension in his *De Scriptis* (1666). In it he refuted the arguments of Daillé in the interests of episcopacy, which he saw as necessary for the fullness or perfection of the Church. Pearson remains a constant reminder to the Church that devotion and loyalty need the undergirding of sound learning in its proclamation of the faith to every generation.

E. Churton (ed.), *Works* and a *Life* (1844), excluding *An Exposition* and *Annales Cyprianici* (1682), in which Pearson collaborated with John Fell. (HM)

Perkins, William (1558–1602), Puritan theologian. Educated at Christ Church College, Oxford, he was elected a fellow and received his M.A. in 1584. In his undergraduate days he was known for his reckless and drunken behaviour before a dramatic conversion experience. Eventually he became known both as an excellent preacher in the university and for his anti-Romanist writings. His writings were largely polemical but noted for their depth of understanding of his opponents' positions as well as his use of scholastic methodology and appreciation of history. He is best remembered for his plain yet learned sermons, his unflinching Calvinism, and his anti-Romanist writing and views. The best examples of his occasional writings are his *Golden Chain* (1590), in which his strident Calvinism was expressed. In it he writes, 'Theology is the science of living blessedly forever. Blessed life ariseth from the knowledge of God and therefore it ariseth from the knowledge of ourselves, because we know God by looking into ourselves.' Seven years later he wrote

Reformed Catholicke (1597), in which he delineated the differences between Protestant and Roman beliefs, and the next year *De Praedestinationis Modo et Ordine* (1598), which provoked a personal reply from Jacobus Arminius. Holy living and sanctification dominate his writings in which he looks for a reformation in the hearts of individuals which will bring about ongoing reformation in the Church. This, with a concern to balance the absolute sovereignty of God in salvation with the responsibility of the human agent to respond with faith and holiness to God's call are prominent themes. His plain and honest style as well as the volume and substance of his works enabled him to be a major force in seventeenth-century Puritan thought.

Oxford Dictionary of the Christian Church, 1064.
J. B. Mullinger in *Dictionary of National Biography*, XLV, 6–9.
Paul R. Shaefer, 1994. 'The Spiritual Brotherhood on the habits of the heart: Cambridge Protestants and the doctrine of Sanctification from William Perkins to Thomas Shepard'. (Oxford: unpublished D.Phil thesis).

Prichard, Harold Adye (1882–1944). Educated at Oxford University, where he received his B.A. in 1906 and his M.A. the following year, he also attended Johns Hopkins University, General Theological Seminary and St Stephen's College, where he was awarded a D.D. in 1926. Prichard was ordained to the priesthood in 1913. He was elected honorary Canon of the Cathedral of St John the Divine, 1920, and served as acting Dean of the cathedral 1924–5. He was a contributor to church periodicals and magazines as well as the author of several books, including *What did Jesus Think?* (1935) and *The Minister, the Method and the Message* (1932). His book *What Did Jesus Think?* revolves also around the experiences which brought Jesus to an understanding of who he was, and what his mission was to be. He taught because of what he felt about himself, he went to the cross and faced death because he internally must have understood that this death would have something to do with the Kingdom. In *The Minister, the Method and the Message*, Prichard focuses upon the minister's manner of life, the development of his devotional life and the mechanics of ministry. His re-evaluation of theological training suggests that time spent learning theological languages is a 'complete and tragic waste of precious time'. The Christian minister, according to Prichard, should spend his time travelling, mixing with people in the smoke rooms of hotels, experiencing life. The greatest training for a minister is 'experience'. The emphasis upon personal experience is also the apologetic for the message of the preacher. Christianity is seen to be true because of the positive experience which has come with the message of Jesus. Christ is greater than Buddha because the world became a better place as a result of Jesus Christ. Prichard's theological writing is deeply speculative, with an emphasis upon subjective experience over objective truth.

The Minister, the Method and the Message (New York: Charles Scribner, 1932).
(With Stanley Brown Serman), *What Did Jesus Think?* (New York: Macmillan, 1935).

Stowe's Clerical Directory of the American Church, 1929–30.

Ramsey, Arthur Michael (1904–88), the 100th Archbishop of Canterbury, was a leading figure in the Church of England and in the worldwide Anglican Communion in the twentieth century. As Archbishop of Canterbury and, therefore, *primus inter pares* of Anglican bishops, he was an important ecclesiastical figure: prominent in ecumenical relations with Roman Catholics, the Orthodox, and the churches of the Reformation; a spokesman for the Anglican Church on social and justice issues in Africa and elsewhere; and a constant traveller to the other national churches of the Anglican Communion, of which he was the spiritual head.

He also made the time, because it was important to him, to be a theologian of depth and substance. He was not a theologian of great originality; he broke no new ground; and he wrote only two major theological books: *The Gospel and the Catholic Church* (1936, 1956, 1990), and *From Gore to Temple: The Development of Anglican Theology between Lux Mundi and the Second World War 1889–1939* (1959, published in the USA as *An Era in Anglican Theology*, 1960). Some would consider his study, *The Glory of God and the Transfiguration of Christ* (1949) also to be a major work in biblical theology. In his ministry he exemplified the ancient theological calling of a bishop, namely, to be a teacher of the Christian faith and pastor of the people of God. It is this unity of theology and pastoral care which marks his importance as an Anglican theologian.

Michael Ramsey was born in 1904 in Cambridge. His father was a Congregationalist and mathematician; his mother was Church of England and was active in liberal political causes. He attended Cambridge, originally to read law, but, after his conversion to Anglicanism (in its Anglo-Catholic form) he switched to theology. At Cambridge he was involved in politics and supported the Liberal Party. He was also impressed by William Temple, then Bishop of Manchester, and by Sir Edwyn Hoskins, the New Testament scholar. Both were to be a major influence upon the development of his own thinking, although he was not uncritical of either. He was ordained in the Church of England, served in several parishes, and then was called to teach at Lincoln, where he wrote his first and, many believe, most important book, *The Gospel and the Catholic Church*. Subsequently, his life followed the usual course for an emerging leader of the Church of England: Canon and Professor of Divinity at Durham, Regius Professor of Divinity at Cambridge, Bishop of Durham, Archbishop of York (during which time he delivered the Hale Lectures in the United States which were to become his second major book, *From Gore to Temple*), and finally, in 1961, Archbishop of Canterbury. He retired from Canterbury in 1974 and continued his pastoral and theological ministry until his death in 1988. During all of his involvement with ecclesiastical affairs he wrote extensively, publishing collections of essays and addresses as well as small books on Christian spirituality and theological themes. His last book, *Be Still and Know* (1982) is regarded as a classic study of prayer.

As has been said, Michael Ramsey was not a highly original theologian. Even when dealing with current theological issues and crises (such as the controversy over J. A. T. Robinson's *Honest to God*, a small book which attempted to shake many religious foundations), he looked to the older sources of Holy Scripture, the Fathers, and Anglican Divines of the past for inspiration and guidance. Central to all his work as a theologian was the incarnation as it had been witnessed to in the Gospel of John and as it was developed doctrinally in the early councils. In fact, he regarded the doctrine of the incarnation as a guiding theological principle in Anglicanism.

In an early essay, written while he was at Durham, Ramsey set out the principle which was to continue to find expression in his later writings. In discussing Richard Hooker, he wrote:

> The method, use, and direction characteristic of Anglican divinity first came into clear light in the writings of Hooker. . . . [His theology] dealt with the whole man, both by its reverence for reason and conscience and by its refusal to draw a circle around the inward personal element in religion and to separate it from the world of external things. It was congruous with all this that the Incarnation, with the doctrine of the Two Natures, was central, and that the Church and the Sacraments were closely linked with the Incarnation. The claim of this theology to be 'catholic' rested not only upon its affinity with antiquity but upon the true 'wholeness' of its authorities and of its treatment of man and his need. It offered him not only justification in his inward self but the sanctification of his whole being through sharing in the divine life. . . . ('What is Anglican Theology?', *Theology*, January 1945)

187

The 'catholic life' expressed in Anglicanism was thus to extend from belief in the incarnation into the sacramental life of the Church: the 'wholeness' of past and present, and the 'wholeness' of the life of Christian people in the world and in their inward life, all of which was made possible through their sharing in the life of God in Christ – what he was to call in many of his later writings (for example, *The Glory of God and the Transfiguration of Christ*) 'Glory': the Glory of God and the Glory of our transformed and transfigured humanity. From this basic theological theme derived Ramsey's spirituality as well as his work for social justice and his personal apostolate for the unity of the Christian Church.

That personal apostolate was first expressed in his early and most influential book, *The Gospel and the Catholic Church*. There Ramsey linked the gospel of redemption in the cross to the spiritual life of the Church and its institutional structures as they had developed in history. Here also, his theme was 'wholeness': that institutional structures, especially the ministry of the episcopate, cannot be separated from the work of God in Christ and that to be 'catholic' was not to adhere to a particular piety or polity, but to see how the Church expresses the gospel of redemption in its on-going life of belief, worship and ministry.

While he there argued finally for a view of the episcopate as essential to the life of the Church – a view which has not received universal agreement in ecumenical conversations – he was later able, in the conversations between the Church of England and the Methodists, to recognize the necessity of adaptation and development in the pursuit of unity. That those conversations failed, he regarded as one of the great failures of his time as Archbishop of Canterbury. His personal witness for unity and wholeness did, however, find expression in his many meetings with Roman Catholics (especially that with Pope Paul VI in 1966, which led to the establishment of the Anglican–Roman Catholic International Commission) and with the leaders of the Orthodox churches. He especially impressed the Orthodox because of his deep sympathy for patristic spirituality. He also participated in the World Council of Churches, more as a theologian, however, than as an administrator. He was not always comfortable with the political conflicts of ecumenical meetings and what seemed to him to be a lack of theological depth.

Ramsey's other significant theological writing was the lectures he gave at Seabury-Western Seminary in Evanston, Illinois – the Hale Lectures – on the development of Anglican theology in Britain, from Bishop Gore and the collection of essays *Lux Mundi* to Archbishop William Temple. In those lectures he elaborated upon the centrality of the doctrine of the incarnation for the development of Liberal Catholicism – Bishop Gore's name for the theological point of view which characterized *Lux Mundi* – but at the same time he recognized the limitations of a theology which, he believed, did not pay sufficient attention to the sinfulness and chaos of a fallen world. He was especially critical of his early mentor, William Temple, for his 'Hegelianism' (although it must be said that Ramsey himself had little understanding or knowledge of the actual philosophy of Hegel): his tendency to 'make sense' of sin by considering it a part of the divine plan. He regarded Temple's theology as neglecting 'the sense of the total dependence of creation upon a Creator perfect in Himself, the sense of sin as an unspeakable distortion of the divine plan, such as cannot be contemplated as capable of rationality or synthesis' (*From Gore to Temple*). Ramsey himself never lost a sense of the depth of human sin, even while proclaiming Christ's victory of redemption in the incarnation.

That victory he saw as expressed in the spiritual life, namely, our calling to union with God in Christ through the grace of the sacramental life and prayer. In his last book, *Be Still and Know*, he gave expression to his theological and pastoral work:

> *Be still and know.* The scene on the mount [of transfiguration] speaks to us today, but we are not allowed to linger there. We are bidden to journey on to Calvary and there to learn of the darkness and the desolation which are the cost of the glory. But from Calvary and Easter there comes a Christian hope of immense range: the hope of the transformation not only of mankind but of the cosmos too. In Eastern Christianity especially there has been the continuing belief that Easter is the beginning of a transformed cosmos. There is indeed a glimpse of this hope in St Paul's letter to the Romans, a hope that 'the creation itself will be set free from its bondage to decay and obtain the glorious liberty of the children of God'. The bringing of mankind to glory will be the prelude to the beginning of all creation. Is this hope mere fantasy? At its root there is the belief in the divine sovereignty of sacrificial love, a sovereignty made credible only by transfigured lives.

Michael Ramsey's importance for the future of Anglican theology and of Anglicanism lies in his vision of 'wholeness': the unity of theology and prayer and of human redemption in the cross and our transfiguration in the resurrection. The human and the divine, the temporal and the eternal hold together in the incarnation of God in Christ.

A complete list of Michael Ramsey's published writings can be found in Owen Chadwick, *Michael Ramsey: A Life* (Oxford: Clarendon Press, 1990), 409ff. This was the first complete biography of Bishop Ramsey, and it contains much information about him which derives from a long personal friendship. Professor Chadwick locates Ramsey's theological work in the context of his public ministry, and it is, therefore, especially helpful in showing the connection between Ramsey the theologian and pastor and Ramsey the statesman and church official. There have been two collections of essays about Ramsey's contributions to theology: Christopher Martin (ed.), *Great Christian Centuries to Come: Essays in Honour of A. M. Ramsey* (London and Oxford: Mowbray, 1978); and Robin Gill and Lorna Kendall (eds.), *Michael Ramsey as Theologian* (London: Darton, Longman and Todd, 1995).

After his retirement from Canterbury, Michael Ramsey spent much time at Nashotah House, a theological seminary of the American Episcopal Church in Nashotah, Wisconsin. A list of his published writings was included in the journal *Nashotah Review* 16 (3) (Autumn 1976): 'Essays in Honor of Michael Ramsey'.

In addition to the principal books cited above, several other of Ramsey's shorter writings ought to be mentioned:

F. D. Maurice and the Conflicts of Modern Theology (1951). Lectures on the nineteenth-century theologian, who was especially influential in the development of Anglican incarnational theology.

Durham Essays and Addresses (1956). Writings from his time as Bishop of Durham, they demonstrate Ramsey's pastoral interests.

Introducing the Christian Faith (1961). Lectures to university students.

Image Old and New (1963). His response to *Honest to God*.

Canterbury Essays and Addresses (1964). Again, a collection of writings and sermons given on various occasions.

God, Christ and the World: A Study in Contemporary Theology (1969). Owen Chadwick describes this as 'a weighty' book. It indicates the development of Ramsey's thinking from an older, more biblical and patristic perspective to a more contemporary one.

The Christian Priest Today (1972; rev. 1985).

Canterbury Pilgrim (1974). More essays and addresses from his years as Archbishop of Canterbury. It is especially interesting in showing how Ramsey responded to the crises of the 1960s. (JG)

Ridley, Nicholas (*c.* 1502–55), came of a gentry family in South Tyndale, Northumberland. In 1518 he was admitted as a student at Cambridge, where he distinguished himself as a classical scholar and disputant.

In 1524 he was ordained and elected a Fellow of Pembroke Hall. It was in these years that Lutheran ideas were circulating in the university. We have no record of Ridley's attitude at the time, but it does seem probable that he became acquainted with Cranmer, some twelve or more years his senior and a Fellow of Jesus College.

Between 1527 and 1530 Ridley studied at the Sorbonne and for a short time at Louvain. He could hardly have avoided the ferment of ideas stirred up by Erasmus and Luther, and on his return to Pembroke Hall, he tells us, he learnt by heart the New Testament Epistles in Erasmus's Greek.

In 1537 he became chaplain to Archbishop Cranmer, an indication of his growing sympathy to Protestant views. The following year he became vicar of Herne. In his study there he later states that he came to an understanding of the presence of Christ in the sacrament as spiritual rather than corporal. 'This Bertram (Ratramnus) was the first that pulled me by the ear, and that first brought me from the common error of the Romish church, and caused me to search more diligently and exactly both the Scriptures and the old ecclesiastical fathers in this matter.'

A Catholic reaction in the latter years of the reign of Henry VIII made life dangerous for Cranmer and his associates. Nevertheless Ridley's career gathered momentum. He had taken his degree as D.D. at Cambridge in 1540 and been elected Master of Pembroke Hall, but his need to support Cranmer kept him away from the university. He became one of the royal chaplains and was appointed to prebends at Canterbury and Westminster Cathedrals. Yet we know little of his movements in those years. He kept his views to himself.

The accession of Edward VI brought great changes, but not immediately, as the Reformers were wary of attacking the Mass directly. Ridley, who was consecrated Bishop of Rochester in September 1547 preached on the issue at Paul's Cross. He attacked those who mocked the sacrament but gave no indication of his own views. But that was soon to change.

He was now an active member of the House of Lords, a confidant of the Archbishop, and caught up in the affairs of church and state. In December 1548 the House of Lords held a disputation on the question of transubstantiation at which Ridley opposed the idea of a corporal presence. The following year he presided at a further disputation at Cambridge and in his decision publicly condemned the doctrine of transubstantiation.

In April 1550 Ridley was installed as Bishop of London. He moved decisively, issuing injunctions to remove any lingering traces of the old religion by suppressing popish ceremonies and gestures and replacing the stone altars by wooden tables. It was a deliberate and public expression of his theological convictions. 'If we come to feed upon him, spiritually to eat his body, and spiritually to drink his blood (which is the true use of the Lord's Supper), then no man can deny but the form of a table is more meet for the Lord's board than the form of an altar.'

At the same time he acted to ensure that Reformed doctrine was taught by appointing able preachers as his chaplains. Ridley himself preached frequently and on many great state occasions, but all that has survived are reports of his sermons. Like Latimer and others he spoke out against the social evils of the time, attributing the 'sweating sickness' that plagued London to divine punishment for covetousness, and condemning the rapacity of the nobility. Such analyses were neither novel nor revolutionary, but they do reflect the concern that Ridley and others felt that the Reformed theology had brought about a new beginning in England which must be reflected in the life of the people.

On 14 July 1553 Ridley preached at Paul's Cross against Mary's claim to the throne. Not surprisingly, a week later he was arrested and for more than two years was to be held in prison. But the charge levelled against him was not treason but heresy, and foremost among the reasons for his protracted imprisonment was the hope that, faced with the choice of 'turn or burn', he would make an abject recantation and so discredit the whole Protestant heresy.

It is to this period that we owe almost all of Ridley's writings. From the beginning he knew there could be only one ending, and he wrote to provide instruction and encouragement for those who would survive him. It was an act of faith and courage matched only by his fearsome death at the stake on 16 October 1555.

Bishop and theologian

'That famous and notable member of the church of God, Nicholas Ridley, doctor of divinity, being of great learning, integrity of life and sincerity of doctrine': so ran a Bill passed in the Elizabethan Parliament posthumously reinstating Ridley in 1559.

Ridley was a formidable exemplum of Reformed Anglicanism with its appeal to the authoritative teaching of Scripture supported by the testimony of the early church fathers and the use of careful reasoning.

Where Scripture was not explicit, he believed that the Church should order its affairs in accordance with tradition and reason. In July 1550 Hooper, a prominent London preacher, was nominated to a bishopric but refused to wear vestments. In the months that followed Ridley engaged in an acrimonious debate, and it was not until Hooper capitulated that he was consecrated. It presaged the Puritan arguments in the Elizabethan church. Authoritarian by nature, Ridley held that although the wearing of vestments was biblically a thing indifferent, nevertheless the laws of the realm must be obeyed.

Hooper's model for a Reformed church was Zurich. In London he had the support of the Strangers' Churches, the continental Protestant refugees who with Cranmer's support sought to maintain their Reformed pattern of worship. Ridley saw in this a threat to his own plans to establish uniformity of worship. It was a clash which uncovered basic questions about the role of the Church in ordering its life and worship. Ridley's stance is significant as it became the model of Reformed Anglicanism.

It was confirmed in the preface 'Of Ceremonies' in the second Prayer Book and reiterated in the writings of Richard Hooker.

Theological progress and clarification are often the result of cooperative endeavours. No one doubts that much of Ridley's most significant work was done in this way, but we are quite unable to document it. If Cranmer took the initiative in the Reformed agenda of Edward VI's reign, Ridley was his closest ally, contributing to the process of Prayer Book revision, the formulation of the Forty-two Articles and the unfinished work on canon law. However, at a first reading the bulk of Ridley's theological writing appears to be narrowly concerned with a refutation of transubstantiation and the Mass as a propitiatory sacrifice. Yet neither party had any uncertainty that on these questions hung all the great theological issues for the church of the day.

In holding to the doctrine of a spiritual not a carnal presence, how much did Ridley, and consequently Cranmer, owe to Ratramnus the ninth-century monk who wrote a treatise on the eucharist, *De Corpore et Sanguine Domini*? The question should be treated with some caution. Ridley saw himself as Cranmer's pupil, not his teacher. To both, the biblical data was basic, and in interpreting it they undertook a wide and diligent study of the early church fathers. As Ridley put it, 'I prefer the antiquity of the primitive church before the novelty of the Romish church.'

As a pastor Ridley was also concerned to convey his understanding of the Lord's Supper in simple and concise terms for the general reader. In 1553 he wrote twice to his fellow prisoner, Latimer, for comments. Smuggled to Europe, it was later published.

In March 1554 a theological disputation on the doctrine of the Mass was held at Oxford. In reality it was a heresy trial, and Ridley, Cranmer and Latimer were arraigned before theologians from both universities. Afterwards Ridley was anxious that his views should not be misrepresented and wrote a lengthy report. His concluding affirmation ran,

> But we behold with the eyes of faith him present after grace, and spiritually set upon the table; and we worship him which sitteth above, and is worshipped of the angels. For Christ is always assistant to his mysteries, as the said Augustine saith. And the Divine Majesty, as saith Cyprian, doth never absent itself from the divine mysteries; but this assistance and presence of Christ, as in baptism it is wholly spiritual, and by grace, and not by any corporal substance of the flesh, even so it is here in the Lord's supper, being rightly and according to the word of God duly ministered.

A further year in prison concluded with a trial in the court of the papal legate presided over by three bishops. The nub of his defence as always was that Christ's body was really present, 'spiritually by grace and efficacy for so every worthy receiver receiveth the very true body of Christ'. It was a theological conviction he was willing to die for.

A brief declaracion of the Lordes supper (Emden: E. van der Erve, 1555).

Certein godly, learned, and comfortable conferences, betwene N. Rydley and H. Latimer (Emden: E. van der Erve, 1556).

Certë godly, . . . Wherunto is added, A treatise agaynst transubstantiation (Strassburg; heirs of W. Rihel, 1556).

John Foxe (ed.), *A frendly farwel, which master doctor Ridley, did write unto all his true lovers and frends in God, a little before that he suffred. Newly setforth* (London: J. Day, 1559).

Miles Coverdale (ed.), *Certain most godly, fruitful, and comfortable letters of such true saints and holy martyrs as in the late bloodye persecution gave their lives* (London: J. Day 1564).

A pituous lamentation of the miserable estate of the church of Christ in Englande, in the time of the late revolt from the gospel. Never before imprynted, Whereunto are also annexed letters of J. Careles (London: W. Powell, 1566).

Susan Brigden, 1989. *London and the Reformation* (Oxford: Clarendon Press).

Peter Brooks, 1965. *Thomas Cranmer's Doctrine of the Eucharist* (London: Macmillan).

Henry Christmas (ed.), 1841. *The Works of Nicholas Ridley* (Cambridge: Parker Society).

A. G. Dickens, 1989. *The English Reformation*, 2nd edn (London: Batsford).

Basil Hall, 1993. 'Cranmer, the Eucharist and the Foreign Divines in the Reign of Edward VI', in Paul Ayris and David Selwyn (eds.), *Thomas Cranmer: Churchman and Scholar* (Woodbridge: Boydell Press).

E. W. Hunt, 1992. *The Life and Times of John Hooper, c. 1500–1555* (Lewiston, Queenston, Lampeter: Edward Mellen Press).

David Loades, 1970. *The Oxford Martyrs* (London: Batsford).

Jasper Ridley, 1957. *Nicholas Ridley* (London: Longmans, Green and Co.). (MB)

Robinson, Donald William Bradley (1922–), Australian churchman and New Testament scholar; Vice-Principal of Moore College, Sydney, 1959–75; Archbishop of Sydney 1982–93.

Donald Robinson was born on 9 November 1922, the son of a clergyman in the diocese of Sydney. His education was interrupted by the Second World War, but in 1946 he was able to complete his classical studies at the University of Sydney (B.A.). A year later he travelled to England to study theology at Queen's College, Cambridge. Here he was profoundly influenced by the careful exegetical method of C. F. D. Moule and the ideas of C. H. Dodd. After successfully completing the Theological Tripos, including a special study of the doctrine of the Church, he returned home and was ordained by the Archbishop of Sydney in 1950. He served his first curacy at St Matthew's, Manly, and then, in 1952, he was appointed as Curate of St Phillip's, Sydney, and simultaneously Lecturer in Old Testament at Moore College. Two years later he was appointed Senior Lecturer at the college, concentrating now on the New Testament. It was in this early period that a lecture series on the Acts of the Apostles developed into a course on biblical theology which remains a distinctive feature of theological education at Moore College.

In 1959 Donald Robinson was appointed Vice-Principal of Moore College, under the new Principal D. B. Knox. It was a partnership which has had an incalculable impact on Anglican Evangelicalism in Sydney and beyond. His own series of articles, on a wide range of New Testament topics, often anticipated later developments in the discipline. His observation of the importance of the Jew–gentile issue for a correct understanding of the New Testament found early expression in his Inter-Varsity Fellowship lecture of 1961. He highlighted the metaphorical nature of much baptismal language in the New Testament in a series of articles and booklets beginning in 1958. He also made an early contribution to the debate over the nature of the genitive in the expression 'the faith of Jesus' in 1970.

Amongst his many contributions during his time at Moore College, two are particularly important. The first of these is his emphasis on a wholistic approach to the Bible which takes seriously both the distinctive emphases of each passage and its place within the overall movement from the Garden of Eden to the New Jerusalem. He expounded each text with a confidence that it was part of a whole and that the whole itself had an intelligible meaning. At first it seemed clear to him that the covenant of God – originally given to Abraham; then developed as it was reaffirmed to Israel at Sinai, to David in Jerusalem, and in the prophets; and finally fulfilled in Christ – provided a basic framework for understanding the Bible's message. However, he soon discovered that the idea of 'promise' was more foundational than that of 'covenant', the latter simply being a mechanism for conveying the former. The whole of the Bible is held together by the promise of God to gather his people around himself. In this way he insisted that the Old Testament be viewed on a trajectory towards the New, and that the New Testament must be understood against the background of the Old. Both testify ultimately to Christ, in whom the promise of God is fulfilled.

Connected to this is his other important, and in some quarters controversial, contribution: his exposition of the New Testament teaching on the Church. Its origins can be traced to his special study of the doctrine of the Church at Cambridge in 1949; however, the ecumenical debate of the late 1950s and 1960s provided an additional stimulus. His study of the meaning of the word *ekklēsia* in the New Testament led him to insist that 'church' is properly a description of the gathering of believers around Christ, for which the assembly of Israel on Sinai had been the prototype. Such an understanding gave enormous dignity to the local congregation and at the same time undermined the suggestion that denominational union would provide an expression of 'the ecumenical Church'. He did not dismiss all possibility of involvement with those outside the local gathering, nor did he deny the fundamental Christian obligation of love; however, he insisted that the word 'church' is never applied in the New Testament to some notion of the sum total of all Christians or Christian bodies.

Donald Robinson produced an impressive series of lectures, short articles and textual notes whilst teaching at Moore College. However, this work was increasingly restricted by his heavy involvement in the wider affairs of the diocese of Sydney. In 1973 he was appointed a bishop, with specific responsibility for the fastest-growing area of the diocese. He played a critical role in liturgical revision in Australia, being largely responsible for the production of An Australian Prayer Book in 1978. His involvement ensured that this new book, unlike so many attempts at revision around the world, would continue to give expression to the theological concerns which underlay Cranmer's work in the Book of Common Prayer. This achievement, built upon such a significant theological contribution through his teaching at Moore College, led to the award of an honorary doctorate in theology in 1979. On 1 April 1982 he was elected Archbishop of Sydney, a post he held until his retirement early in 1993.

Amongst the written work of Donald Robinson, the following deserve mention: *Jew and Greek: Unity and Division in the Early Church* (Inter-Varsity Fellowship Lecture, 1961); 'Who were "the saints"?', *Reformed Theological Review* 22 (1) (1963); 45–53; *The Church of God: Its Form and Unity* (1965); 'The Distinction between Jewish and Gentile Believers in Galatians', *Australian Biblical Review* 13 (1965); 29–48; 'Towards a Definition of Baptism', *Reformed Theological Review* 34 (1) (1975); 1–15; *Faith's Framework: The Structure of New Testament Theology* (1985). In 1992 a collection of essays was published in his honour: D. G. Peterson and J. Pryor (eds.), *In the Fullness of Time*. (MT)

Romaine, William (1714–95), preacher and theologian. Educated at Christ Church College, Oxford, he received his M.A. in 1737. His earliest published works show him to be solidly orthodox, and he made a solid contribution to the critical study of Scripture by editing a new edition of the Hebrew concordance by Marius de Calasio in 1748. For a short while he was attracted through the Evangelical revival to Wesley's view of the atonement, but by 1755 he was firmly entrenched in the Calvinist views of Whitefield. He remained a high Calvinist until his death and was one of this school's champions. In his letter to his sister 'Dialogue concerning Justification' (*Works*, VIII, 125), he holds Wesley's views of free will and the righteousness of Christ as being a shrewd adaptation of the Roman theory of justification by works. He was appointed to several lectureships in London parishes but his committed Calvinism and popularity with the poor brought persecution. He was refused the pulpit of St Mary's in Oxford after criticizing the university for teaching justification by moral rectitude not by faith. His difficulties in London continued until he was confirmed in the living of St Anne's, Blackfriars, which he held by himself until John Newton came in 1780. His preaching attracted crowds, and a gallery had to be erected to hold them. Reported to have prayed for everyone in his parish church every day, he started at the beginning of his ministry praying for twenty people and ended up praying for over five hundred people daily. Apart from his extreme views on the doctrine of predestination, his three treatises on the spiritual life convey his conception of theology well: *The Life of Faith* (1763); *The Walk of Faith* (1771); and *The Triumph of Faith* (1795).

Oxford Dictionary of the Christian Church, 1194.
H. L. Bennett, 'Romaine, William', in *Dictionary of National Biography*, XLIX (1897), 175–7.
W. B. Cadogan, *Works and Life* (London: James Clarke).
J. C. Ryle, 1869. *The Christian Leaders of the Last Century* (London: James Clarke) 149–79.

Ryle, John Charles (1816–1900), Bishop of Liverpool and Evangelical theologian. Educated at Christ Church, Oxford, where he held several prestigious posts, he graduated M.A. (1871), and eventually D.D. (1880). In 1842 he was ordained to the priesthood, which he pursued after his father's bankruptcy forced him to abandon his earlier plans to stand for Parliament. Ryle was strongly influenced by William Wilberforce and his book *A Practical View of the Prevailing Religious System of Professed Christians* (1797). Subsequently he went on to serve three parishes, in Hampshire, Winchester and Suffolk, the last being at Helmingham, where he stayed until 1861. A few years later he was made a rural dean of Hoxne (1869), honorary canon of Norwich (1872), select preacher for Cambridge (1873–4), select preacher for Oxford (1874–6, 1879–80), and dean of Salisbury in 1880. Immediately he was advanced to the see of Liverpool, which had just been created, and he served as bishop there until his death. Ryle strongly supported the various Evangelical associations which fought against Old Testament higher critical views. The strong support he gave to the Evangelical party within the Church is well known, and his writings have been popular enough to be translated into foreign languages. Perhaps his most famous work is his book on *Holiness* (1879), which is an Evangelical devotional classic. Other important works include: on doctrine *Old Paths* (1877) and *Knots Untied* (1874); on past Evangelical leaders *Christian Leaders of the Last Century* (1868); and on reformers and puritans (e.g., Hugh Latimer, Richard Baxter and George Whitfield) *Light from Old Times* (1890). *What do we owe the Reformation?* (1877) and *Principles for Churchmen* (1884) were also well received, as they were Ryle's attempt to preserve the Protestant theology and character of the Anglican Church at the height of the Ritualist movement.

Oxford Dictionary of the Christian Church, 1215.
M. L. Loane, 1953. *John Charles Ryle 1816–1900* (London: James Clarke).
J. M. Rigg in *Dictionary of National Biography, Suppl.,* III (1901), 334f., s.v.
P. Toon and M. Smout, 1976. *J. C. Ryle, Evangelical Bishop* (Cambridge: J. Clarke).

Simeon, Charles (1759–1836). Born at Reading on 14 September 1759, Charles was a foundation scholar at Eton. In 1779 he went up to King's College, Cambridge, as a scholar. The Provost of King's sent him a customary note informing him that he would be expected to attend Holy Communion at the College. Though Simeon was a gay, conceited, affluent and somewhat foppish young man, he had a very sensitive side and a strong sense of duty. Convinced that he was not worthy to receive communion, he commenced a personal spiritual quest. After much reading and prayer, he came, three months later, to the realization that all his guilt had been borne by Christ and that what he had to do was to trust in Christ alone. His life was transformed, although, as he would freely admit, his character changed only gradually. He was ordained in 1782, while still an undergraduate. After a brief, informal curacy, he was appointed (through the influence of his father) as vicar of Holy Trinity, Cambridge, in the same year. There he remained until his death in 1836. He had to overcome considerable opposition: the churchwardens encouraged the pew-holders to lock their pews; they threw out extra seats he brought into the church; they bolted the church doors when he proposed to hold an evening service aimed particularly at the poor of the parish; and, in the university, he was, in his own words 'an object of much contempt and derision'. But he came to be accepted and even revered in Cambridge and beyond.

Simeon was a preacher, pastor, strategist and an immensely practical and innovative leader. Though not an academic, he retained a lifelong contact with the often not very academic university world of his times. He was a Fellow of King's College, where he lived for the whole of his life at Cambridge. He held many of its offices, including that of Vice-

Provost. He was the select preacher at the university on ten occasions. His theological influence came primarily through his preaching ministry and through his teaching of generations of undergraduates. A reflection of this is the fact that his chief writing legacy is the twenty-one volumes of 2,536 sermon outlines (*Horae Homileticae*) covering the whole Bible, which were published between 1796 and 1832. These reflect his clarity of mind and his deep spirituality.

First and foremost he was a leader of the Evangelical Revival within the Church of England. Though his conversion was the result of a very personal search, he fairly quickly came under the influence of Evangelical leaders such as Henry Venn and his son John, John Thornton and John Newton. He was a close friend and almost contemporary of that other great Evangelical leader of the period, William Wilberforce. His emphases were those of contemporary Evangelical Anglicanism: justification by faith in the saving work of Christ on the cross was the heart of the Christian life and needed, in his words, 'to be experienced in your own soul'; the Bible was central, and hence the importance of carefully listening to what it said and accurately expounding it and in a way that appealed to both mind and heart; preaching was a key to effective ministry, always with the aim of allowing the Holy Spirit, as he put it, to 'humble the sinner, exalt the Saviour and promote holiness'; the Prayer Book was second only to the Bible, and liturgy was one of God's greatest gifts to the Church; pastoral care as much for the body as for the soul was a non-negotiable part of the gospel and hence his energy in meeting the needs of the poor in his parish through special service, through an elaborate system of parish visiting by the laity which he devised, through appropriate relief and through education. In this last respect, however, it has to be said that, though he acted locally, he never acquired the passionate and global social conscience of his many Evangelical friends more intimately connected with the Clapham Sect.

What raises Simeon above a growing number of clergy with similar emphases was not only his ability and spirituality but the fact that he used his privileged position at Cambridge to the full; that he had a strategic vision that went far beyond Cambridge and that he very deliberately steered a moderate course through the various controversies which dogged Evangelicalism through most of his life.

Simeon's influence was most obvious on students. Through his preaching and through his 'conversation party' in his rooms when he answered their questions, he helped to form the Christian outlook of thousands of undergraduates. Their effect in every corner of Britain and its empire remains incalculable, but undoubtedly they did much to form and shape the seriousness with which Victorians conducted their religious and moral lives. But his greatest impact was on ordinands. Specialist ordination training for undergraduates was a development yet to come. Simeon, as early as 1792, set up 'sermon classes', where those who contemplated ordination were taught the kernel of their faith and how it should be preached. His classes were extremely practical, concentrating on sermon construction and delivery and on the leading of worship. His following grew slowly, but it became immense. He also made provision for wives of ordinands, inviting them to ordinands' conferences where they 'compared their own schemes for local usefulness' while their husbands discussed 'biblical and parochial subjects'. However it may seem today, in the context of his time this was a far-sighted step. His followers were often known as 'Simeonites' or 'Sims'. Simeon emphasized a disciplined, sober and hard-working lifestyle and was extremely critical of the sort of spiritual enthusiasm which belittled academic study.

His influence, however, stretched far beyond the student world of Cambridge. It was of course felt in the formation of Evangelical Anglicanism. He was an active member of the Eclectic Society founded in 1783 by John Newton. He was a prolific correspondent and had a strong commitment to missionary outreach. He encouraged many of his best students to go to India, mainly as chaplains because, until 1813, there were severe restrictions on missionaries. He was a founding member of the Church Missionary Society (1799). He had a particular concern for the conversion of Jews.

Simeon's leadership was crucial in helping Evangelicalism to consolidate its position within Anglicanism, moving from rebellious irritation to enthusiastic, if always critical, support and involvement. He genuinely loved the Church of England – its structures, its emphasis on the sacraments and its liturgy. Though this new Evangelicalism was willing to work with Nonconformists for certain limited objectives, it was also prepared (as many of the earlier Evangelicals had not been) to abide by Anglican conventions and discipline, for example about preaching outside of parish boundaries, even when these seemed irksome. He did, however, want to change the Church of England, though from the inside, and the setting-up of what became known as Simeon's Trust with the object of purchasing patronage is the best example of this. He looked in particular for what he called 'spheres of influence', and by his death there were some forty livings, including Bath Abbey. Simeon was a man of breadth, and the Trust was not conceived with narrowly party objectives; indeed the word 'Evangelical' is not mentioned in his charge to the Trust – rather it was couched in wide-ranging, spiritual terms, the primary stipulation being that the person presented should be 'a truly pious and devoted man, a man of God in deed and in truth'. The Trust quickly grew to a major body with, currently, involvement in 150 livings.

He was above all a man of moderation. He said of himself that he was 'no friend of systematizers in Theology' and he carefully eschewed an Arminian or a Calvinist label. He was content to see truth in apparent polarities if there were scriptural grounds for both. And, though Scripture was always his rock, he was not a literalist and readily acknowledged that it contained 'inexactness in reference to philosophical and scientific matters'. He had little time for the new harder, more unbending, Calvinistic, aggressive and controversial tone which emerged among Evangelicals such as Alexander Haldane and the *Record* in the late 1820s. He opposed them on many issues, including their bitter and successful campaign to overturn the Bible Society's policy of printing some editions of the Bible with the Apocrypha in order to ensure its distribution in Roman Catholic countries. He was very disturbed by the prophetic, millennialist, charismatic emphases of Edward Irvine, Henry Drummond and others. He, again against the majority of his fellow Evangelicals, supported Catholic Emancipation.

His achievements in bringing an Evangelical heart-religion to Cambridge, in ensuring that Evangelical Anglicanism came to terms with the reality of the Church of England, in re-establishing the place of preaching, in planning strategically for evangelism in England and beyond, in commending his faith attractively through his obvious pastoral concern and evident spirituality, were immense.

Evangelical Anglicanism has nearly always been an 'uneasy coalition'. If, for a short period, under the leadership of Charles Simeon, John Venn and William Wilberforce, a softer, more accommodating, less abrasive brand was in the ascendancy, it was not to be for long, and well before his death, warring, divisive forces were again in evidence. In particular an intolerant and frenetic sort of Evangelicalism grew in strength and influence while, perhaps partly in reaction, some of its brightest leadership hopes were beginning their journey through the Oxford Movement towards Anglo- or Roman Catholicism. And yet Simeon's influence lived on, inspiring those who wanted to be faithful to Scripture and committed to preaching the whole counsel of God, while accepting that much of the Church was not as Evangelical as they would wish it to be and that this reality was often best dealt with through a measure of accommodation rather than through endless unbending confrontation and criticism. Probably no Evangelical leader until, in recent years, John Stott, has acquired the respect and stature which he achieved.

Horae Homileticae, 21 vols. (London: Richard Watts, 1832).

Wesley D. Balda, 1981. '"Spheres of Influence": Simeon's Trust and Its Implications for

Evangelical Patronage' (University of Cambridge Ph.D.).

Abner William Brown, 1863. *Recollections of the Conversation Parties of the Rev. Charles Simeon, M.A.* (London).

W. Carus, 1847. *Memoirs of the Life of the Rev. Charles Simeon, M.A.* (London: Hatchard and Son).

Hugh Evan Hopkins, 1977. *Charles Simeon of Cambridge* (London: Hodder and Stoughton).

H. C. G. Moule, [1892] 1948. *Charles Simeon* (London: InterVarsity Press).

Charles Smyth, 1940. *Simeon and Church Order: A Study of the Origins of the Evangelical Revival in Cambridge in the Eighteenth Century* (Cambridge: Cambridge University Press).

James Stephen, 1860. *Essays on Ecclesiastical Biography* 4th edn (London: Longman).

Max Warren, n.d. *Simeon: An Essay on the Revd Charles Simeon, M.A., 1759–1836, Fellow of King's College and Vicar of Holy Trinity Church, Cambridge* (London: Church Book Room Press). (PW)

Shepherd, Massey Hamilton (1913–), priest, liturgical scholar, church historian. Born in Wilmington, North Carolina, he was educated at the University of South Carolina (B.A., 1932; M.A., 1933), the University of Chicago (Ph.D., 1937), and Berkeley Divinity School (B.D., 1941; S.T.D., 1951). He was ordained deacon in 1941, and priest later the same year. A lecturer at the University of Chicago (1937–40), he held other prestigious posts including: Professor of Church History, Episcopal Theological School, Massachusetts (1940–54), and Professor of Liturgies, Church Divinity School of the Pacific, California (1954–81). A theologian from the Catholic tradition, Shepherd is one of the foremost American liturgical scholars of the twentieth century. In its time, Shepherd's *The Oxford American Prayer Book Commentary* (1950) was considered the definitive study on the history and theology of the 1928 American Book of Common Prayer and is still regarded a classic by many traditional Episcopalians. During his career, Shepherd took quite an interest in the modern liturgical movement, especially as it related to the cause of ecumenism. He was an Anglican observer at Vatican II in 1964, and took part in the Roman Catholic Liturgical Commission from 1966 to 1970, and the Anglican–Roman Catholic Joint Preparatory Commission from 1967 to 1968. On the other side of the ecumenical spectrum, he sat on the Worship Commission for the Consultation on Church Union (COCU) from 1966 to 1968. A representative sample of his works includes *The Worship of the Church* (1952), *The Eucharist and Liturgical Renewal* (editor, 1960), and 'The Origin of the Collect' in *Ecclesia Leiturgia Ministerium* (1977). A popular visiting professor in liturgics and church history at various universities and seminaries throughout his career, he was awarded the Berakah Award by the North American Academy of Liturgics in 1978 for his scholarship and contribution to the study and practice of Christian worship.

The Oxford American Prayer Book Commentary (New York: Oxford University Press, 1950).

The Episcopal Church, USA, *The Clerical Directory* (1995).

Stott, John Robert Walmsey (1921–), pastor, teacher, author and Evangelical leader. Scholar of Trinity College, Cambridge, with a double first in modern languages and theology, John Stott trained for the ordained ministry at Ridley Hall, Cambridge, to serve as assistant curate (1945–50), rector (1950–75) and rector emeritus in the central London parish of All Souls, Langham Place.

Under his leadership, All Souls was distinguished by an innovative (and much-copied) strategy of parochial evangelism; by the growing influence and diversity of ministry, ordained and lay; and by the 'double-listening' (to the Word and to the world) which has been a fulcrum to all his theological thinking. Yet it was not primarily his transforming vision of parish work which lay behind the award of a Lambeth D.D. (1983), the Templeton Foundation prize (1985), nor the assessment by Dean David Edwards (1988) that, with the exception of William Temple, Stott was 'the most influential clergyman in the Church of England during the twentieth century'.

Stott's wider ministry as an Evangelical leader began in the 1950s with student missions in many countries, effectively building fruitful evangelism upon a biblical and theological foundation. *Basic Christianity* (1958) based on these addresses has never been out of print (though revised, 1971) and is translated into over fifty languages. In 1960 Stott founded the international Evangelical Fellowship in the Anglican Communion (EFAC), with the Church of England Evangelical Council as its English member; his influence was felt in most of the larger Evangelical groupings, notably Inter-Varsity Fellowship (later Universities and Colleges Christian Fellowship), Scripture Union, the Evangelical Alliance with its TEAR Fund, etc., together with newer bodies such as Latimer House, Oxford. Through a revived 'Eclectic Society', some hundreds of younger Evangelical clergy looked to Stott as their natural leader; and he was the moving spirit of the two historic National Evangelical Anglican Congresses (Keele, 1967 and Nottingham, 1977) which brought the thinking of Evangelicals into a new engagement with the contemporary world.

Meanwhile his ministry of writing (nourished by his speaking and lecturing in many parts of the world) became increasingly influential. Never offered an English bishopric (though approached about others, and appointed in 1959 a chaplain to the Queen) and still unmarried (somewhat to his own surprise), the years following 1975 saw a further extension of his worldwide teaching ministry and his participation in movements such as Lausanne, through which, in the words of Dr Billy Graham, he 'helped shape a whole generation of evangelical thinking and action'.

His own writings reveal the theological and pastoral concerns which undergird his Evangelicalism; *Essentials* and *Christ the Controversialist* (among others) make clear his firm stand on the authority of Scripture and its divine and human authorship. *The Cross of Christ* argues convincingly for a substitutionary understanding of the atonement. *The Contemporary Christian*, as well as earlier studies, reveals his concern (constantly renewed by his ministry in the Third World and in Eastern Europe) for authentic Christian mission to embrace both Christian social action and the proclamation of the gospel. Such convictions found personal expression in his founding of the Evangelical Literature Trust (supported by his own royalties) and the bursary programme for Third World scholars run by the Langham Trust and by EFAC. Other books underline his concern for preaching; for biblical exposition (notably the Bible Speaks Today series) and for the application of biblical principles to today's world; a cause served also by the London Lectures and the London Institute for Contemporary Christianity (now Christian Impact).

Behind the mantle of acknowledged leadership there lies a disciplined devotion and a humble genuine concern for individuals, attested to by many of every race and background but perhaps notably by students and pastors. His theology should therefore be seen not primarily as an academic study (though lacking neither reading nor rigour) but as the foundation for a ministry of the Word, lovingly applied to the real worlds of individuals, churches and cultures, who recognize in turn a caring and authentic pastor in the apostolic mould, committed to self-giving in the service of Jesus Christ.

Primary sources

A very wide range of books, articles, chapters in symposia, interviews, etc., is listed in: Timothy Dudley-Smith, 1995. *John Stott: A Comprehensive Bibliography* (Leicester and Downers Grove, Ill.: InterVarsity Press).

See, especially, for example, the following by John Stott:

Basic Christianity (London: Inter-Varsity Fellowship, 1958; rev. 1971. Grand Rapids: Eerdmans/InterVarsity Press, 1958; rev. 1971).

Christ the Controversialist (London: Tyndale, 1970; Downers Grove, Ill.: InterVarsity Press, 1970; rev. 1991).

The Lausanne Covenant: An Exposition and Commentary (Charlotte: Worldwide Publications, 1975 and other imprints).

I Believe in Preaching (London: Hodder and Stoughton, 1982; Grand Rapids: Eerdmans, 1982 as *Between Two Worlds: The Art of Preaching in the Twentieth Century*).

Issues Facing Christians Today (London: Marshalls, 1984; Old Tappan: Revell, 1985 as *Involvement*, 2 vols. Revised and enlarged, London: Collins/Marshall Pickering, 1990; Old Tappan: Revell, 1990 as *Decisive Issues Facing Christians Today*).
The Cross of Christ (Leicester and Downers Grove, Ill.: InterVarsity Press, 1986).
The Contemporary Christian (Leicester and Downers Grove, Ill.: InterVarsity Press, 1992).
And see in the 'Bible Speaks Today' series (London and Downers Grove, Ill.: InterVarsity Press, 1968–), of which Stott is New Testament editor. He contributes studies of Galatians, 1968; 2 Timothy, 1973; The Sermon on the Mount, 1978; Ephesians, 1979; Acts, 1990; Thessalonians, 1991; Romans, 1994; 1 Timothy and Titus, 1996.
Also:
David L. Edwards and John Stott, 1988. *Essentials – a Liberal–Evangelical Dialogue* (London: Hodder and Stoughton, 1988; Downers Grove, Ill.: InterVarsity Press, 1989 as *Evangelical Essentials*).
Timothy Dudley-Smith (ed.), *Authentic Christianity* – a personal selection from the writings of John Stott (Leicester and Downers Grove, Ill.: InterVarsity Press, 1995).

Secondary sources
The best of these is the entry by Peter Williams in Walter A. Elwell, *Handbook of Evangelical Theologians* (Michigan: Beker Books, 1993), 338–52.
See also:
Christopher Catherwood, 1984. *Five Evangelical Leaders* (London: Hodder and Stoughton).
Timothy Dudley-Smith, 1991. 'John Stott: an Introduction', in Martyn Eden and David F. Wells (eds.), *The Gospel in the Modern World: A Tribute to John Stott* (Leicester and Downers Grove, Ill.: InterVarsity Press, 1991).
Donald English, 'John Stott – Christian Communicator Extraordinary', *Epworth Review* 20 (2) (May 1993): 31–8.
Marcus L. Loane, 1988. *These Happy Warriors* (Blackwood, S. Australia: New Creation Publications, Inc.).
A number of postgraduate dissertations have been written, but no major study. See for example:
Geoffrey Laurence Clark, 1994. 'An Examination of the Work and Writings of John Stott and an Assessment of his Influence on Evangelical Spirituality in English Church Life from 1967–1989' (School of Theology, Westminster College, Oxford, September 1994).
William Arthur Groover, 1988. 'The Theology and Methodology of John R. W. Stott as a Model for Pastoral Evangelism' (Southern Baptist Theological Seminary, December 1988).
An authorized biography is in preparation. (TDS)

Stringfellow, William (1928–85) was an attorney, an active lay member of the Episcopal Church, an ardent spokesman and, when his health permitted, an activist on political and social issues, and a theologian. In all those capacities he offended many people by stirring the waters. He also became for many other people a voice of Christian conscience. Consequently, anything that might be said of him will be controversial, both as to his writings and his actions. With his companion of many years, Anthony Towne, he gave hospitality to Fr Daniel Berrigan, SJ, who was being sought by the FBI because of his protests against the war in

Vietnam; he defended Bishop James Pike when he was charged with heresy; and he protested over and over again in his writings against 'the principalities and powers' which, he believed, governed both church and state, conservative and liberal institutions, and Christians and secularists. Karl Barth, on a visit to the United States, praised him as an important voice, one to whom Americans ought to listen, but not many other academic theologians or ecclesiastics did.

Stringfellow wrote many books and articles, usually on the relationship between Christian faith and politics, and occasionally on more personal subjects: his illness, for example, his friendship with Daniel Berrigan and Bishop Pike, and the death of his companion Anthony Towne. Throughout all of his writings there are three major theological themes: reading and hearing the Word of God, the Church, and the principalities and powers of this world.

In *An Ethic for Christians and Other Aliens in a Strange Land* (1973), he explained what was always a major theme of his work:

> This book is necessarily at once theological and political for the good reason that the theology of the Bible concerns politics in its most rudimentary meaning and in its most auspicious connotations.
>
> The biblical topic *is* politics. The Bible is about the politics of fallen creation and the politics of redemption; the politics of the nations, institutions, ideologies, and causes of this world and the politics of the Kingdom of God; the politics of Babylon and the politics of Jerusalem; the politics of the Antichrist and the politics of Jesus Christ; the politics of the demonic powers and principalities and the politics of the timely judgment of God as sovereign; the politics of death and the politics of life; apocalyptic politics and eschatological politics.

He was harsh in his judgement of the Church, especially the Episcopal Church, which he believed too often yielded to the ideologies of the principalities and powers of the present time. And yet he also saw the Church and its sacramental, liturgical life as the best sign we have of God's work in the world.

> Sacramentally, we have in the liturgy a meal that is basically a real meal and that nourishes those who partake of it as a meal. At the same time, this meal portrays for the rest of the world an image of the Last Supper, of which Christ himself was host, and is also a foretaste of the eschatological banquet in which Christ is finally recognized as the host of all humanity. The liturgy, therefore,

wherever it has substance in the gospel is a living, political event. The very example of salvation, it is the festival of life that foretells the fulfillment and maturity of all of life for all of time in *this* time. The liturgy *is* social action because it is the characteristic style of life for human beings in this world (*Dissenter in a Great Society*, 1966).

Stringfellow has been disregarded for many years, and all of his books are out of print. He is now at the end of the twentieth century, however, being rediscovered as the Episcopal Church and the other churches must deal with fundamental changes in American society and with the loss of their privileged social and economic status. Stringfellow stands in the tradition of other Episcopalians in the USA who have deeply questioned the accommodation of the Church to the dominant political order.

A complete bibliography of Stringfellow's writings can be found in *A Keeper of the Word: Selected Writings of William Stringfellow*, edited by Bill Wylie Kellerman (Grand Rapids: Eerdmans, 1994). Because all of Stringfellow's book are out of print and his articles are scattered among many small journals, this volume is the most accessible source. It contains selections from all of his major books and from many of his articles.

Only one major study of Stringfellow's work has so far been published: Andrew W. McThenia (ed.), *Radical Christian and Exemplary Lawyer: Honoring William Stringfellow* (Grand Rapids: Eerdmans, 1995). Another collection of essays edited by Robert Slocum and to be published by the Church Hymnal Corporation of the Episcopal Church is planned for 1997. (JG)

Studdert-Kennedy, Geoffrey A. (1883–1929). An Anglican priest from Leeds, Kennedy was one of the best-known preachers of the 1920s in England. He came to renown through his writings from the trenches in World War I. An army chaplain, he was impressed both by the troops' personal qualities, and their impatience with orthodox religion. He gained the nick-name 'Woodbine Willy' from the cigarettes he offered them – a policy he later regretted. The sufferings ordinary men and their women experienced led Kennedy to rework traditional incarnational doctrine, in journal form (*The Hardest Part*), apologetic (e.g. *Lies, Democracy and the Dog Collar*), theological writing (e.g. *The New Man in Christ*), and above all in poetry (collected in *The Unutterable Beauty*). His popular style, employing startling, even violent metaphors, frequently took on a romantic tinge, especially in writing about men, and the dream of Christian socialism. After the war he worked in the Industrial Christian Fellowship, travelling all over England to speak to working men. He died relatively young, at the height of the Depression, having made a marked impression on many of the leaders of the Church of England in mid-century.

Kennedy's thought focused on two key points: the suffering of God, and the social dimensions of faith. These came together 'in terms of the continual actual correspondence between the sufferings of men and the suffering of Christ' (J. K. Mozley). God's power is thus known only in and through the cross, the focus of Christ's rule of suffering love: all triumphalism is rejected. Kennedy refused to divide material from spiritual reality: 'body and blood' take on many shades of meaning. As a priest in the Anglican tradition, he felt deeply the presence of the suffering Christ in the eucharist. As a prophet in the Christian socialist tradition, he felt the suffering of Christ in the despair, pain and hope of the ordinary man and woman. Kennedy turned English theology towards a more personal, Christological understanding of 'impassibility' (e.g. J. K. Mozley): in recent years his work has been taken up by theologians such as Moltmann. Kennedy offers a resource for men who are seeking to explore what it means to be male. Though his romantic ethos has not endured, his ability to inspire Passion-ate theology endures: his poetry remains in print.

> The sorrows of God mun be 'ard to bear
> If 'e really 'as Love in 'is 'eart,
> And the 'ardest part i' the world to play
> Mun surely be God's Part.

(CS)

Taylor, Jeremy (1613–67), was born in Cambridge, the son of a barber. He attended the Perth School, then located in the centre of Cambridge, and then Gonville and Caius College, Cambridge, helping to pay his costs by serving as a sizer for wealthier students. After he received his M.A. and ordination in 1633–4, Taylor's preaching ability gained the attention of William Laud. Laud became Taylor's patron, arranging Taylor's appointment as a Fellow of All Soul's College, Oxford. Laud made Taylor his chaplain and made him a chaplain to Charles I.

In 1638, Taylor was instituted to the rectory of Uppingham, Rutland.

Around 1644, Taylor supported Charles I against Parliament and was imprisoned for his efforts. After his release, Taylor spent the years of the Protectorate as chaplain to Richard Vaughan, Second Earl of Carbery, and his household at Golden Grove in Wales. Most of Taylor's influential writings, e.g. *The Liberty of Prophesying*; *The History of the Life and Death of the Holy Jesus: The Great Exemplar*; *Holy Living*; and *Holy Dying* date from this period. In addition to serving as chaplain, founding and teaching in a secondary school and writing, Taylor discreetly supported groups loyal to the Church of England by personal visits, spiritual guidance and celebrations of the Holy Communion using the Book of Common Prayer. From 1657 to 1658 Taylor officiated to a small congregation of Episcopalians in London.

In 1639 Taylor married Phoebe Langsdale. She died in 1651. In 1667, he married Joanne Bridges. Taylor had five children with his first wife and two with his second.

After restoration of the monarchy, Charles II made Taylor a bishop in Ireland. He was consecrated in 1661. First assigned the diocese of Down and Connor, Taylor was additionally given jurisdiction over the diocese of Dromore. Taylor also brought order to the administration of Trinity College, University of Dublin.

Taylor's ministry as bishop in Ireland was made increasingly difficult by attacks from both Presbyterians and Roman Catholics there. He repeatedly requested reassignment to a diocese in England. His requests were denied, however, probably because of concern over theological views on original sin which Taylor expressed in his writings.

Taylor died in 1667, from an infection probably received while visiting a sick parishioner. He was buried in the cathedral of the diocese of Dromore, pursuant to his own request. In the funeral sermon, George Rust ascribed to Taylor 'the good humour of a gentleman, the eloquence of an orator, the fancy of a poet, the acuteness of a schoolman, the profoundness of a philosopher, the wisdom of a chancellor, the sagacity of a prophet, the reason of an angel, and the piety of a saint'.

Taylor's historical influence

Taylor was an outstanding example of a remarkably large number of contemporaries in the Church of England, thinkers and leaders usually referred to as seventeenth-century 'Caroline Divines'. The Caroline Divines combined wide learning, deep Christian faith and piety and influential writings. Their writings appealed to Scripture, tradition and reason. Their lives and works embodied, during the century after the Elizabethan Settlement and the writings of Richard Hooker, for the Church of England, a third alternative between Protestant extremism – represented in England by Puritans and Presbyterians, and especially the Independents – and Roman Catholic claims. Thus, Taylor, with the other Caroline Divines, defended the Catholic polity of threefold ministry of bishops, priests and deacons, the legitimacy of the theological inheritance of the patristic and medieval theology and piety, and the centrality of baptism and eucharist, while at the same time affirming Protestant teachings on justification and the centrality of the Bible.

Among these Caroline Divines, Jeremy Taylor, with others like Joseph Hall and Robert Sanderson, form a special group of 'moral Divines' because of their special concern for the Christian moral life. Although he, like other Caroline Divines, wrote on theological themes against Puritans and Roman Catholics, Taylor stressed the moral significance of all aspects of Christian faith and sacramental practice. Taylor stands out among all the Caroline Divines for his rhetorical eloquence. Though his style often seems prolix and florid to modern readers, Taylor applied his literary gifts to an understanding of human nature and of moral persuasion informed by the Greek, Roman and Renaissance rhetorical traditions. Taylor's writings richly mix rhetoric, theology and ethics, and this mixture, combined with the example of his own dedication and piety, deeply impressed later Anglicanism.

Taylor, along with the other Caroline Divines, served as an historical model of Anglican identity for the leaders of the Oxford Movement in the nineteenth century, as evidenced in E. B. Pusey's Tract 81, among the *Tracts for the Times*. Also, Taylor's eloquent focus on holiness of life has been influential. John Wesley started the Holiness Club at Oxford after reading Taylor's *The Rule and Exercises of Holy Living*.

In addition to Taylor's influence on the eighteenth-century Wesleyan movement and the nineteenth-century Oxford Movement, his constitutional inclination against doctrinal dispute in favour of emphasis on moral behaviour corresponded deeply with the emphasis of the later seventeenth-century movement of Cambridge Platonists on the practical implications of Christian faith. Thus, Taylor was also an intellectual source of the Broad Church school in the Church of England.

Thus, Taylor stands out as one of the most influential of the seventeenth-century Caroline Divines.

Significance of Jeremy Taylor today

The following theological themes and motives in Taylor's writings are important for Anglicanism today.

Emphasis on Holiness.

Taylor's writings on the moral life presupposes the centrality in the Christian life of holiness. By holiness Taylor meant a single-minded, consistent orientation of human appetites, understanding and will toward, and a shaping of these by, the will of God as revealed in God's commandments but most persuasively – because concretely and winningly – expressed in the example of Jesus of Nazareth, the incarnate Word of God. Taylor's preoccupation with holiness of life presupposes the claims of God's holiness on us, and this, in turn, presupposes a God-centred attention to God's righteousness, transcendence and grace. In our age, overemphasizing God's immanence and tending to reduce God to a support for human moral projects, Taylor's preoccupation with holiness of life stands as a healthy reminder of the biblical theme of God's transcendence, and of God's will as an end in itself, with all this means for Christian moral teaching and moral leadership in the Church.

C. F. Allison has correctly criticized Taylor's writings (in contrast to Taylor's prayers) for overemphasizing the role of human moral effort in justifying righteousness. In part, Taylor's Arminianism was a product of his high estimation of reason in theology and ethics and of his reaction against the laxism and antinomianism of some emerging movements in English Independent movements and in Roman Catholic moral theology. If one replaces Taylor's chronological model of God–human relationship, implying a 'first, humans must do this, then God will do that' logic, with a covenantal model in which human effort is included in God's prior, gracious initiative, Taylor's emphasis on moral effort might be reappropriated today. (See Jeanette R. Rollins, 'Recovering Holiness: Jeremy Taylor and the Christian Life' (M.T.S. Thesis, Virginia Theological Seminary, 1995.)

Natural Law as Element in Moral Theology.
Taylor was critical of an over-reliance on speculative reason in theology. But he affirmed the roles of human appetites and natural moral law in Christian ethics. He taught that revelation does not contradict the deepest appetites of unfallen human nature but elevates and satisfies these. Likewise, he believed that revelation of God's truth and will in Jesus Christ do not destroy the deepest instincts of reason and will but complete these aspects of human nature. (See the Preface to *The Great Exemplar.*)

Taylor's emphasis on human appetites and reason are important today. Christian ethics can and should be in dialogue with ethical discourse outside the Church. God's moral will, while conflicting with fallen human nature, does not contradict human nature as God originally created it. Taylor's qualified affirmations of natural human appetites and of natural moral law are important antidotes to the one-sidedness of some, otherwise legitimate, contemporary emphases on revelation as the only source of the moral life and of the Church as the only context for Christian ethics.

Grounding of moral theology in trinitarian-incarnational faith.
Taylor is important today because he recalls the contemporary Church to the theological foundations of Christian morality. Taylor, like classical

Christian theology, grounds the moral life in the reality of God as Holy Trinity and the incarnation of the Word of God in Jesus Christ. Ultimately for Taylor, the Christian moral life is a mode of participation in God's own life as an imitation of, in the sense of a participation in, Jesus Christ through the power of the Holy Spirit. As much as Taylor stressed the conformity of God's will with human nature as God intended it, he understood the moral life as oriented and keyed to God's eternal life of love in the Trinity. Thus, Taylor serves the Church today as a corrective whenever contemporary Christian ethicists reduce the moral life to the promotion of a secular utopia, as legitimate as a concern for justice, mutuality and equality is for Christian ethics. Henry R. McAdoo's scholarly reappropriation of Taylor's moral theology has correctly highlighted Taylor's grounding moral theology in spirituality, i.e. in faith, hope and love of God, the Trinity, manifested in the gracious work of creation, reconciliation and perfection in Jesus Christ through the Holy Spirit in the context of the preaching, worship, service and fellowship of the Church as the Body of Christ. Taylor's writings all tried to further 'the great designs of the gospel, that is, a life conformable to God, a Godlike life, and an imitation of the holy Jesus'.

Episcopacy Asserted; full title: *Of the Sacred Order and Offices of Episcopacy by Divine Institution, Apostolical Tradition and Catholic Practice*, 1642. Uses biblical and patristic sources to affirm the divine origin and apostolic tradition of the episcopate in dialogue with the Reformed churches.
A Discourse on The Liberty of Prophesying, 1646. Stressing the role of reason in theology, the fallibility and finitude of human teaching, Taylor called for religious toleration and search for unity in the 'common term' of the Apostles' Creed.
The Great Exemplar, 1649. Dedicated to Christopher Hatton, Laud's cousin. 'The earliest life of Jesus in English'; a narrative, devotional, moral theological work based on events in Jesus' life. As a key source for Taylor's moral theology, see the secondary works on Taylor by McAdoo and Scott, below. For the possibility of the influence of English Franciscanism as background for this work, consult Patrick Grant, *The Transformation of Sin: Studies in Donne, Herbert, Vaughan and Traherne* (London and Montreal: McGill-Queen's University, 1974).
Apology for Authorized and Set Forms of Liturgie, 1649.
The Rule and Exercises of Holy Living, 1650. Taylor's most influential work, combining prayer and ethical teaching. Originally separate works, *Holy Living* and *Rules and Exercises for Holy Dying*, 1651, were later often printed together. See the excellent edition by P. G. Stanwood (ed.), 2 vols. (Oxford: Clarendon Press, 1989).
Clerus Domini, 1651. An exposition of priesthood based on Scripture and antiquity.
A Discourse on Baptism, 1652.
The Real Presence and Spiritual of Christ in the Blessed Sacrament, 1654.
The Golden Grove, 1655. Illustrating the weaving of spirituality and moral theology in Taylor's works.
Unum Necessarium: Of the Doctrine and Practice of Repentance, 1655. This work evoked criticism from Taylor's friends, including Robert Sanderson, for taking a strongly

Arminian position on the question of original sin. See the studies of C. FitzSimons Allison below.

Sermons, 1655.

A Treatise on Friendship, 1657.

Ductor Dubitantium or the Rule of Conscience, 1660. Taylor called this 'my great endeavour'. Its prolixity and ponderousness assured its lack of popularity.

The Worthy Communicant, 1660. An important source for Taylor's sacramental theology.

Dissuasive to Popery, 1664–7. An acrimonious anti-Roman Catholic tract which Taylor was disinclined to write but did so because asked by his fellow bishops in Ireland.

Bibliography

Robert Gahorne-Hardy, 1971. *A Bibliography of the Writings of Jeremy Taylor to 1700: With a Section of Tayloriana* (Dekalb: Northern Illinois University Press).

Collected works

Thomas K. Carroll, 1990. (ed. and Introduction), *Jeremy Taylor: Selected Works* (New York: Paulist Press).

Margaret Gest, 1954. *The House of Understanding: Selections from the Writings of Jeremy Taylor* (Philadelphia: University of Pennsylvania Press).

Reginald Heber (ed.), 1928. *The Whole Works of the Right Reverend Jeremy Taylor*, 15 vols. (London).

Key secondary works

C. FitzSimons Allison, 1966. *The Rise of Moralism: The Proclamation of the Gospel from Hooker to Baxter* (New York: The Seabury Press).

Sister M. Salome Antoine, 1946. *The Rhetoric of Jeremy Taylor's Prose: Ornament of the Sunday Sermons* (Washington, D.C.: The Catholic University of America Press).

Nancy Lee Beaty, 1970. 'The Rule and Exercises of Holy Dying' in *The Craft of Dying: A Study of the Literary Tradition of the Ars Moriendi in England* (New Haven and London: Yale University Press).

Paul Elmen, 1962. 'The Fame of Jeremy Taylor', *Anglican Theological Review* 44: 389–403.

Edmund Gosse, 1904. *Jeremy Taylor* (London: Macmillan & Co. Ltd.).

B. Harvey Hill and Allen S. Davidson, 1994. 'Literary Art in the Moral Theology of Jeremy Taylor', *Anglican Theological Review* 76: 27–43.

Trevor H. Hughes, 1960. *The Piety of Jeremy Taylor* (London: St Martin's Press).

Kevin Kelly, 1967. *Conscience: Dictator or Guide? A Study in Seventeenth Century English Protestant Moral Theology* (London: Geoffrey Chapman).

Henry R. McAdoo, 1949. *The Structure of Caroline Moral Theology* (London: Black).

Henry R. McAdoo, 1983. 'Anglican Moral Theology in the Seventeenth Century: An Anticipation', in Paul Elmen (ed.), *The Anglican Moral Choice* (Wilton, Conn.: Morehouse-Barlow Co.).

Henry R. McAdoo, 1988. *The Eucharistic Theology of Jeremy Taylor Today* (Norwich: Canterbury Press).

Henry R. McAdoo, 1994. *First of its Kind: Jeremy Taylor's Life of Christ: A Study in the Functioning of a Moral Theology* (Norwich: Canterbury Press).

Harry Boone Porter, 1979. *Jeremy Taylor, Liturgist* (London: SPCK).

David Scott, 1991. *Christian Character: Jeremy Taylor and Christian Ethics Today* (Oxford: Latimer House).

Timothy Sedgwick, 1981. 'Revisioning Anglican Moral Theology', *Anglican Theological Review* 63: 1–20.

C. J. Stranks, 1952. *The Life and Writings of Jeremy Taylor* (London: SPCK).

Thomas Wood, 1952. *English Casuistical Divinity during the Seventeenth Century: With Special Reference to Jeremy Taylor* (London: SPCK). (DS)

Temple, William (1881–1944). At Temple's funeral in 1944 it seemed to many that the Church of England itself was being laid to rest. Temple carried so many hopes: he represented the hope of a credible gospel for the modern world, the hope of an ecumenical future and the reunion of the churches, the hope of a better society after the war. He embodied in his ample person profound scholarship lightly worn, robust good sense and a gift of humour that imparted a sense of proportion. Church people trusted Temple while they remained wary of Gore. While Gore was brilliant, volatile and somewhat aloof, Temple was luminous, steady and one with whom one could feel a sense of fellowship. If Gore was a meteor blazing across the heavens leaving burning debris in its wake, Temple was a rotund heavenly body imparting a wholesome light and warmth.

Biographical sketch

William Temple was born to the purple and destined for Lambeth Palace: his career had an aura of inevitability. His father Frederick (who was sixty when William was born) had then been Bishop of Exeter for twelve years, but in 1869 there had been a concerted attempt to prevent his consecration. Frederick had been one of the contributors to the notorious symposium *Essays and Reviews* in 1860 which had caused a row greater than *Honest to God*, Bishop David Jenkins and the ordination of women priests rolled into one!

In his essay 'The Education of the World', published only a year after Darwin's *The Origin of Species*, Frederick Temple had assumed the truth of the theory of evolution and had elaborated a progressive, developmental view of salvation history which had entailed some relativization of the Bible and the creeds. He placed the Old Testament alongside ancient Greek, Roman and Far Eastern culture. All these had mediated divine revelation in their different ways. The New Testament contained not formulated doctrines but the normative divine–human life of Christ and of the early Church. The Bible was to be interpreted in an historical way which recognized its discrepancies and errors. The trust deeds of the Christian faith were to be investigated with scholarly rigour. This essay anticipated by thirty years some of the characteristic positions of *Lux Mundi* (q.v. Charles Gore), but also contained a dash of old fashioned rationalism that was alien to Gore and his colleagues.

William Temple assumed the mantle of his father in a number of ways: as headmaster (of Repton instead of Rugby); as (eventually) Archbishop of Canterbury; but also as a daring, radical young scholar who contributed to a controversial symposium. William had always wanted to be ordained, but in the early years of the twentieth century, while at Balliol College, Oxford, he felt that his own questioning approach would make that inappropriate. At this time, the doctrine of the virginal conception of Jesus was not the main problem, though Temple was ambivalent about it. He could not give unquestioning assent to the physical resurrection of Jesus. By 1908, as a fellow of Queen's College, Oxford, he had satisfied the Archbishop of Canterbury, Randall Davidson, as to his essential orthodoxy, and Davidson ordained him himself to avoid embarrassment elsewhere. Temple went from his Oxford Fellowship to be Headmaster of Repton (to which he was ill-suited) and thence to be Rector of St James's, Piccadilly, an important and fashionable London church, from where he published his first major philosophical-theological work *Mens Creatrix* (Creative Mind). Temple resigned his living to devote himself to the Life and Liberty movement, campaigning for limited self-government for the Church of England (which came to fruition in the Enabling Act of 1919). He was then briefly a canon of Westminster Abbey before beginning his episcopal career.

Meanwhile, Temple had contributed two essays to the symposium *Foundations* in 1912. The essays, on the divinity of Christ and on the Church, were unobjectionable, but objection was taken to the company Temple was keeping in this volume. Its subtitle was *A Statement of Christian Belief in Terms of Modern Thought* and it clearly stood in the tradition of *Essays and Reviews* and *Lux Mundi*. The editor, the New Testament scholar B. H. Streeter, worried his colleagues by his essay, which proposed that the resurrection of Jesus could be understood in terms of objective or externally generated visions. In reply to both humorous and serious criticism by Ronald Knox, then an Anglo-Catholic, soon to be an illustrious convert to Rome, Temple explained that while he accepted such miracles as the virginal conception and the physical resurrection, he could not find much theological significance in them and his faith was independent of them.

Neither his radical campaigning for the rights of the Church nor his provocative association with Streeter could prevent the rise of this multi-talented man, already the author of numerous worthy volumes, who bore such a distinguished name and had from boyhood mixed on equal terms with the great personages of church and state. In 1921 Temple was made Bishop of Manchester, at thirty-nine the youngest diocesan of the day. From Manchester he published his second major work of philosophical theology *Christus Veritas* (Christ the Truth).

In 1929 he was elevated to York and as an archbishop was able to make a notable contribution to the social, educational and economic questions of national life and to the international affairs of the Church, especially in the ecumenical sphere, where Temple became a leading light in the Faith and Order and the Life and Work movements and a shaper of the future World Council of Churches. It was as Archbishop of York that Temple gave the prestigious Gifford Lectures in the University of Glasgow in 1932–4 which were published in 1934 under the title *Nature, Man and God*. It is his finest work. It embraces a lifetime of reading, reflection and prayer. It repays careful study today.

The report *Doctrine in the Church of England*, commissioned by the Archbishops of Canterbury and York in 1922, which Temple had chaired since 1925, was published in 1938 with an important Chairman's Introduction. Temple also called and presided over the Malvern Conference of 1941 at which, in those dark days of the Second World War, Anglicans took counsel on the crisis of modern civilization and addressed the reconstruction of society after the war.

When Archbishop Cosmo Lang eventually took overdue retirement in 1942, Temple was appointed by Prime Minister Winston Churchill to succeed him. Churchill was reluctant to appoint this prominent critic of the capitalist economy and exponent of social (if not quite socialist) change, but was constrained to choose 'the half-crown article in a penny bazaar'. Temple's reign at Canterbury lasted a mere two and a half years. Although he reached a wider public (as 'the people's archbishop' and through his Penguin Special *Christianity and Social Order*) than at any previous period of his national ministry, administrative pressures, of which he conscientiously but misguidedly shouldered too many himself, together with the exceptional demands made upon his pastoral and theological leadership in time of war, took their toll of his health and led to his death, just after his sixty-third birthday, at the height of his powers. It is not too much to say that the Church of England has never fully recovered from the loss.

Temple's philosophical and theological thought

As a child, growing up in his father's episcopal and archiepiscopal residences, Temple had naturally been ineradicably imbued with the Bible, the creeds and Anglican worship according to the Book of Common Prayer 1662. Everything else – Hegel, Aquinas, Gore – had to be grafted on to that genuinely filial piety.

Taught Hegelian philosophy by Edward Caird at Balliol (to whose memory he dedicated *Nature, Man and God*), Temple constructed his philosophical theology on the principles of Personal Idealism, a version of Hegelian Absolute Idealism which was assimilated to Christian theism.

Though as a young Fellow of Queen's, Temple was rather too enamoured of Platonism, regarding the Christian revelation as merely the crowning glory of Idealist philosophy, he steadily matured into an orthodox Christian theist, achieving a balance and synthesis of divine transcendence and immanence.

A creative Mind was the source of the universe, and the nature of this Mind was love. Thought, not matter, was the ultimate stuff of reality. Matter was the sphere of the outworking of mind and could become sacramental of it. Through creation, incarnation and the Church's sacramental life and worship, Christianity was actually the most materialistic of the world religions. Though the Spirit of God was at work far and wide in all cultural expression and scientific discovery, the prevenient grace of God was paramount, and Pelagianism (the doctrine of human moral sufficiency and autonomy) was 'the only heresy that is intrinsically damnable'.

Temple sought an integrated theology – one that today would be called 'holistic'. He believed that faith and reason complemented each other and that grace brings nature to perfection. He was convinced that the unity of thought was achievable and that all knowledge and insight pointed to Jesus Christ. He rejected Descartes' dualism of mind and body ('The Cartesian *Faux-Pas*') and distrusted empiricist epistemology. Through the physical medium of nature, as well as in the realm of thought, mind can commune with Mind. Temple achieved a synthesis which is irradiated by the glory of God in the universe, in the human mind and, above all, in Jesus Christ and his Church.

As the storm clouds of war gathered, Temple took stock of this theology in his Introduction to the report *Doctrine in the Church of England* (1938). He felt that too much energy had been devoted, in recent Anglican theology like his own, to interpreting the world, and too little to transforming it. While he and others had succeeded in elaborating a 'Christocentric metaphysic', the world was crying out for the gospel of redemption. Like Augustine in his *Retractiones*, Temple was having second thoughts and was humble enough to admit it.

Temple on Anglicanism

Temple was famous for his ability to reconcile conflicting points of view. He was temperamentally, as well as academically, inclined to the Hegelian synthesis. This conditioned his understanding of Anglicanism. In a paper 'The Genius of the Church of England' (1928), he claimed that the attempt to hold together divergent forces was typically Anglican because it was typically English. Anglicanism combined unbroken continuity with earliest Christendom with the characteristics of that 'new birth' of Christianity which we call the Reformation. Anglicanism therefore required a twofold loyalty:

> If a man sets out to be loyal to the Catholic tradition, so understood as to rule out all that is distinctive of the Reformation, he cannot also be fully loyal to the Church of England. If a man sets out to be loyal to the Reformation, so understood as to rule out any elements of the Catholic tradition which were not universally retained by the reformed Churches, he cannot also be loyal to the Church of England. The Church of England has always bridged the gulf (or sat on the hedge, if you like) that divides 'Catholic' and 'Protestant' from one another.

Temple added that 'nowhere was the Reformation accomplished with so little assertion of abstract principles as in England'. Like the British constitution, it was weak on theory but strong on practice: it worked. The aim, under Elizabeth at least, was the practical one of including as many as were willing to be included in the 'comprehension' of the national church. The 'spiritual essence' of the Reformation was that it was a search for spiritual purity, like every religious revival; but the historical forms that it took were determined by two other factors – the rise of national self-determination and the right of private judgement, both of which Temple was careful to affirm.

Temple went on to discuss the tension and conflict between Anglo-Catholics and Evangelicals in the Church of England, commenting that no other church possessed these two strands in such fullness and strength. Temple aligned himself with neither, but his capacious spirit had absorbed much from both. On the one hand, his theological formation was deeply shaped by his sustained reading of St Thomas Aquinas and his was a sacramental spirituality. Furthermore, when it was proposed that the Church of South India should be created out of the immediate union of episcopal and non-episcopal churches, Temple insisted that the Church of England's and the Anglican Communion's commitment to the historic episcopate should determine its relations with that church during the period in which new ministries were being incorporated into the historic threefold order. On the other hand (as his popular *Readings in St John's Gospel* testifies), in his personal devotion to Christ as Saviour and Lord and in his love of the sacred text, Temple conceded nothing to the Evangelicals. His zeal for evangelism – from schoolboy beach missions to archiepiscopal university missions – confirms this. He revealed his own churchmanship location when, in reply to a clergyman's question as to which tradition he identified with, Temple invited him to consider his girth for the answer – Broad!

Temple's social thought

Like Westcott and Gore, Temple was impelled by a Platonic theology of the incarnation towards social reflection and action. Temple wrote extensively on social, economic and educational matters. His philosophical theology was certainly not confined to the realm of theory: it issued in a social vision. 'He set out a theological system which would support his overall social aim of a redeemed, organic, national community expressing itself religiously through the Church of England' (Kent 1992: 37).

Temple's social activity was expressed in his early involvement in the Workers Educational Association; his initiative in bringing about COPEC (the Birmingham Conference on Christian Politics, Economics and Citizenship) in 1924 which produced twelve substantial reports on various aspects of social life from a Christian perspective; the Life and Work arm of the ecumenical movement; the Malvern Conference (see above); and his Penguin Special in which he distilled a lifetime of social thought.

In this short paperback Temple claimed that it was not for the Church to pronounce on particular policies. It was, however, the Church's role to enunciate basic moral, theological and spiritual principles. Christians together could go further and articulate the 'middle axioms' which lay between uncontroversial platitudes and concrete political programmes. So Temple began with the fundamental Christian world-view: God as creator and redeemer; humanity as the child of God, destined for eternal fellowship with God. Love was the dominant Christian impulse, and the form that love took in social organization was justice. From these axioms Temple derived certain basic human rights: adequate housing, education and employment; times of recreation; liberty of worship, speech, assembly and association; a say in the way one's labour was used. Where Temple went further than this, commenting critically on aspects of current policy, he strove to make it clear that he was speaking purely as a private individual. But the distinction between the Archbishop of Canterbury and the private Christian citizen was precarious.

Temple's social thought is open to criticism (see, for example, Suggate 1987). How can an axiom be in the middle? Should not these key concepts be drawn from the empirical study of economics or sociology, as well as from theological principles? Temple's approach is methodologically weak. On the other hand, Kent has claimed, in a rather backhanded way, that 'in the long run, Temple's own theological critique of western capitalism was more significant than his work in the philosophy of religion'. The Penguin Special shows that, however much Temple may have begun to hearken to the European theologians of catastrophic

judgement and redemption (notably, of course, Karl Barth), he maintained to the end 'his strong belief that Anglicanism must discharge its
role as the established form of Christianity in England by bringing pressure to bear on the state in favour of specific social changes' (Kent
1992).

Assessment and influence

William Temple dominated the Church of England for twenty years
before his death. As Gore's influence waned in his old age, Temple's filled
the vacuum. Gore's militant Anglo-Catholicism, that was unable to
recognize non-episcopal churches as true churches of Christ with
authentic ministries of word and sacrament because they lacked the
'apostolic succession', gave way to Temple's genuine ecumenical outlook,
which strengthened the Protestant churches of northern Europe
through the Second World War and the Cold War.

Under Temple, the Church of England attained a buoyancy and
confidence unmatched for fifty years on either side of his death. While
adulation of Temple is misplaced, and a reading of John Kent's study will
correct the balance, Temple's memorial is all around us. The synodical
structures of the Church of England go back ultimately to the Enabling
Act of 1919 which Temple did much to bring about through the Life
and Liberty movement. Anglican social thought received an impulse
from him which sustained it until comparatively recently. The ecumenical
movement – specifically the World Council of Churches – owes much
to his pioneering vision.

Temple had the rare gift of being equally at home in high-powered
philosophical argument or in giving a simple but profound homily from
the pulpit of a country church. His philosophical theology belongs to a
different world, but the model of an apologetics that engages with all
that is most creative in contemporary culture, while not wavering in its
loyalty to the cross of Christ, remains impressive. Sadly, however, Temple
is one of the last examples of a time when the ministry of the Church
could attract and motivate the most gifted individuals and the greatest
intellects of the day.

Select bibliography of works by William Temple
'The Divinity of Christ' and 'The Church', in B. H. Streeter (ed.), *Foundations: A
Statement of Christian Belief in Terms of Modern Thought* (London: Macmillan, 1912).
Mens Creatrix (London: Macmillan, 1917).
Christus Veritas (London: Macmillan, 1924).
Christian Faith and Life ([1931]; London: SCM, 1963).
Nature, Man and God (London: Macmillan, 1934).
Readings in St John's Gospel (London: Macmillan, 1939–40).
Christianity and Social Order (Harmondsworth: Penguin, 1942).

Religious Experience and Other Essays and Addresses, ed. A. E. Baker (London: James Clarke, 1958). Includes 'The Genius of the Church of England'.

Books about William Temple
F. A. Iremonger, 1948. *William Temple, Archbishop of Canterbury: His Life and Letters* (London: Oxford University Press).
J. Kent, 1992. *William Temple: Church, State and Society in Britain, 1880–1950* (Cambridge: Cambridge University Press).
J. F. Padgett, 1974. *The Christian Philosophy of William Temple* (The Hague: M. Nijhoff).
A. Suggate, 1987. *William Temple and Christian Social Ethics Today* (Edinburgh: T. & T. Clark). (PA)

Thorndike, Herbert (1598–1672). 'The learned Mr Thorndike' may fairly be described as the intellectual's theologian. An expert in Oriental languages who participated in the production of Brian Walton's *Polyglot Bible* (1653/7) and a patristic scholar, his style is at times tortuous, his meaning often involved and elusive. Some of his contemporaries distrusted his opinions, but Simon Patrick testified that Thorndike's works led him to episcopal ordination. A friend of Ussher and of George Herbert, he shared the concern of Sheldon and others concerning the episcopal succession as he shared with them deprivation for his unflinching loyalty to a persecuted church. A Fellow of Trinity College, Cambridge (1620) and Hebrew Lecturer, his election as Master of Sidney Sussex College was prevented by Cromwell. He then became rector of Barley (1644) but was shortly deprived of this and of his Fellowship, after which he was reduced to poverty. None of this silenced Thorndike's pen, and he had produced a succession of works, influential and often (as witness his *Right of the Church in a Christian State* (1649)) very pointedly relevant to the current religious and political situation, by the time of his reinstatement to Barley in 1661 and his appointment as Prebendary of Westminster. He attended the Savoy Conference, during which he wrote his *Just Weights and Measures*, setting out conformity to the primitive Church as basic. This is a recurring theme throughout his work, as in his *Of the Government of Churches* (1641), but Thorndike's use of the appeal to antiquity has a striking variation. He insists that the Church of England 'had not in all points carried out her own principle'. In certain respects the Reformation needs 'to be reformed anew' and he instances penance and discipline, prayer for the dead, the *epiclesis* and presbyters as a council with the bishop. In other words, the appeal is not to be used as a mantra but applied without exception and in reason. This stress on an aided reason and on 'common sense' and on consensus are foundational elements in Thorndike's *Epilogue to the Tragedy of the Church of England* (1659), a massive work described by T. A. Lacey as a *summa de ecclesia*. In reality it is no epilogue but, as Hadden observed, 'the prologue to the renewed life of a Church more vigorous than ever' (*Life*: 220), a plan for reconstituting the Church on the basis of the primitive Catholic Church. Divided into three books, *The Principles of Christian Truth*, *The Covenant of Grace* and *The Laws of the Church*, to summarize is an impossibility here. Suffice it to say that there is much of value for Anglicans today in Thorndike's handling of consensus and tradition, of baptism and the covenant, of the role of the Spirit and of the centrality of the eucharist in the Church's life: 'the frequent celebration and communion of the eucharist, which is indeed the crown of public service' (*Of Religious Assemblies* (1642), ch. 8). This is true of many areas in Thorndike's learned, involved and digressive works, as for instance in his theology of the eucharistic presence and sacrifice in *The Laws of the Church*. Indeed it is striking to see him making the same conclusion as ARCIC I on the 'two complementary movements within an indissoluble unity' (*Final Report*: 22):

> If this were agreed upon . . . that the Body and Blood of Christ become present in the sacrament by the institution of our Lord, by celebrating the sacrament, whereby His institution is executed by consecrating the elements to the purpose that the Body and Blood of Christ may be received: – the whole dispute concerning the manner of presence in the nature of the formal cause might be superseded. For then all parties must agree, that they are present sacramentally, as the nature of a sacrament requireth. And that . . . so it would still require living faith to make that presence effectual . . . which all parties are obliged to require to the effect, as much as they are obliged to require consecration to the sacramental presence of the Body and Blood of Christ in the sacrament. (*Reformation of the Church of England* (1670/2), XXV, 6).

Anglican theology today would be enriched by a critical *Selection* from his works. The most complete evaluation of Thorndike known to me is an Oxford University doctoral thesis (1990) by E. C. Miller, which it is to be hoped will be published, and see also Kenneth Stevenson *Covenant of Grace Renewed* (1994), 139–49. Thorndike's *Works* are in the Library of Anglo-Catholic Theology edn (1855) with a *Life* by A. W. Hadden. (HM)

Thornton, Lionel Spenser (1884–1960), Anglo-Catholic priest, monk, author, and philosophical theologian. Graduated first in theology, Emmanuel College, Cambridge in 1907, M.A. in 1911, B.D. 1929, and D.D. 1943. He was ordained deacon in Southwark diocese in 1908, and priested in 1909. A member of the Community of Resurrection,

Mirfield from 1915, where his earliest work *Conscience and the Supernatural* (2nd edn, 1916) established him as a theologian who was keen to address the problems of the modern world from both moral and philosophical perspectives. *The Incarnate Lord* (1928) reflected his large debt to the work of the philosopher Whitehead and the view of an evolving universe finding its fitting climax in the incarnation. Thornton himself never deviated from the Christian understanding a transcendent and sovereign God who was independent and all-sufficient. He would eventually find it necessary to distance himself from Whitehead's later view that God evolves along with the universe in a mutually dependent relationship. Although he never strayed from the strictest Catholic doctrine, Thornton's *The Common Life in the Body of Christ* (1942), was appreciated by Anglicans and Nonconformists alike and established him as a worthy biblical scholar as well as theologian. His later interest in biblical typology and attempts to employ the allegorical method of the early Fathers in New Testament exegesis was not as well regarded. However, he did in this respect encourage his students to get to the mind of the original writers of Scripture, rather than uncritically cling to the methodologies and assumptions of modern biblical criticism.

Conscience and the Supernatural (Westminster: Dacre Press, 1916).
The Incarnate Lord (Westminster: Dacre Press, 1928).
The Common Life in the Body of Christ (Westminster: Dacre Press, 1942).

'Father Lionel Thornton', an obituary. *The Times* (23 July 1960).

Underhill, Evelyn (1875–1941) created a distinctive place for herself in the Church of England on the basis of an education completed at the 'Ladies' Department' of King's College, London (of which she was made a Fellow in 1927) with the accomplishments of botany, philosophy and history and more than a fistful of languages to her credit. Baptized and confirmed, not until 1921 did she publicly identify herself with the life of the Church, by then with a formidable reputation established in independence of it, but which enabled her to move with confidence within it. No more than a minor poet and novelist, she had turned to the writings and teachings of those who throughout the centuries and in varying contexts had taught others how to pray and who had dared to believe that they had experienced the love of God. Publications of biographical and textual studies had in the pre-Anglican phase of her life a centrepiece in *Mysticism* (1911). Had it not been for her fiancé's distress at the prospect, and in 1907 (the year of their marriage) the papal condemnation of 'modernism', she might have become a Roman Catholic. Inchoate discomfort with the place of women in the Church of England may have played its part both in keeping her clear of it for so long, and then in setting her own agenda within it. A series of 'spiritual directors' both Roman Catholic and Anglican steered her towards and through her eventual vocation of retreat and spiritual director for others, including male clergy. She sought for them what she sought for herself – both intimacy with God and freedom within that intimacy. A 1933 letter which refers to Barth is revealing (and she had read him on *Romans* as well as Otto on *The Holy*). She recognized the need for 'gentle and penetrating intimacy' to balance that sense of 'over-againstness' which she so much valued in his work. At the end of her life, she was too ill to go in person to accept her honorary D.D. from Aberdeen, but not so ill that she could not continue to write and teach the pacifism which for her came to be the necessary issue of her prayers.

Apart from *Mysticism*, her other major publication comes from her life as an Anglican: *Worship* (1936). The first defies summary, although her materials are arranged thematically. The gist of it is to insist on the genuinely cognitive character of prayer, and on the sanity, sobriety and sheer practical energy of mystics. She argued that any account of human experience which excluded mystical experience (which crowned even the achievements of artists and scientists) could not be adequate. She understood the proper place of asceticism, not least the practice of poverty, as breaking the habit of things less than God (210). She was an advocate of the 'affective', that of the lover, poet, mourner, convert, with Christ himself an object of intimacy, emotion and desire (128) and notes that the Kingdom of heaven is 'taken by violence, not by amiable aspiration' (147). She draws on a very wide range of resources, including some of the mystics of Islam, the Benedictine women of Helfta, and Angela of Foligno. Margery Kempe's *Book* was rediscovered in its entirety too late for her to consider, and the identity of the author of *The Mirror of Simple Souls* was not conclusively identified until 1965 (Marguerite Porete), so much remained to be done by Evelyn Underhill's successors, notable though her scholarship was for her day. She used the work of poets, notably Blake and Dante (to be followed by Charles Williams and Dorothy L. Sayers). She admired the 'virility' of those who made an impact on the politics of their day (St Bernard, St Catherine of Siena, Joan of Arc). She had clear likes and dislikes, such as the 'weathercock' spirituality of Mme Guyon, the vulgarity of those whose 'corporeal visions' included roses, rings and jewels (291) and the 'superstition' of certain visions of the demonic (270). In 'Mysticism and Magic' she analyses the work of the heirs of the Magi. She delights in natural beauty, including that of the very small scale, and the cyclical rhythm of nature. She helpfully gives instruction in a beginner's exercise in contemplation

(301–2). *Mysticism* is barely explicitly Christian (see the references to Emmaus (449) and to cross, tomb and new life). A woman who can write that the parable of the Prodigal Son is to the mystic 'the history of the universe', interpreted as union with the One, the 'return to the Father's Heart' (41) is interpreting Scripture and other texts through the 'mapping' of Awakening, Discipline, Enlightenment and Self-Surrender rather than, for instance, the creeds.

For Anglicans, her re-emphasis on the importance of taking prayer utterly seriously is of lasting importance, notwithstanding her intellectual discomfort with 'symbols' with which she simply had to come to terms in the liturgical life of the Church. Engaging with ritual, with sacrament, and with sacrifice (the transmutation of her discussion of pain in *Mysticism*) she found herself distinguishing between symbol as representation by way of 'significant image' and sacrament as 'significant deed', something which actually makes a difference. Ever hospitable to 'homely pieties', the cycle of the natural year is here transposed into that of the liturgical year (and with the Book of Revelation providing illumination as to the significance of liturgy). The specifically Anglican tradition (as she understood it) finds its place not simply in the concluding chapters of the book, written after the controversy over the proposed 1928 Prayer Book revisions, but in her chapters on corporate worship, the eucharist and personal worship, which re-presents some of the themes of *Mysticism* in this new context. She takes a long, cool look at Evangelicalism as well as Tractarianism and what they had to offer to her time. She rejoiced in the rediscovery of the importance of cathedrals, and the growth of the retreat movement. A remarkable concluding paragraph expresses her hopes for the transfiguration of the whole universe. If she is still to be criticized for being God- or Spirit-centred rather than 'Christo-centric', then such criticism has to be sustained in the fact of her meditations on the creed, entitled *The School of Charity*, especially Part II (Incarnate, Crucified, Glorified). As a 'cradle-Anglican' who became Anglican as an adult with a passion which puts many to shame, and who turned herself into a considerable theologian in the process, she remains an inspiration, not least to those who think they need an 'official' position to be authoritative for their own generation.

A bibliography is included in the back of Christopher J. R. Armstrong, *Evelyn Underhill* (London: Mowbrays, 1975).

Key publications
Mysticism continuously reprinted since 1911, 12th edn, rev. 1930 (Oxford: One World, 1995).
Worship (London: Nisbet, 1936) and many reprints.
The School of Charity: Meditations on the Christian Creed (1934) and *The Mystery of Sacrifice:*

A Meditation on the Liturgy (1938) were reprinted together (London: Longmans & Green, 1954).
The Essentials of Mysticism and Other Essays (Oxford: One World, 1995).

In addition to Armstrong, above, see
Dana Greene, 1991. *Evelyn Underhill: Artist of the Infinite Life* (London: Darton, Longman and Todd).
Todd E. Johnson, 1994. 'Pneumatological Oblation: Evelyn Underhill's Theology of the Eucharist', *Worship* 68 (4): 313–32.
Michael Ramsey and A. M. Allchin, 1977. *Evelyn Underhill: Two Centenary Essays* (Fairacres: SLG Press, 1977).
Susan J. Smalley, 1988. 'Evelyn Underhill and the Mystical Tradition', in R. Bauckham and B. Drewery (eds.), *Scripture, Tradition and Reason: A Study in the Criteria of Christian Doctrine. Essays in Honour of Richard P. C. Hanson* (Edinburgh: T. & T. Clark).
Kenneth Stevenson, 1986. 'Re-Review: Evelyn Underhill's *Worship*' *Modern Churchman* 28 (3): 45–9. (AL)

Ussher, James (1581–1656), member of a prominent and long-established Dublin family, became Archbishop of Armagh in 1626, the one hundredth bishop of the see from St Patrick, having previously been bishop of Meath from 1621. Evelyn frequently refers to him in the *Diary* – 'that pious and learned man'. Ussher's reputation as a scholar in England and in Europe was such that contemporaries regarded him as 'a giant among giants'. As theologian, chronologist and student of antiquities his learning was immense. He had read the whole of the fathers in nineteen years, and his reputation in patristics was high on the continent. Considered a pioneer in Irish history he was first and foremost a scholar, refusing to be Provost of Trinity College, Dublin, as the post would interfere with his studies. As a bishop, some held that he lacked drive, and Burnet remarked that 'he was not made for the governing part of his function' (*Life* of William Bedell, 86–7).

Ussher's early upbringing was Calvinist, and he was influenced as a student by Trinity's Provost Travers, Hooker's opponent. His Calvinism became clear in the matter of the Irish Articles, though later his views changed, as attested by Hammond, Walton, Gunning and Thorndike. Certainly his contribution to defining the Anglican ethos was positive and designedly characterizing as he insists in work after work on doctrinal agreement with the primitive Church, 'we bring no new faith, nor no new Church' (*Works*, vol. II, 493, 497). This identity-affirming appeal to antiquity is the basic theme of Ussher's *Answer to a Challenge made by a Jesuit in Ireland* and of his *Discourse on the Religion Anciently Professed by the Irish and British* (1631). In this fundamental regard, he considered his first book, *The Succession and State of the Churches of Christ* (1613) as a continuation of the *Apology for the Church of England* (1562) by Jewel, whom he calls 'a gem among theologians'. His astounding knowledge of the fathers is everywhere and always the criterion is '*quod ubique, quod semper, quod ab omnibus*'.

He achieved international repute by his *Polycarpi et Ignatii Epistolae* (1644), in which, working from two Latin versions discovered in England, he was able to establish the authentic text. His researches were confirmed by a Greek manuscript in Florence which was printed by Voss. Hailed in his own day, as by Oxford University, his restoration has stood the test of modern scholarship and the Ignatian letters stand in Ussher's redaction, an early witness to monarchical episcopacy. The same can be said of his researches into the original form of what is now known as the Apostles' Creed.

The affair of the Irish Articles of 1615 in which Ussher, then a professor at Trinity College, Dublin, had inserted the Lambeth Articles (1595), the Calvinism of which had been rejected in the final form of the English Thirty-nine Articles, created a problem not only in this respect but because the Irish Articles were defective on church and ministry. The result was an exclusive document as compared with the English Articles, described by Bramhall in the Irish Convocation as having 'that latitude that dissenting persons in those things, that concerned not the Christian faith, might subscribe' (Vesey's *Life* of Bramhall). In spite of Ussher's opposition and piloted by Bramhall supported by Strafford's insistence, the English Articles were adopted in 1634. Much could be written about Ussher's numerous other works and notably his *Reduction of Episcopacy into the form of Synodical Government received in the Ancient Church*, seen now to have been as prophetic as it was ironic then. His piety and devotion were known to all, and throughout his exile in England he had prayers four times a day and 'the full service in his chapel before dinner and supper'. Fittingly, though strangely at the insistence of Cromwell, this great Irishman with a European reputation is buried in Westminster Abbey.

Collected Edition, 17 vols., ed. C. R. Elrington (1864). (HM)

Wesley, Charles (1707–88). The lifelong friend and partner of his elder brother John in the formative days of the Methodist Revival, Charles was the youngest son and eighteenth child of Samuel and Susanna Wesley of Epworth. He entered Oxford in 1726 with a Studentship at Christ Church, becoming on graduation a tutor of his college and leader (in John's absence as their father's curate) of the 'Holy Club'.

In 1735 Charles was ordained deacon and priest on successive Sundays and sailed with John to the new colony of Georgia. This brief and unhappy interlude revealed to the brothers the inadequacy of a ministry based on eighteenth-century High-Anglicanism to communicate a living faith in Christ; but proved significant also for their shipboard acquaintance with some Moravian missionaries. On his return to London Charles was befriended by Count Zinzendorf, leader of the Moravians, and by the young Peter Böhler, who helped sow the seed of Charles's Evangelical conversion, on Whitsunday, 21 May 1738. From his sick-bed Charles wrote in his journal: 'I now found myself at peace with God and rejoiced in hope of loving Christ . . .' He had long been a poet: two days later with 'Where shall my wond'ring soul begin' he began to be the hymn-writer we know today. Three days later his brother John was in Aldergate Street and entered into the same experience.

A brief curacy followed at St Mary's, Islington, including much ministry to prisoners in Newgate awaiting execution; but by May 1739 Charles had joined John in the unheard-of innovation of field-preaching; and continued for more than twenty years to travel in the cause of the gospel, constantly supporting the pioneer work of John, often amid tumult and violence. In April 1749 he married Sarah Gwynne: a wonderfully stable and happy marriage, even though five of their eight children died young. In 1771 they removed from Bristol to London, where Charles became the revered father-in-God of its many Methodist Societies and Chapels; and, as the 'sweet singer of Methodism', a legend even in his lifetime. John Wesley's *Collection of Hymns for the Use of the People Called Methodists* of 1780 was only a culmination of the hymns Charles had published, almost annually at times, from the *Hymns and Sacred Poems* of 1739 to the *Hymns for Children* of 1787. Through all these Charles's theological position is simply biblical, often with the use of strong sacramental imagery. Within the cross-currents of his day he used his pen to assert, for example, a universal redemption (cf. 'Thy undistinguished regard / Was cast on Adam's fallen race; / For all Thou hast in Christ prepared / Sufficient, sovereign, saving grace'); and his satirical verses on his brother's ordination of Dr Thomas Coke are well-known: 'So easily are Bishops made / By man's, or woman's whim? / W------- his hands on C---- has laid, / But who laid hands on him?' Charles never thought of himself as other than a son of the church in which he had been baptized and ordained. 'Sir,' he said to his local vicar, 'whatever the world may have thought of me, I have lived and die as a communicant of the Church of England, and I wish to be buried in the yard of my parish church.' And so he was.

Although Charles Wesley gave himself unstintingly to the cause of the Methodist Revival, it is as a hymn-writer that his influence endures. Many of his 9,000 hymns and poems were written on horseback with his pencil, in shorthand on a card kept for the purpose; and first sung by whatever congregation he was due to visit. The distillation of this huge output, sometimes emended by John and a variety of later editors, continues to be a major resource for Christian devotion. Through the year we turn constantly to the Wesley hymns: at Advent to 'Lo, he comes'; at Christmas to 'Hark, the herald angels sing'; at Easter to 'Love's redeeming work is done'; and so on. Add to these the great universal hymns of praise and discipleship: 'Soldiers of Christ, arise', 'O for a thousand tongues', 'Jesu, Lover of my soul', 'Love divine, all love's excelling' – and many, many more.

There remain some small uncertainties over a few of the Wesley hymns, as to which are by John and which by Charles. Many studies have been published showing their astonishing adherence to the text – sometimes the Greek text – of the scriptures. In J. E. Rattenbury's vivid phrase, 'They contain the Bible in solution'. Others have studied their classical construction, their variety of metre, their use of metaphor and rhyme, their relationship to the best literature of their day, their remarkable ease, 'smoothness', and suitability for congregational song.

By nature cheerful, warm and affectionate, a straightforward person possessed of wit and humour, Charles would not have considered himself a theologian; but to that great company of believers who imbibe their theology from the hymns they sing, Charles has been for 250 years a faithful pastor, a continuing inspiration and a sure guide.

Primary sources

*Thomas Jackson (ed.), *The Journal of the Rev. Charles Wesley*, 2 vols. (London: Methodist Book Room, 1849).

G. Osborn (ed.), *The Poetical Works of John and Charles Wesley*, 13 vols. (London: Wesleyan-Methodist Conference Office, 1868–72).

*Frank Baker, *Representative Verse of Charles Wesley* (London: Epworth, 1962). The valuable introductory chapters were published separately, 1964; and in a revised edition as: Frank Baker, *Charles Wesley's Verse: An Introduction* (London: Epworth, 1988).

Secondary sources

*Henry Bett, 1945. *The Hymns of Methodism* (London: Epworth; rev. and enlarged edn, 1945).

Frederick C. Gill, 1964. *Charles Wesley: The First Methodist* (London: Lutterworth).

John Lawson, 1987. *A Thousand Tongues: The Wesley Hymns as a Guide to Scriptural Teaching* (Exeter: Paternoster).

W. F. Lofthouse, 1965. 'Charles Wesley', in Rupert Davies and Gordon Rupp, *History of the Methodist Church in Great Britain*, vol. I (London: Epworth), 115–44.

Bernard L. Manning, 1942. *The Hymns of Wesley and Watts* (London: Epworth).

*J. Ernest Rattenbury, 1938. *The Conversion of the Wesleys* (London: Epworth).

John Telford, 1900. *The Life of the Rev. Charles Wesley*, rev. and enlarged edn (London: Wesleyan Methodist Book Room).

*See also other Charles Wesley studies by this author. (TDS)

Wesley, John (1703–91), along with his brother Charles, is remembered chiefly as the founder of Methodism. He was educated at Charterhouse and Christ Church, Oxford. He was then elected to a Fellowship at Lincoln College in 1726. Around this time, Wesley began to organize the meetings which subsequently became known as the 'Holy Club', on account of their earnest and methodical approach to Christian living and devotion. In May 1738, Wesley underwent some kind of conversion experience as a result of attending a meeting in Aldersgate Street, at which Martin Luther's Preface to Romans was read aloud. As a result of this experience, Wesley embarked on a major programme of evangelization, generally involving preaching in the open air. His experience with the established church of his day was less than happy, and he found himself excluded from church circles on account of his 'enthusiasm'. Perhaps the most famous such exclusion order was served in August 1739 by Joseph Butler, who was then bishop of Bristol. Butler's refusal to tolerate Wesley's evangelistic activity in his diocese reflected a general hostility towards Wesley within the establishment.

Although Wesley is intimately associated with the establishment of Methodism, it is important to appreciate that this development rests largely upon the hostile attitude of the established church to his ideas. Wesley remains a significant resource for Anglican theology in a number of respects, two of which may be singled out for special mention.

1. The importance of experience

Wesley's own conversion experience, in which he felt his heart to be 'strangely warmed', highlights the importance of what Wesley termed 'experimental religion' – that is, an approach to the Christian faith which recognizes the need to relate it to the subjective world of the individual. Wesley's emphasis on 'affection' (which shows strong parallels with the views developed in North America by Jonathan Edwards around the same time) corrected the sometimes rather formal and dry approach to Christianity which was associated with a number of Anglican writers at this time, including Bishop Butler himself. Wesley may be regarded as an important dialogue partner for contemporary Anglicanism as it seeks to ensure that Christian theology relates to the experience of individuals, and not simply to the world of ideas.

2. The importance of evangelism

Wesley's practical commitment to evangelism serves as a reminder of the importance of this activity to the mission and ministry of contemporary Anglicanism. It also serves to stress the need for theology and evangelism to relate to one another. Although Wesley's contribution to the theology of evangelism perhaps lies more in his insistence that evangelism should be done, rather than critical reflection on its presuppositions and implications, there can be no doubt that he remains a powerful stimulus to think more on this increasingly important theme.

Henry Abelove, 1990. *The Evangelist of Desire: John Wesley and the Methodists* (Stanford, Cal.: Stanford University Press).

Albert Brown-Lawson, 1994. *John Wesley and the Anglican Evangelicals of the Eighteenth Century* (Edinburgh: Pentland).

David Butler, 1995. *Methodists and Papists: John Wesley and the Catholic Church in the Eighteenth Century* (London: Darton, Longman and Todd).

Gregory S. Clapper, 1989. *John Wesley on Religious Affections: His Views on Experience and Emotion and Their Role in the Christian Life and Theology* (London: Scarecrow).

Henry H. Knight, 1992. *The Presence of God in the Christian Life: John Wesley and the Means of Grace* (London: Scarecrow). (AM)

Weston, Frank (1871–1924), theologian and Bishop of Zanzibar. Educated at Trinity College, Oxford, he spent four years working in the slums of London. In 1898 he joined the Universities Mission to Central Africa, and was assigned to Zanzibar, where he spent nine years. As the Principal of St Andrew's Training College in Kiungani, he developed his unusual cross-cultural skills. Despite being in Africa, he was able to write *The One Christ* in 1907, which expressed an orthodox if adventurous kenotic theory which paid particular attention to patristic kenotic theories. It was considered by Dr Sanday as having the merits of being both new and totally consistent with the creeds and Chalcedonian formularies. Weston was consecrated Bishop of Zanzibar in 1908. Several years later he played a significant role in a controversy with the Bishops of Mombasa and Uganda when he denounced their agreement with several Protestant denominations which intended to set up a Protestant federation over Rome. This same year he published *Ecclesia Anglican*, which set out his concerns with the Modernist movement. In 1916 and 1919 he published *The Fullness of Christ*, and *The Christ and His Critics*, which delineated his views on the Church and the Modernist controversies respectively. During this time he also wrote a short book *Conquering and to Conquer* (1918), which was written to comfort those who were experiencing the horrors of war, through examining the sufferings of Christ. Subsequently he wrote *Serfs of Great Britain* (1920), in which he attacked the government policy which was encouraging forced labour in Africa. Three years later he presided at the second Anglo-Catholic Conference, and the force of his personality made a great impression. At this conference he sent greetings not only to the

Bishop of Canterbury but also to the Pope and Ecumenical Patriarch. This act of apparent spontaneity was widely misunderstood though it was fully in accord with the Lambeth resolution.

Oxford Dictionary of the Christian Church, 1473.
H. M. Smith, in *Dictionary of National Biography, 1922–30*, 902–3.
D. W. Weston, OSB, 1983. *Frank Weston, 1871–1924* (London: The Church Literature Association).

Whately, Richard (1787–1863), Archbishop of Dublin. Educated at Oxford, he received his B.A. four years before he received his M.A., in 1812. In 1811, he was elected to the coveted position of Fellow at Oriel. He graduated D.D. and B.D. in 1825. Along with E. Copleston, E. Hawkins, and R. D. Hampden, he was a member of the Oriel 'Noetics', a mocking term that described a group of intellectuals who examined traditional religious orthodoxy under the scrutiny of their understanding history and reason. Their party was at its height in the decades prior to the Oxford Movement. In *Historic Doubts relative to Napoleon Buonaparte* (1819), he demonstrated that Hume's scepticism, taken to its logical conclusion, caused greater improbabilities than simple belief. Two years later he attacked Calvinists and their views on predestination in *The Right Method of Interpreting Scripture* (1821), and the following year he delivered *The Use and Abuse of Party Feeling in Matters of Religion* as the 1822 Bampton Lectures. Unwittingly the anti-Erastian *Letters on the Church by an Episcopalian* (1826), though never claimed by Whately, might have been his most important work. In arguing for the separation of church and state, he did so by appealing to the doctrine of apostolic succession, an historic doctrine of the Church which many in his day were unaware of. Newman credits Whately for teaching him this doctrine, and it became a unifying principle in the early Oxford Movement. His *The Errors of Romanism traced to their Origin in Human Nature* (1830) clearly reveals that he had no sympathy toward so-called Catholic principles, and he remained an enemy to the Tractarian party. In 1831 he was appointed the archbishop of Dublin. In this position he was diligent but involved in many difficult issues that his English birth, anti-Evangelicalism, and various aspects of his theology, which were often suspect of heresy, did not help.

J. M. Rigg, in *Dictionary of National Biography*, LX, 423–9.
Oxford Dictionary of the Christian Church, 1474.

White, William (1748–1836), bishop. Graduated from the College of Philadelphia in 1765. He became rector of Christ Church and St Peter's

Church, Philadelphia in 1779, where he also served as Chaplain to the Continental Congress and later the Federal Congress. White had tremendous influence upon many early American leaders, many of whom, like George Washington, attended Christ Church. White had little tolerance for revivalism, finding it necessary in the nineteenth century to distance himself from the emerging Evangelical party. Yet his tact, diplomacy and administrative propensity were vital to the survival of Anglican churches after the Revolution in the new anti-British, pro-democracy republic. White's proposal for presbyterial oversight in *The Case of the Episcopal Churches Considered* (1782) was largely rejected, but his idea for organizing the Protestant Episcopal Church on the principles of lay representation and the division of powers became the basis of the denomination's constitution. He served as president of the first General Convention in 1785. With William Smith, he drafted the *Proposed Book* (1785–86), an American adaptation of the Book of Common Prayer, which though failing in adoption exerted considerable influence on the American liturgy. Ironically it was adopted by the Reformed Episcopal Church, a separate episcopal body founded in 1873 by Bishop Cummins and his group of dissenting Evangelicals. Consecrated first Bishop of Pennsylvania at Lambeth in 1787, White saw his task clear to ensure the survival of the infant denomination by establishing full unity with New England Anglicans, and so joined with Seabury of Connecticut to constitute the House of Bishops in the first united General Convention of the Protestant Episcopal Church in 1789. White published several books, including *Memoirs of the Protestant Episcopal Church in the United States of America* (1820).

Dictionary of American Biography, X.
Dictionary of American Religious Biography.
Dictionary of Christianity in America.
A. C. Guelzo, 1994. *For the Union of Evangelical Christendom: The Irony of the Reformed Episcopalians* (University Park: Penn State University Press).
F. V. Mills, 1978. *Bishops by Ballot: An Eighteenth Century Ecclesiastical Revolution* (New York: Oxford University Press).

INDEX

234

The Society for Promoting Christian Knowledge (SPCK) was founded in 1698. It has as its purpose three main tasks:

- **Communicating the Christian faith in its rich diversity**
- **Helping people to understand the Christian faith and to develop their personal faith**
- **Equipping Christians for mission and ministry**

SPCK Worldwide serves the Church through Christian literature and communication projects in over 100 countries. Special schemes also provide books for those training for ministry in many parts of the developing world. SPCK Worldwide's ministry involves Churches of many traditions. This worldwide service depends upon the generosity of others and all gifts are spent wholly on ministry programmes, without deductions.

SPCK Bookshops support the life of the Christian community by making available a full range of Christian literature and other resources, and by providing support to bookstalls and book agents throughout the UK. SPCK Bookshops' mail order department meets the needs of overseas customers and those unable to have access to local bookshops.

SPCK Publishing produces Christian books and resources, covering a wide range of inspirational, pastoral, practical and academic subjects. Authors are drawn from many different Christian traditions, and publications aim to meet the needs of a wide variety of readers in the UK and throughout the world.

The Society does not necessarily endorse the individual views contained in its publications, but hopes they stimulate readers to think about and further develop their Christian faith.

For further information about the Society, please write to:
SPCK, Holy Trinity Church, Marylebone Road,
London NW1 4DU, United Kingdom.
Telephone: 0171 387 5282